CW01081663

Indigenous Roots of Feminism

Indigenous Roots of Feminism
Culture, Subjectivity and Agency

Jasbir Jain

Los Angeles | London | New Delhi
Singapore | Washington DC | Melbourne

First published in 2011 by

 SAGE Publications India Pvt Ltd
B1/I-1 Mohan Cooperative Industrial Area
Mathura Road, New Delhi 110 044, India
www.sagepub.in

SAGE Publications Inc
2455 Teller Road
Thousand Oaks, California 91320, USA

SAGE Publications Ltd
1 Oliver's Yard,
55 City Road
London EC1Y 1SP, United Kingdom

SAGE Publications Asia-Pacific Pte Ltd
3 Church Street
#10-04 Samsung Hub
Singapore 049483

Published by Vivek Mehra for SAGE Publications India Pvt Ltd, typeset in 10/15 Times New Roman by Diligent Typesetter, Delhi.

Library of Congress Cataloging-in-Publication Data
Jain, Jasbir.
   Indigenous roots of feminism: culture, subjectivity, and agency/Jasbir Jain.
      p.cm.
   Includes bibliographical references and index.
   1. Women—India.   2. Feminism—India.   3. Class consciousness—India.
   4. Gender identity—India.   5. Self—India. I. Title.
HQ1742.J35   305.420954—dc22   2011   2010053793

ISBN: 978-81-321-0439-1 (HB)

The SAGE Team: Rekha Natarajan, Aniruddha De, Sanjeev Kumar Sharma
          and Deepti Saxena

*For my grandmother, Beji, who struggled alone
with a six-month-old girl child;
my mother, who passed on her creativity to
eight children;
and to the men who made all the difference—
Papaji, Ram, Pranay and Saachi.*

Thank you for choosing a SAGE product!
If you have any comment, observation or feedback,
I would like to personally hear from you.

Please write to me at **contactceo@sagepub.in**

Vivek Mehra, Managing Director and CEO, SAGE India.

Bulk Sales

SAGE India offers special discounts
for purchase of books in bulk.
We also make available special imprints
and excerpts from our books on demand.

For orders and enquiries, write to us at

Marketing Department
SAGE Publications India Pvt Ltd
B1/I-1, Mohan Cooperative Industrial Area
Mathura Road, Post Bag 7
New Delhi 110044, India

E-mail us at **marketing@sagepub.in**

Get to know more about SAGE

Be invited to SAGE events, get on our mailing list.
Write today to **marketing@sagepub.in**

This book is also available as an e-book.

CONTENTS

LIST OF PHOTOGRAPHS

1. Sita's *swayamvara*—Rama wins her hand.
2. Celebrating the destruction of evil: A view of the Dussehra festival.
3. Crushing all opposition: Hanuman on his way to Ayodhya with Rama and Sita.
4. After the victory: Rama and Lakshmana return to Ayodhya—a Ramlila procession.
5. Ramlila performance.
6. Draupadi's *chirharan* in the *Mahābhārata* and the benevolence of Krishna.
7. Kathakali mask.
8. A dome depicting the *Rāmāyana* in Shekhawati region.
9. Continued histories of the *Rāmāyana*: Worshipping through art.
10. Understanding good and evil at a young age.
11. Śakuntalā and Duhsanta in the hermitage.
12. Durga Mata in all her glory.
13. Worshipping Mata Vaishno Devi amidst domestic bliss.
14. Hansa Wadkar.
15. Women protestors arguing with the police.
16. C.S. Lakshmi speaking on oral narratives at Jaipur with Gitanjali Chatterjee in the chair.

PREFACE

In 2003, I happened to lecture in several colleges and universities in the United States. It was the month of March, the month earmarked for women's history. Most of the talks I gave dealt with women either in history or in politics. I discussed the Bhakti Movement, the impact of reservation for women at the panchayat level, the legislations that followed the Roop Kanwar sati case and the Bhanwari Devi rape case. I also discussed the meaning of modernity and its impact on women. There were references to women's economic worth in society at large and within marriage in particular.

Moving away from history and politics, literary representations in texts as widely different as Tagore's *Home and the World*, Attia Hussain's *Sunlight on a Broken Column* and Anita Desai's *Clear Light of Day* were also discussed. The first novel was concerned with the twin issues of women's freedom and the nation's independence, while the second and third were partition narratives from two different perspectives, two different kinds of families and two different centres of minority culture—Lucknow and Delhi—both vibrant with Muslim culture.

One talk was specifically on 'Women and History: Memory, Resistance and Agency', in which I attempted to give my listeners a glimpse of the range and multiplicity of issues of both methodology and historical recording. At the end of it, several members wished to know where they could locate the details. But I was in no position to give any single reference as the ideas and perceptions were directly related to my culture, my reading and my experience and interpretations. Several of them had shaped themselves over a period of time through an accumulative process—something which cannot be passed on mechanically. I also realised that my own reading in ancient history was limited and based on second-hand sources, or on modern representations of myths and epic narratives. It was then that I decided to fill in the gaps in my own knowledge and grapple with areas I had not explored in depth earlier.

Very often, in academics, one is called upon to contrast and compare, analyse and explain. The debate on the Western impact/origin of feminism has been an ongoing one. I have been convinced that culture has a much greater role in the formation of one's ideas than we credit it with. Since women in India view their bodies, their roles and their social structures differently, there is no way the origins of the movement in two different cultures could have been the same. In the 1980s, we were in the midst of discussions on the report *Towards Equality* as well as on the New Education Policy; many of us were members of the Rajasthan University Women's Association and actively participated in the demonstrations during the Roop Kanwar and Bhanwari Devi cases. We were greatly enthused by the activities of the NGOs around us and, in general, by being part of the change, representations and legal battles that engaged our attention. The successes and failures of the Women's Studies Centres were also part of this period. As we worked towards raising consciousness, our own consciousness expanded; the sharing sessions opened out many a closed door.

The scenario was, however, limited. Literature had a minimal role in Women's Studies, except for a few centres where recovery of lost texts was undertaken. Thus, a requirement was felt to break language barriers and interweave a pattern out of our multilingual discourses. This project has had multiple origins: the lacuna in my own learning, the lack of availability of any consolidated material, misconceptions and growing

disaffection from feminist concerns in society at large and a divide between feminists and non-feminists that was increasingly beginning to
be visible were only some of these. There was, in addition, a growing
need to rescue feminism from a secondary status both in society and in
academics. The attempt has been to connect the past with the present.
As part of this effort I have worked with contemporary interpretations,
retellings and rewritings as a continuation or a questioning of the past at
the same place where I have discussed the texts of the past. Thus, it was
also easier to see where the shifts were and why they had taken place.

I have worked through the formation of patriarchal and religious structures in the first chapter and the concept of the 'self' these generated. The
second chapter looks at the two epics—*Rāmāyana and Mahābhārata*—
and at some of the significant rewritings of the epics. The third goes on
to analyse *Manusmriti* as closed space and *Nātyaśastra* as open space
and the divisions in the categories these expositions brought about. Here
again, the concern has been to bring it right up to the present. The fourth
chapter deals with the Bhakti Movement and transgressive rebellions
of the women Bhakti poets. The fifth is concerned with the tracing of
the nineteenth-century resistance narratives while the sixth works more
closely with the caste question, the state role, the impact of the freedom
struggle and the beginnings of the present resurgence. The final chapter
is a modest effort at a restatement of my main thesis: the indigeneity and
the difference. The methodological approach is dominantly literary, even
as it uses the methodology of sociology, psychology and other related
disciplines. During the course of this research, I have depended heavily
on the scholarship of several friends well grounded in their own disciplines. Basant Jaitly, Ranbir Sinh and Kusum Jain have been of immense
help.

This project would not have been initiated if I had not lectured in
the United States. Friends who made this possible and facilitated the
sessions—Nancy Pierce, Sharada Nayak, Prem and Amritjit Singh, Vijay
and P.S. Chauhan, Manju Gupta and her family, Linda Dittmar and Pavel

and his young wife, Mita—my thanks to them. There are many more who offered me hospitality, rescued me from the snowstorms and shared an hour or two over a cup of tea.

My debts are to many and are manifold. To my various hosts and the host organisations who invited me, the different departments ranging from Economics, Political Science, Philosophy to Religion, Women's Studies and Literature in Bard College, Skidmore, St Lawrence University, Boston University, Wellesley College, Arcadia University, Brown University, Community College, Philadelphia and the Association of American Colleges and Universities, Washington. Closer home, Renuka Pamecha, Mamta Jaitly, Aruna Roy and Gerda Unnithan are among my many educators who taught me the meaning of activism and solidarity, my colleagues in the Department of English and the organisers and audiences of various seminars and conferences who became ready sounding boards. These debts are the pleasures of scholarship. There are many others—the Women Studies Department of SNDT University, Mumbai and Vidyut Bhagwat, Pune—I need to acknowledge my gratitude to all of them.

And it would not have been possible without the UGC grant, which allowed me the luxury of buying books and researching to my heart's content. This research has been possible mainly because of the grant attached to the UGC Major Research Fellowship.

Let me add a note on the spellings. Mythological names are spelt in several different ways in India, depending upon the regional differences; even last names may often vary. In the main, I have tried to be faithful where quotations have been used or with reference to a particular text. Diacritical marks have been used only for proper names. Elsewhere, the variations have been used, as for instance Antherjanam is also spelt as Antarjanam and Warkari as Varkari, depending upon the use made by a particular writer.

A People without a History?

Every society has a concept of its past and therefore no society can be called ahistorical.
—Romila Thapar ('The Tradition of Historical Writing' 238)

The feminist movement is a sociopolitical reality that has grown and developed over a period of time in a variety of different ways: protest against oppression, legal reform, nationalistic concerns, education and social change being only a few of these. Somehow, its growth and development have been attributed mainly to Western influence. Time and again, one hears or reads that it, like the concept of 'nation' and the creative form 'novel', has Western origins. Such a belief (in all three cases), dismisses the past as irrelevant or as oppositional to the present. Such a belief also misreads traditional concepts and goes on to minimise the reality of evolving patterns rooted in Indian history and culture. Further, it ignores cultural differences and seeks to read history in universal terms.

Culture is one category that goes on to influence all facets and aspects of life—behaviour, relationships, identities, responses and epistemologies. How we 'know' and respond to the outside world is governed in large measures by cultural constructs. If the Indian woman's attitude to her body is different, then this too will affect her self-image. The emphasis on family and community still continues to persist, as does the belief in marriage as sacrosanct. Changes have occurred; nuclear families and

1

reversal of traditional hierarchy have taken place due to urbanisation and employment compulsions; divorce is increasingly becoming acceptable and 'live-in' relationships are also catching on in urban areas. But the values with which one grows up are still rooted in traditional culture wherein myths and concepts are reflective mainly of ideas and aspirations not prevalent in actual practice. Perhaps there were always variants. What is recorded or is interpreted emanates from temporal contexts. And interpretations are guided by ideological beliefs, locations and compulsions contemporaneous to that interpretation.

For nearly two centuries, there has been a heightened awareness of and a concentrated public concern with women's issues—a concern which runs parallel to the British rule and its aftermath. First, there was the imperial focus on women-related legislation, and then there was the absorption of both the issues and women in the rhetoric of the freedom struggle. The latter has also resulted in them being used as cultural counters, which has drawn a disproportionate attention to their 'representative' role at the cost of their individuality (P. Chatterjee, *The Nation* 118–121).

For all practical purposes, the women's movement in the present work will be used as a term which includes and is synonymous with the feminist movement. The difference is more in terms of time than of degree. Women's movement is a social happening, which at a later stage developed into feminism; honed by its self-consciousness and interlaced with ideology, it came to be supported by sophisticated theory. The forces that generate the two are often similar if not exactly the same. A 'movement' is group activity and seeks to base itself on solidarity, a coming together for a common cause. It is likely to bridge class, educational and generational differences. Feminism has deeper roots in the individual consciousness than the basic fact of being a woman. Both self-image and social image come together in this. The perception of the outer reality is guided by this. The two terms—'woman' and 'feminine'—feed on each other.

Feminism, in itself, is a term in dire need of a restatement as it has acquired a negative connotation through its association with protest and resistance. Feminism is also, if not primarily, an issue of identity, sub-jecthood, space and freedom. Thus, it includes the freedom to choose and to be recognised as a 'countable' human being. The use of the word 'countable' is to assert that there is need for us to discard terms that once were inclusive of both the genders like *purusharth* or the pursuits of hu-man existence.[1] Feminism insists on recognition of agency, of a separate space, but does not refute relationships. Being fully aware of the social construction of gender, the attempt for the time being is to free feminism from the underpinnings of ideology and relate it to the relationship be-tween the biological body and its location in a social environment, and to go ahead to examine the nature of this gendered reality.

The growth of feminism/women's movement has not been a tale of linear progression but of struggles (collective as well as individual), in-terruptions, setbacks, embroilment in religious conflicts, return to patri-archal constructs, especially during times of national crises, and even resort to male models of heroism and leadership. There has been a con-stant need to negotiate cultural myths which are part of the socialisation of the girl child and to retell and reinterpret them. In the last few decades the reinterpretative act has been widely spread, thus emphasising the re-lationship between culture and self-image.

Projections of women's images, both by men and women, have un-fortunately polarised female identity between the *Devi* image and the public woman—both exclusionary images. Again, identities are fixed in the image of the sacrificing mother, the supportive wife and the young virgin. This morning as I opened an old file, a newspaper cutting from 1984 stared me in the face with the title 'The Blessed and the Damned'. It also carries a photograph of 'Portrait of a Hindu Girl, 1880' and states, 'Hindu society has not changed its attitude to women substantially in the past 1500 years.' This article then proceeds to examine the role of biology (with reference to sex and sexuality), Darwin's impact on West-ern religious constructs, the formulating ideology behind patriarchy and religious construction of gender-based morality. In the process, it seeks

3

to deconstruct some commonly believed assumptions about women and tries to connect the two extreme views of the 'blessed' and the 'damned'. At the same time, it succeeds in underlining some main constructs that need to be opened out—patriarchy, religion, morality and sexuality—and thereafter located within an evolutionary pattern (Parikh). It proceeds to indicate the dominance of popular discourse that continues to work with polarities. Ironically enough, these very images are used to build up a feminist discourse of power. The absence of a middle ground calls for attention.

Feminism in India cannot be treated in the singular; there is not one but several feminisms, having their origin in social conditions, religious traditions and caste backgrounds. Codified traditions have, in the main, belonged to elitist societies. There are parallel traditions in rural and tribal societies, which work differently and, at times, frame morality differently. The varied history of Indian women makes it clear that feminism is not necessarily an ideology of resistance to patriarchal control but a movement that seeks integration of the public and the private space and the collapsing of the divisions between two different kinds of sexuality and moral values. It is expressive of the need to be heard, to have a choice as well as the freedom to act in accordance with that choice.

The distinction between 'identity' (and its dependence on economic and social conditions) and 'self' (with its base in human perception and awareness) is an important one, not only for the construction of the female self-image but also for the relationship (and its embedding) in institutional frameworks like marriage, family and education. At one point, I had held the view that true equality can only be attained when women are able to rise above the body and move about less conscious of themselves as 'bodies' to be seen, that is, the 'object' image. Freedom of the body would allow the intellect to gain supremacy. Also, it would liberate a woman from the *triya jaal*, the wily artfulness, which is forced upon them if they want to obtain their objectives. Two examples

4

come immediately to mind: Kakeiyi's withdrawal into her chamber in order to get Daśaratha to comply with her wishes in the *Rāmāyana* and Savitri's in R.K. Narayan's *The Dark Room.* I have chosen these two examples, which are centuries apart, in order to demonstrate the cultural unconscious and its load of images. Both the women—Kakeiyi and Savitri—protest, but in their protests they resort to indirections and use their relationship. Pressure tactics often work in a similar manner, even in workers' strikes, for they exploit the indispensability of their work/relationship. But women got trapped in the term *triya jaal.*[2] Why not use debate or argument? We have examples, in various narratives of the past, of the debates in which women have participated. Draupadi used both—argument and pressure.

Again, why should women have to rise above the body in order to demand respect for their mind? Can the body and the mind not go together? By conceding to a separation, there is the danger of falling into the trap of valorising asceticism and accepting polarisation. This is self-defeating. The body needs to be recognised with all its desires and unconscious drives as much as the feelings and thoughts which inhabit the human mind.

Feminism is the recognition of this 'wholeness' of existence that encompasses all three—body, mind and soul. And for this recognition it also forces a rethinking on the idea of masculinity. Men, both in tales of yore and in more realistic narratives, have given sufficient evidence of being gentle and caring. Why then is a single dominant image of power employed to frame them? Patriarchy, despite the power vested in it, has its own compulsions. It is these compulsions, the myths of superiority and the need to protect them, which drive it. No man has been able to come up to the ideal role model—not Rāma, nor Yudhisthra, nor any of the others. Why? Is this not a question we ought to raise and proceed to re-examine the notion of masculinity? Feminism demands exactly this—that the construction of masculinity be based on the wholeness of man rather than on power and authority.

Working with the premise outlined before, briefly that: feminism is not characterised solely through resistance; the concept of self is rooted in culture traditions and both phenomenological and epistemological constructs are impacted by it; no reconstruction of feminine space can come into being in a one-sided manner, it has to interact with the notion of masculinity; there are many cultural narratives and their retellings that trace a history of feminist standpoints and idea of the self and hence we are not a people without history. As Romila Thapar has pointed out, 'historical writing on ancient India goes back for more than two centuries' ('Interpretations' 1), everything cannot be linked to the coming of the West or the cultural encounter of two cultures. British recordings were motivated by ideological and administrative goals. There was a disproportionate reliance on 'pandits' and many 'ideological prejudices … were often incorporated' in the interpretations of the past. The Indians who followed also adhered to Western approaches and were hesitant to question the Western models (3–10). In another article in the same volume, Thapar argues that when India is said to lack history, the idea is located in a definition of history. She goes on to offer a new definition:

> A sense of history can be defined as a consciousness of past events, which events are relevant to a particular society, seen in a chronological framework and expressed in a form which meets the needs of that society…the historical tradition can be culled from existing literature, whether specifically historical or not. ('The Tradition of Historical Writing' 237–238)

Thapar then proceeds to look at mythology, genealogy and historical narrative as the three constituents of a historical tradition. My procedure is going to be somewhat different for two reasons: I am not a historian but a student of literature, and my concern is with a tradition of cultural constructs that have moulded the role of women and affected their relationships, status and position. Further, I would also like to explore their self-images, their strengths and their resistance to decisions adversely

6

affecting their lives. Whether their ethics, moral values and social roles are passively constructed or do they exercise some agency? This is one of the questions that interest me. Beginning with this, it is proposed to work through literary constructs in order to trace both continuities and discontinuities and attempt to locate the 'traces' (in the Derridean sense) of the origin of our present location in the feminist debate. There are several ways of reading the past and they of necessity are bound to be selective. One, we read and interpret from our context; two, the narrative of the past works within its own context, that is, nothing is context-free. Further, when the past is written, even if it is documented (and not oral), it has travelled to us through a variety of interpretations made to suit those particular contexts. Traditions and realities can be viewed from multiple angles depending on the various perceptions that have affected them. And oral traditions have a habit of accruing over a period of time. The past is thus always difficult to read. The relationship between oral traditions, the social event which is a prelude to the formation of thought, and other unrecognisable currents working through the whole process are of great significance. Pashaura Singh provides 'a theoretical schema for various hermeneutic techniques' in *The Guru Granth Sahib: Canon, Meaning and Authority* in which he refers to three kinds of interpretations: first, the doctrinal where the interpreter is approaching the text with preconceived intentions; the second is the historical reading, where the reader/historian is 'trying to make sense of the world behind the text' and is interested in exploring what went on to its making; the third is the literary reading where one sets out to explore the many possibilities of its meaning and 'confronts the world in front of the text' (259–260). Each locates the reader and the text in a different position. Singh describes them as world before the text, behind the text and in front of the text respectively. To this, I may add that in the first category the reading does not really come into a live contact, the self goes out to locate itself in it: it illustrates a point one wants to make. The Vedas were projected in this manner in the nineteenth century and all policies and positions against the interrogation of sacred texts (adopted from time to time by religious bodies) lead to this, just as a single-stream, selective interpretation of the past does. The historical links up with the present; the literary, on the other hand, projects a constantly living relationship with the text/past/culture and admits the dynamic relationship that the present has with the past. Fixities of location, of meaning, of perspective are all rejected in this method.

When we begin to analyse the gender issue from our point in time, we tend to read it through the present socioreligious situation as it affects gender issues. In between then and now a large number of readings, interpolations and alterations have taken place due to historical and political interventions. There are several markers to choose from in order to identify our present location—the UN Resolution on International Women's Day; the report *Towards Equality*, Government of India, 1974; the New Education Policy of 1986, where for the first time education for equality is mentioned; the Mathura rape case, which set off the protest movements; the rise in dowry deaths in the 1970s, the establishment of Women's Studies as a discipline and state support of gender-related welfare and empowerment activities. They run contemporaneous to the Second Wave of Feminism, as the post-1970 movement is referred to (it has also been identified as the third phase, if male contribution to the reform phase of the early twentieth century is taken into account). Other protest movements like the anti-Vietnam movement and the Black militancy in the United States, the students' movement in France and the dalit upsurgence in India surfaced in the 1960s as if they constituted a wave passing through the whole world—a world that was simultaneously postmodern and postcolonial. Surely, there is something in the atmosphere of those times that ignited and inspired them all. It is not a matter of sheer coincidence. The women's struggle and the feminist movement also need to be seen in this context—not linearly alone, placed in a chronological history, but within a simultaneity of resistance movements and demands for equality on grounds of race, gender, class or generation. It needs to be located firmly in the political environment.

Women's movement has ordinarily been collectively identified on the grounds of collectivity and continuity, or when an issue has transgressed personal space to become a public concern. The first phase is identified as the social reform movement, initiated and propagated by at least three different agencies: male intervention in public issues and desire for reform; the government's initiatives and legislation in this connection; and women themselves. Khullar, Gandhi and Shah see it as a long period spanning almost a century: from the 1850s to 1940s, a period actually divisible into two phases—first, when male initiative dominated the reform movements; second, when women themselves acquired an agency and actively participated in social and political matters. The third phase is located in the 1970s when the Indian government in accordance with the United Nations' mandate appointed a Committee on the status of women in India and this Committee produced a report entitled *Towards Equality* in 1974, which in its turn rendered a whole society conscious of the inequalities at work in almost every sphere—education, employment, economic rights as well as the manner in which these inequalities impinged on domestic space, women's perception of themselves and male perception of women.[3] For the sake of convenience, one may follow the more common division into waves and treat the 1970s and after as the second wave of feminism, clubbing the first two phases into one. The second phase is different from the first on several counts. The first worked against a foreign legislative authority and political considerations weighed on both sides. A large number of initiators in this were men. This was also closely associated with religion and caste. From the women's point of view, in retrospect, one can discern its uneven progress where women themselves were concerned. The 'home and the world' cultural divide which Partha Chatterjee points out to in *The Nation and Its Fragments* had in itself a further stultifying effect on women. The 1970s and after have a large number of active and academic women and the issues are more focused on violence against women, and customs and practices which have built-in gender discrimination. Both rural and

9

urban women come into this fold. It is the perception of the female body which, however, is central to both these phases. In one, the inherited cultural model is still very powerful even as a few cosmetic changes are effected; in the second, the physicality (rather than the sexuality) of the female body, its biological roles, its violation and control are much more centrally placed, partly also because of government policies and the development of technology. With the increased emphasis on education, women's participation in decision-making is also natural.

The attempt is not to trace the development in isolation from the rest of the world but to trace the differences in tradition, value structures, political history, social concerns and the nature of resistance. If a female body was to be nailed down as Gulliver was by the Lilliputians, the different nails would be the projected religious and mythological role models, the issue of purity (inclusive of virginity and fidelity), marriage, lineage, caste and economic status.[4] Thus, violence, rape, abduction and control become the necessary associates to produce a docile body and control its labour.[5] Whatever role the mind and the soul have, in the way a woman is imagined, is seen as marginal or peripheral. This is the natural fallout of a patriarchal structure but it can also be partly blamed on a continued selective projection of cultural values. From time to time, there have been interventions and resistance movements, but there have also been recessions into even more restrictive measures evident in things as different from each other as the retelling of a received myth, narrative or story, religious reform or fundamentalism or ideological stance. Ironically enough, these contrary movements draw their sustenance from the same accounts, only each reads and interprets them differently.

Patriarchy begins with creation myths, and one of the reasons behind this is that women have been seen as a secondary creation, born out of the male body. The story of the Genesis is common to Judaism, Islam and Christianity. In them, as in Hinduism, Buddhism and Sikhism, the Word is supreme. They all emphasise the creative act as an imposition

10

of order on nothingness or chaos. In the Rig Veda, dismemberment and incest are both projected as creation myths. O'Flaherty writes:

> The most basic form of cosmogony is implicit in many early hymns, though never explicitly described: it is the formation of distinct elements out of the primeval cosmic flux, the evolution of order out of chaos, the propping apart of heaven and earth. This concept of creation as separation remains at the heart of much of later Hindu mythology (as well as Hindu social thought) and forms the animating spark of the conflict between gods and non-gods (demons or human beings). (25)

Natural elements are also created by Prajapati, and the cause of these generations is loneliness, the desire to have companion/s and progeny. Creation myths, fall from a paradisical state, good and evil—all highlight desire, longing for the 'other', power, control and separateness. The fall from a paradisical state also announces the arrival of death. The practice of asceticism conserves energy and generates power. Time and again Hindu myths underline this—men and women both acquire extraordinary powers which they employ either to curse or to confer boons on others. Asceticism also stresses control of both body and mind. It is these elements and emotions which dominate human life. Desire is not only attraction, love or the aspiration to become immortal but it is also a desire for power and authority and the impulse to control others and intervene with the course of events. *Kama*, *krodh*, *lobh*, *moha* are not only states of emotion to be avoided or kept under control but also the active agents of human life and its motivating agents. Unfortunately, they are often framed within the male perspective, and woman's visibility in the whole discourse is indeed very limited. But the energy that can be earned through the practice of asceticism or concentrated devotion is available alike to men and women as several narratives demonstrate in both the epics, in Jain stories as well as in other religious and folk narratives.

If one were to ask the question: whether there is a principle of gender equality in the dominant religious discourses in India, one is likely to get a whole range of answers for a number of reasons. First, versions differ; then there is a multiplicity of myths, especially creation myths; third, the origins are not contemporary in time, as for instance Sikhism, with its base in the Bhakti Movement, is a much younger religion and its conceptualisation has to be seen in its historicity. One of the views that the Upanisads present is of the origins in sacrificial rites and self-division. In the *Bṛhadāraṇyaka-Upaniṣad*, the creation of the world is described in the following way:

> There was nothing whatsoever here in the beginning. By death indeed was this covered, or by hunger, for hunger is death. He created the mind, thinking 'let me have a self' (mind). Then he moved about, worshipping. From him, thus worshipping, water was produced. 'Verily', he thought, 'while I was worshipping water appeared, therefore water is called *arka* (fire). Water surely comes to one who thus knows the reason why water is called *arka* (fire). (Radhakrishnan 151)

And the 'froth of the water became solidified' as earth, and the heat was produced by 'Prajapati's practice of austerity' (151). This self-generation and division lie at the heart of all creation. First the conscious self divides itself, creates the sun, fire and water. Then it experiences fear of death and loneliness, desires companionship and creates a woman. All species of animals were created later through a series of metamorphosis (165). Then the nature gods (Indra, Agni and others) were created. In all processes of creation, sacrifice and will are required. Thus it is the 'self' which has primacy over all else. Even for a woman for whom the 'husband is dear for the sake of the self' (197). Nothing—progeny, weath, castehood, gods—is dear on its own count; all are of value to the self:

> Verily, not for the sake of all is all dear but all is dear for the sake of the Self. Verily, O Maitreyi, it is the Self that should be seen, heard of, reflected on and meditated upon. (197)

12

S. Radhakrishnan, the philosopher-translator of the version I am using, comments on this section (*Fourth Brahmana*) that 'this section indicates that the later subjection of women and their exclusion from Vedic studies do not have the support of the Upanisads' (201). The 'Self' is immortal, it is *Brahman*. It is the means of knowing, of understanding, of desire and its fulfilment. It is in a relationship with the other that one transcends the self. The physical union between man and woman is not 'mere physical satisfaction but a psycho-spiritual communion…many mystics employ this as the symbol of divine communion' (262–263). This is also the kind of desire that surfaces later in the Bhakti Movement—the centrality of the Self to all forms of knowing, experience and attainment of goals. The *Bṛhadāraṇyaka-Upaniṣad* in Bk VI, Sec. 4, v. 15 lays procedures for a large variety of desires ranging from hatred for the wife's lover to the sex and complexion of the progeny. One of the desires includes a daughter who is learned (Radhakrishnan 326).[6]

One interesting passage is in *Kausītakī-Brāhmana Upanisad*, which identifies the masculine with the vital breath, the neuter with the mind and the feminine with speech (Radhakrishnan 759). And a later passage goes on to read: 'This *Brahman* shines forth, indeed, when one speaks with speech; likewise it dies when one speaks not, its light goes to the eye; its vital breath to the vital breath' (770).

But even as speech and thought are necessary for existence, the 'superior excellence' of the vital breath, that is, the masculine, is recognised (771). And nature, on which order has been imposed, is a thing to be enjoyed, says the *Maitri Upanisad* (Radhakrishnan 824). Thus, even as a certain gender neutrality is maintained, a gender hierarchy is subtly reinforced by projecting one source for all secondary creations and emphasising the superior power of the creator.

Buddhism relatively offers greater equality, but it too has its own discriminations. Buddhism and Jainism admitted nuns and allowed them to preach, but it was a path of struggle for women. Yet the concept of the self is gender-neutral. Buddha's concept of 'self' has been the subject of much controversy and debate. Beginning with the premise of a non-self, an *anatman* being, he rejects the idea of a transcendental, permanent self. Instead, it is a nonegoistic self that has to be achieved through *dharma* and the Eightfold Path. *The Dhammapada* states, 'Your own self is your master; who else could be? With yourself well controlled, you gain a master very hard to find' (Easwaran 121).

Jainism was divided on the issue of salvation for women. While Śvetāmbara Jains did not exclude women from the possibility of attaining salvation, Digambara Jains did. Buddhism conceded that salvation was attainable, but the Buddha admitted nuns into the order only after a great deal of persuasion by his foster mother. After having given them the permission to join, 'a more rigorous discipline than monks' was made requisite for them. And several other discriminatory practices came in along with the permission (Altekar 208–209).

Sikhism, clearly a religion born out of a different socio-historical context, and with roots in the Bhakti Movement, concedes greater equality to women in its creation theory. It traces origins to the sound. The 'Word' is supreme. The *vak*, that is, the commandment/speech, is perceived as the source of all creation and a manifestation of the Supreme Creator, and the Sikh scripture—the *Guru Granth Sahib*—is the centre of all religious rituals like worship, congregation, marriage and devotional singing. The importance of the congregation lays emphasis on social behaviour and relationships (Grewal, *Guru Nanak*).[7] The possibility of spiritual attainment across social barriers is also emphasised (171). Pashaura Singh goes on to explore the strategies, policies and spiritual thought behind the editing of the *Guru Granth Sahib* and recognises the impact of the social forces. He goes onto observe, 'The inclusive ideal of the *Adi Granth* is the culmination of its effort to transcend conventional forms of Hindu tradition and Islam. Its message is open to all people regardless of their caste status, vocation or religious affiliation.' Inward meditation and not any external religious observation is the route to liberation (167). The

Guru Granth Sahib in addition to its resistance to hegemonic structures also incorporates within it the *bhagat bani* prevalent across languages, castes and regions, that is, a 'pan-Indian' representation, thus rendering it both accessible and comprehensible to a wider audience (171–173).

Religions, like resistance movements, are immediately linked to two processes: one is the need to express oneself, a need born out of personal circumstances and search for solutions; and the other, to reach outward and assert. Even the idea of 'difference' is based on this, for difference resists anonymity and claims individuality/independence/identity. Sikhism proceeds along the same lines. Guru Arjan Dev specifically asserts, 'I do not keep Hindu fasts or [the Muslim fasts during] the month of Ramadan. I serve him, and him alone, who is my ultimate refuge.... We are neither Hindu nor Musalman.' There is also no unquestioning acceptance of other strands of thought. The hymns of the Gurus, very often, express disagreement with the views of the *bhagat*s (*bhakta*s) and define their world-view differently (178). Sikhism privileges the householder's life against asceticism, and a non-ritualistic inward meditation as against ritualistic observances and sacrifices.

In view of the continuously present resistance movements in Indian culture such as Buddhism, Jainism, Sufism, the Bhakti Movement and Sikhism, it is a mistake to construct Indian culture dominantly through Hindu culture, *shruti*, *smriti*s and reform movements, especially when we wish to trace the histories of resistance, the relationship of the individual—whether man or woman—to social institutions. By persistent marginalisation, we tend to construct monolithic notions of culture as well as of oppression and fall prey to the idea that passivity and renunciation are the major characteristics of our society where sacrificial ideals dominate.

The creator is *nirgun* and *sagun* at one and the same time, both transcendent and immanent. God is gender neutral and created both man and woman. If the world is *maya* (illusion), even the idea of impurity is a delusion. Guru Nanak rejects any blind following of social practices.

15

The Guru also does not uphold renunciation and asceticism: devotion is a separate thing altogether and can be practised/internalised by the householder. Both purity and impurity are of the mind. J.S. Grewal in his monograph on *Guru Nanak and Patriarchy*[8] points out that the idea of devotion to a personal god was common to Vaishnava *bhakti*, the Sant tradition and Sufism (16). The *bhakta* often adopted the female devotional voice.

The Upanisads have some rituals that go on to exclude women. The *smriti*s further stress this kind of exclusion. The exclusionary rituals are related to the female body, which because of its beauty is seductive as well as vulnerable; its flow of menstrual blood and the act of giving birth are seen as impure. Other practices piled themselves on this initial exclusion, which, it is obvious, is directed not only at the body, but becomes a base for other social and mental exclusions. It is a power strategy and is contrary to the belief that there is nothing pure or impure in itself and that all life has emanated from self-division and dismemberment. Altekar in *The Position of Women in Hindu Civilization* has discussed in detail how women's participation in Vedic sacrifice gradually declined and men began to substitute for women in these rituals (202). Additionally, the introduction of child marriage pushed them to the margins as an early marriage excluded them from access to education.[9]

India's past is also contained in another stream, outside the Vedas and the Sastras. This is the 'narrative' stream of practical advice imparted through fables and 'kathas'. *Tales from the Kathāsaritsāgara* credited to Somadeva, *Panchtantra*, the *Jataka Tales*, the medieval Jain stories and *Hitopedesha* are only some of them. They depict a variety of everyday situations and a wide range of human desires, emotions, deceptions and failures, raising questions related to the common man, moral values and social practices. Many of these include animal fables and this allows the narrator to reach the essence of human mind through an oblique narrative which is slightly distanced from human life and yet very close to it. Birds and animals also function as messengers and commentators.

16

Arshia Sattar in the Introduction to the 1994 translation of Somadeva's *Kathāsaritsāgara* observes that the tales are only marginally didactic. The work 'celebrates earthly life with all its joys and sorrows, its triumphs and defeats, its petty ambitions and noble aspirations' (xvi). Its slightly distanced from human life and yet very close to it. Its worldly, non-religious aspect also makes it much more accessible across gender, education and caste. In fact, the caste hierarchy is dismissed. Rather than reinforce 'a Brahminical aspect, such stories work to democratise the values of Hindu society by privileging a contingent social dynamic over an "ideal" one' (xxvii).

These narratives are populated by different kinds of characters, susceptible to all kinds of emotions and feelings—revealing the interconnectedness of life. These stories are never-ending ones. In fact, in order to add to the meaning or to explain a point they launch into another narrative, each expanding in turn to contain another. The segment is never fully self-contained. In both *Hitopedesha* and *Kathāsaritsāgara*, the continuity is maintained throughout as earlier births, forgotten lives or episodes and parental memories are remembered, retold, reenacted and a fresh inference drawn.

These narratives, even as they give examples of strong women—women capable of looking after themselves and at times their husband and families, enduring stress, resisting parental authority or reprimanding the husband, bringing a recalcitrant son to book and taking decisions—still uphold the ideal of the *pativrata* and the rewards and punishments are worked in accordance. A clear division between worldly life and heavenly life is impossible as curses and boons act as external agencies that push them into different worlds. What is remarkable is that even these external agencies stress the role of individual action and conduct, that is, they concede the role of individual choice and decision. Another factor worth noting is that aggrieved women—daughters, wives or mothers—also have the power of controlling other people's action through a curse or a boon. For Sati, the choice is between her loyalty to

17

her husband and to her father. At one level the question is with whom does she identify herself—father or husband? When her husband Śiva was neglected, Sati sacrificed her life in order to break connections with her father (Somadeva 2–3). When she is reborn as Parvati, Śiva accepts her proposal of marriage for his 'own benefit' (3).

In another cycle of stories beginning with the 'The City of Unchaste Women', Ratnadhipatti, the king, realises that none of his 80,000 wives is found to be chaste. When a servant woman, Silavati, is able to prove that she is chaste, the king expresses the wish to marry a woman of her family. He marries her sister Rajadatta, and leaving her all by herself, he comes back to attend to his kingly duties. On his return he finds her in another man's arms. As the story of the curse and its redemption is told, the moral that emerges stresses the self-generation of virtue: 'Thus it is true that a woman cannot be guarded by force in this world. But young women from good families are protected by their own virtue' (91).

In the stories collected in *The Forest of Thieves and the Magic Garden*, a collection of Jain medieval stories (edited by Phyllis Granoff), there is apparently no difference between the 'knowing' ability of men and women. Granoff, in his Introduction (1–20) to the collection, points out that the narrators of these stories belong to both the sexes. The folktale model is handy as a way of communication. At times, the wisdom and knowledge of women is greater than that of men as in the story of Kuberadatta and Kuberadattā, brother and sister, children of a courtesan, Kuberasena, who had got separated as children and, later, were married to each other. Realising the relationship, Kuberadattā becomes a nun. Her brother/husband finds his way to the courtesan Kuberasena, who also happens to be his mother. A child is born out of this union. In this very Oedipus-like story, it is the sister who is stronger than her brother and also wiser. She had perfected her knowledge to the extent that she now had the ability 'to know some things that were beyond the range of the senses' (Granoff 130). The agency of a woman is prioritised here. Kuberadattā assesses, decides and also acts.

Mohadatta's narrative progresses on similar lines with twins being separated at birth and getting married, and with the son committing patricide. The only way to do penance is to abandon everything and become a monk (Granoff 166). Human action is guided by *karma*, and the only way to conquer or destroy it is through conquering one's desire and by being able to resist the temptations of delusion. Knowledge is defined in an extensive sense—knowledge of the 'self', of the world, of nature, of duty and of relationships—the kind of perception that is inward directed and flows in the passage of time which moves from one life to another, one world to another and between past, present and future. Devotion to god and the Superior Being is often personified in the loved one—be it man or woman. Devotion in itself implies sacrifice and moving out of self-concern.

The story of Nala and Damayanti illustrates this mobility between different worlds in great detail. Damayanti acquires knowledge, becomes a 'pious lay Jain' (178) and wins her parents to the faith. Her *swayamvara* is remarkable for the degree of freedom she exercises in her choice. Instead of a trial of masculine strength and indulgence as in the case of Draupadi and Sītā, Damayanti assesses her prospective suitors with reference to their qualities of judgement and control. The king of Kasi is rejected because his people deceive others, the lord of Kumkana because his people have a reputation for being short-tempered and the list grows as her suitors are rejected on account of their age, location or some such thing, until she comes to Nala. They get married but their life is also subject to the vicissitudes of life, especially of royal life. Desire for extension of power is followed by wars, jealousies and rivalry, and one day Nala, like the Pandavas, gambles away his kingdom to his brother and along with it Damayanti and the rest of his harem. This condition of exile and loss of power is a recurring theme in several narratives including *Rāmāyana* and *Mahābhārata*. Their recurrence draws attention to their significance. The change of circumstances is a test of both adaptability and endurance, it is a test of human worth and a shifting out of worldly concerns to the forest or an ashram, a forced isolation which separates one from the other and draws upon inner energies.

When in the forest, Nala, in sheer desperation, decides to abandon her, unwilling to seek his father-in-law's help. But again, it is not an inconsiderate act; he keeps a watch over her throughout the night and leaves a message for her before leaving. Damayanti, he assures himself, will be protected by her own chastity (191), a conviction that displays an enormous amount of trust. But both before and after this abandonment by Nala, Damayanti displays supernatural power and authority. She is able to ward off wild men, dacoits and thieves, displays great fortitude and singleness of purpose (190–196) and devotes herself to severe penances. Asceticism, singleness of purpose, physical endurance and penance—all get interlinked in the purpose of strengthening human character. In the nineteenth-century novels of Bankim Chandra Chatterjee, *Debi Chaudhurani* and *Durgeshnandini*,[10] one sees the reenactment of such penances. Meditation confers power not only over oneself, but over the elements as well. As Damayanti experiences different kinds of adventures, trials and travels, Nala also has his own share to bear during the 12 years of exile and is turned into a hunchback. Thus shorn of outward beauty, his power can only emanate from his deeds. In the Jain version, the winning back of Nala by Damayanti from the hands of Death is not recounted but there is apparently no discrimination in the kind and degree of devotion or asceticism that is required of both men and women. It is 'virtue' in the sense of correctness and steadfastness that goes to generate power.

Another important issue is how does one 'know'? Knowledge in these stories is acquired through a number of means, some of which are: upbringing, education and training, devotion, penance, meditation and gifted knowledge—a carry-over from the previous birth. In addition to these, experience and the trials of human life are essential. One learns through experience, the knowledge of one's past sins/life. Knowledge, in these stories, is also acquired through supernatural power. Thus, while agency is not totally denied—for self-effort and direction are essential to achieve one's goals—it is also not vested entirely in the individual as external circumstances and agencies also play a role.

The recurrence of themes like reward and punishment, exile, curses, boons, penance and asceticism, continuation of *karma* across birth and death and self-generation of an 'other' power or energy go on to define the web of human life. The marginal hierarchy symbolised by the creation of the 'sexual' other from the male is rigidified only later into gender inequality as rituals begin to dominate meditation and as social institutions such as marriage and caste begin to acquire a stronger hold. There is a gap between the Upanisads, which advise restraint and spiritual life, and the epics and other religious narratives which depict a more equal, free and dialogic life, but the gap between the ideal person and the 'ideal' woman come into being as a result of the hardening of rituals which gradually went on closing options, choices and alternatives such as we find in the oral tradition. Women such as Draupadi are further trapped in clan histories of revenge and war.

They have been 'frozen' or turned static on account of a variety of reasons, some of which are ignorance, political goals, ideologies and power. The national movement, despite its liberating effect, was also a restrictive influence as it trapped women further in the images of 'custodians of culture', 'motherhood' and *Devi*. Indian feminisms are questioning and deconstructing these in myriad different ways—in their day-to-day practices, family relationships, transforming rituals and resisting other barriers imposed on them by decontextualised role models. All meaning is context sensitive, as A.K. Ramanujan has pointed out, and Indian cultural constructs are even more so, as they have been negotiated by external factors over a long period of time and fundamentalisms have often worked disguised as religious reform.

One concept which needs further consideration is *purusharth,* which is conceptualised as a framework for human goals. This is defined as a fourfold course of *dharma, arth, kama* and *moksha. Dharma* is the most complex of these and cannot be equated with merely duty or religion. It encompasses an ongoing negotiation between one's own intuition, sense of ethics and potential on the one hand, and on the other with the outside social world with its contrary demands. It also involves living constantly in two timescales—the immediate present where action has to take place and the long-term relationship with the self and one's conscience. Thus, it may cover divided loyalties, conflicting demands and choice between self-interest and self-sacrifice. Even this does not cover all meanings and aspects of *dharma*, but it will perhaps suffice as a working definition. *Arth* is the science of economics. Etymologically, one of the meanings of *arth* is also 'meaning' (inference). This relates the individual to employment, to economics and to the acts of production. *Kama*, which comes next, is desire inclusive of sexual desire, love, attraction, attachment and procreation. *Moksha*, the final goal, is working towards salvation. At one level, these also coincide with the four *ashrama*s: *brahmacharya*, a period of controlled sexuality or celibacy, education and training; *grahastha ashram*, the life of a householder which includes both *arth* and *kama* as well as a participation in social life; *sanyas*, which approximates renunciation, a shift in the social role and moving towards a more reflective and meditative life; and the last is *vanaprastha*—an ascetic's life in the forest based on detachment and withdrawal. Where and in what measure these *purusharatha*s and *ashrama*s are available to both the genders becomes a major question in itself. Theoretically, the *purushartha*s can be accessible to women. *Dharma* is more than necessary; a disproportionate emphasises on *stree-dharma* (a woman's duty) has gone on to lead to discrimination. But it is considered indispensable. *Moksha*, the final goal, is conceded in some religious constructs as traced in the foregoing analysis. But despite the contribution to economic productivity as well as to the act of procreation, women have been marginalised in both *arth* and *kama*. Similarly, of the four *ashrama*s, they as followers and conjuncts are largely confined to the role of a householder and even the initial phase of early educational training is adversely affected. We have several examples of educated women both in the Upanisads and the epics, but they can at best be treated as symbolic representations or exceptions. The difference between religious precepts and their practice is apparently grounded on biological difference, but the need to hold power is also a major reason for women's exclusion from knowledge, choice and freedom.

Most of the ancient texts—Upanisads, Vedas and the two epics *Mahābhārata* and *Rāmāyana*—are ascribed to an all-encompassing narrator, such as generic figures like Manu, Ved Vyas or Valmiki. Their compositions inscribe accounts already existent in the oral tradition. Several of them are in Sanskrit. They have also been composed by men of the upper castes—either brahmin or kshatriya—and are composite creations, even the more modern *Guru Granth Sahib*. As such, they can also be read as assertions of power and constructs which consolidate it. What then is of significance is the need to inquire whether there are dialogic patterns, juxtapositions of contrary behavioural code, exceptions to the rule and other alternative structures which may open out other codes of behaviour, and whether there is a questioning by disciples, listeners and characters or not. As several of them are in the form of dialogues or of subnarrative, multiple openings are embedded. Therein lies the importance of rereading and reinterpreting the past, and of rewritings, of which the epics have several; then there are commentaries and interpretations which explicate meanings variously.

Feminist thought is multilayered and works in a variety of ways. In the last two centuries, it has not been unidirectional; instead, it has (*a*) questioned practices and texts, (*b*) resisted hierarchy, (*c*) reinterpreted myths and tradition and (*d*) focused on the woman's body. But, admittedly, the journey to this phase itself has been a winding, meandering one.

The following chapters intend to look at the two epics and the variations in their retellings, and work with *Nātyaśastra* and Kālidāsa, the women *bhakta*s, the *Manusmriti* with its emphasis on closed space, the reform movements and the present reinterpretations of myths, deconstructing their meanings in order to trace the feminist tradition.

II

The Body and the Soul:
Epics—The Living Tradition

❧❧

One group of reality consists of the earth, the sky, the invisible, and the four directions. Another group consists of water, vegetation and herbs, the space, and the body. They are the material groups. The spiritual group of reality exists in the human body and its faculties: the eyes, the ears, the mind, the speech, and the touch. Although these three groups are distinct, they are intimately connected with each other and form an unbroken unity. Whatever is, is unity; the outer completing the inner, the inner completing the outer.

—*Taittiriya Upanisad* (Badrinath 43)

A fairly prevalent perception of women, across cultures, has framed them as matter and as such subordinate. Their physical beauty, role in the procreative process and use as objects of pleasure and sexual satisfaction has thrown their other faculties into the background. Cultural role models, as they have percolated down the ages, have emphasised this, thus depriving the women of agency. But the 'human' is a composite being. The word *adhyatma* relates to the 'human body and its attributes' (Badrinath 43). Chaturvedi Badrinath stresses that Patanjali's *Yoga-Sutra* demonstrates the innate unity of the body and the mind, of the physical and

24

the spiritual (44). Again, as we have seen in the creation myths, one with-out the other is incomplete. If the male is the vital breath and the female is the speech, apparently each is essential to the existence of the other. The *Samkhya* philosophy states this as *Purusa* and *Prakrti*. The soul is, in itself, without parts and qualities: it is consciousness (Dasgupta, 'The Samkhya').[1] The idea of self may be an abstract one in itself but it does act as a force in the cognitive process in the human mind. Feeling, as a category, comes to play a role in this. Dasgupta, elaborating upon this, states that thought and matter are the 'ultimate substances of which con-sciousness and gross matter are made up' (243).

In Indian philosophy, the origin of the world is explained through two different sets of ideas. One theory of creation is believed to be atomic—a coming together of two substances or atoms, and the other projects an evolutionary explanation that the transformation implies a change in the primal substances. *Prakrti* is thus perceived as the first cause of the phys-ical universe and is thus 'one and complex'.[2] It has its attributes which are reciprocal to each other. Thus, it is fluid and evolutionary in itself; it responds to outer reality/environment. It is 'specific to each individual and…accompanies him throughout his worldly existence or *samsara*' (Hiriyanna 44). But the element of awareness (sentience) is attributed to *purusa*, which is seen as the final cause.

This dualistic philosophy, which at heart is not descriptive of gender roles, has been taken as definitive of them in most cultures and has im-pacted knowledge systems.[3] The division between Mind and Matter has also been applied to cultures as is perceptible in imperial positions when conquered cultures have been labelled as feminine and non-modern (primitive). The logicality of the evolutionary theory cannot be refuted at one level—for, there is change even within an organic entity. But, at another level, its indispensability to sentience is proof enough of the sentience's dependence as matter for any kind of partial or full realisation. Thus, it is not the separateness but the interdependence which is important, and in a much greater degree for mind than for matter (which, in any case, is organically whole). Hiriyanna points out that *Prakrti* and *Purusa* virtually act as one. There is no 'spirit without a living organism or a living organism without spirit' (45). Experience is a product of the two coming together. *Tapas*, asceticism and penance, can be seen as attempts at acquiring the transcendent self, controlling bodily desires and impulses, and arriving at a stage of detachment from the external empirical world.[4]

Accessibility to any kind of knowledge is neither perfect nor complete for any one individual. The Samkhya system allots equal importance to both the subjective (response based on emotion and feeling) and the objective (the rational apprehension) and concludes that all knowledge, as we realise it, is personal and fragmentary. No one can speak for others at all times. This recognition explains inconsistencies of life and action and, if rightfully responded to, teaches us humility as well as tolerance (46–47). Even the recognition of a true ideal is based on the consciousness of this imperfection (48), which becomes the base for the questing/aspiring self. Patanjali thus projects a belief in the existence of God, a Supreme Being higher than *Purusa*. And this Being supplements His consciousness with compassion and mercy, 'He is a perfect Purusa and has always been so' (51).[5] And as such Patanjali recognises, in addition to *yoga*, the possibility of *bhakti* also as a means of liberation—a route which works in both a social as well as a personal way. The Bhakti Movement, which continued for several centuries and covered almost the whole country, crossing the barriers of religion, caste and gender is demonstrative of this belief.

It is obvious that to affiliate gender differences to the concepts of *Purusa* and *Prakrti* (or Male Principle as Mind and Female Principle as Matter) is an explanation of the creative process. But various theories regard it as equally obvious that these frameworks are not absolute and do not work as such, at least not in the case of an individual of any particular gender and also not in accordance with what the theories of the human mind illustrate. What should be attributed to hormones, genes and environment cannot be treated as an absolute difference in mental and creative faculties; biological roles do not necessarily stunt their social and intellectual roles.[6] Towards this end, that is, the reaching for the mind and soul (spirit) in women, the male perception of women needs to be explored and one is compelled to look at the epic tradition, which permeates Indian culture even across religious beliefs—so widespread is its influence.

The *Mahābhārata* and the *Rāmāyana*, the two major epic narratives of ancient India, continue to be a living tradition to this day. They have been retold, rewritten and reinterpreted, both in oral and written traditions as well as in the various performing arts. They, or their part narratives, have been made into films, TV serials, plays and dance forms. In some ways they are complementary to each other and are family sagas. They deal with valour, trial, rage, war (between good and evil) and revenge. The *Rāmāyana* is believed to be existent in oral tradition prior to the *Mahābhārata* but the *Mahābhārata*, as it contains the story of the *Rāmāyana* in an embryonic form, is likely to have been composed first. Their narrators are also participants in their narratives. Yet they are different from each other. The *Rāmāyana* upholds the ideals of harmony, obedience, hierarchy and virtue. It is a conformist narrative. Rāma, its protagonist, is *maryada purshottam* Rāma (the ideal man exemplary in his adherence to tradition). The *Mahābhārata* is about sibling (cousins) rivalry, power (division of the kingdom) and near-total annihilation. It is nonconformist in every way—marriage, customs and practices, births and the polyandrous marriage of Draupadi with the five Pandavas; it also does away with the relationship between sister-in-law and younger brother-in-law, such as the one we have in the Sītā–Lakshmana relationship in the *Rāmāyana*.

Both deal with periods of exile, but in the *Mahābhārata*, the exile periods are a recurrent feature, a constant threat and counterbalanced by the threat of recognition. The price of return to power is to be paid first through anonymity. The significance of this needs to be reviewed for its emphasis on humility and transformation. The *Mahābhārata* additionally does not project a single hero—instead we have a multiplicity of heroic figures from Bhishma down to Abhimanyu. If a specific agency has to be identified, it will have to be Krishna, who acts as Arjuna's charioteer in the eighteenth *adhaya*, an *adhaya* which has acquired an independent entity as the *Bhagavad Gita*. It contains the philosophy of life and a discourse on duty, *dharma* and detachment.

The *Rāmāyana* functions with polarities—Rāma and Rāvana. But the *Mahābhārata* works with multiplicities and a closer relationship between weakness, jealousy and evil, as also between virtue and vice. The two epics are a rich material for tragedy as one comes across difficult choices, moral dilemmas and death, but have not been (except in segments) treated as such, primarily because they both culminate in the victory of righteousness and individual human lives are a mere episode in the continuum of time.

The epics are defined as *itihasa puranas*, that is, historical narratives. But in the absence of detailed chronology and records, they do not fulfil the requirements of Western concepts of history. Romila Thapar suggests a definition of history 'as a consciousness of past events, which [*sic*] events are relevant to a particular society, seen in a chronological framework and expressed in a form which meets the need of that society' ('The Tradition of Historical Writing' 237). But she qualifies this by observing that this definition maybe the product of modern thinking. In ancient cultures, history is 'not a consciously thought-out philosophy of history but the result of an individual and rather analytical mind applying itself to historical narrative' (237–238). Thus, it should be possible to trace the historical past from existing literature as 'every society has a concept of its past and therefore no society can be called ahistorical' (238). Another scholar, K.S. Singh, commenting on the *Mahābhārata* writes, 'This may be bad history but it is good myth and therefore good anthropology. It reflects people's perception which is also a resource for history' (3).

Together, the two epics through the myths, role models and debates they have generated, constitute the collective unconscious of the Indian

28

people. Images drawn from them permeate written and oral cultures, political interpretations, man–woman relationships and perpetuate role models of every kind of human behaviour—father–son, husband–wife, brother–brother, mother–son—and project patterns of behaviour across caste, class and religious barriers. Gender construction in India has its roots in Sītā's *agnipariksha*, Draupadi's *chirharan* and Damayanti's adherence to the *pativrata* code. It is from this point of view that the two epics and their many variants and retellings acquire importance. What concerns us here is not only how women have been portrayed in them but also how men have been projected both in the patriarchal roles as well as in their masculinites.[7] Gender is constructed by an interplay of both femininity and masculinity. Further, the manner in which retellings have altered them is equally relevant, for the change marks either a resistance or a shift in the social perception of the role, or it may even signify a shift of focus because of social location (caste or class) of the narrator/narrators. Modern interpretations like Pratibha Ray's *Yajnaseni* and Chitra Banerjee Divakaruni's *The Palace of Illusions* or Saoli Mitra's play, 'Five Lords, Yet None a Protector', are attempts at psychoanalyses, social criticism and deconstruction. These readings—I extend the term to all three: retellings, variants and interpretations—are an additional evidence of their continued impact. It needs to be added that resistant interpretations acquire an ideological base or at least work from one. The narrative dramatic voice is that of a woman and as female psychologies are unveiled, both the victimisation of these women and their resistance, or strategic bypassing of male control, are also made visible. They are also simultaneously engaged in resisting contemporary stereotypical gender constructs which pervade not only the media but have also rooted themselves in language.[8]

As the epics are retained in popular memory in images, the details of cause and effect, the language, debate or argument are not necessarily recollected. Instead, the images are crystallised and reduplicated without all attendant subtleties. For the purposes of this analysis, my main

29

source is the Hindi translation of the *Mahābhārata* (abridged) published by Gita Press, Gorakhpur, which is an accepted standard translation.[9] And my focus will be only on a few episodes and relationships, which I consider relevant to my argument and which I propose to build upon at a later stage. Among these are the depiction of women's roles, their relationships with each other and with the men in their lives and Draupadi's *chirharan* and her desire for revenge.

The *Mahābhārata* states, right at the beginning, that it relates the ethics both for the *devta*s (heavenly beings) as well as for human beings, in some measure acknowledging the difference between the two. It is a realistic world that it seeks to represent where the heavenly intervention acts as an impelling force or a controlling one. The *Mahābhārata* is full of subnarratives and stories which take us in different directions. In fact, it is a compendium in its own right. Looked upon as the fifth Veda, it is said to include some part or the other of the other four Vedas and its intention (of its audience) does not discriminate on the basis of any division or exclusion. It does not profess either to be original or a single author composition. Ved Vyas, himself a delegated author, chooses Lord Ganesha as the scribe. Ganesha accepts on the condition that there should be no interruption in the telling, to which Vyas poses a counter condition that nothing should be recorded without understanding it. Consequently, by the time Lord Ganesha completes the process of 'understanding', Vyas is ready with the next shloka. I draw attention to this for, even in an ordinary process of 'understanding' any event, saying or narrative, there has to be a period of grasping it, opening it out and seeking its many layers. The *Mahābhārata* is no exception to this as it guides the reader from ignorance to knowledge (3). Right at the beginning, it lists its main concerns: the history of the Kaurava dynasty, Gandhari's adherence to *dharma*, Vidur's learning and wisdom, Kunti's endurance, Duryodhana's evil way and the truth of the Pandavas.

Working within this larger framework, the *Mahābhārata* does not hesitate to question and, if necessary, reverse every kind of behaviour—

even the caste of birth; the curses of the sages including those of the wronged animals; the relationship between guru and disciple, master and slave; marriage and kinship expectations. Self-interest, more often than not, dominates behaviour as well as choices and there is a fair amount of deception; thus, there is gap between appearance and reality. The central episode of the Pandavas losing their all in the dice game is a symbol of all human action. Even Nala loses all his possessions in gambling. Men gamble in order to seize an opportunity from the hands of the unknown and the unforeseeable future. The dice is also perceived as a symbol of the 'yuga'. Romila Thapar in her discussion of the various perceptions of time and the four yugas in Puranic cosmology writes that the four yugas *Krta-yuga*, *Treta-yuga*, *Dvapara-yuga* and *Kali-yuga* are called after the throw of the four-sided dice (*Time as a Metaphor* 17–18).[10]

In the subnarrative of Kaccha and Devayani, one perceives a split in Kaccha's behaviour. He is not hesitant to use deception with his guru in order to acquire the mantra of immortality, but when Devayani proposes marriage to him, he refers to the ethics of relationships stating that they are like brother and sister (38–39). Devayani's boldness should not cause any surprise to the reader. She openly proclaims her attachment for Kachha to her father and bases it on a recognition of sexuality. There is no gender difference in this. Men too proclaim their sexual demands. Yayati falls into this category at a later stage in the same story, which is worth analysing for the following reasons: it is a reflection on human nature irrespective of gender; it reveals the gap between one's beliefs in terms of received ideas and conduct and in terms of behaviour; caste and status differences are marked, but marriages between brahmins and kshatriyas are accepted in some cases; curses and boons fly from one to the other with great freedom; and attachment to someone or something in particular motivates action.

Devayani's second proposal is to Yayati, and she takes her former friend and now slave Sharmishta along with her. Sharmishta, on sensing his desire, expresses her own desire to Yayati, justifying it on the basis of her birth and father's position. When Yayati's extramarital relationship with Sharmishta is discovered by Devayani, Devayani's father curses him with loss of his youth for transgressing the prescribed ethical code but later adds that the curse can be passed on to some other willing recipient. Yayati, who has already failed in his duty to his wife and in the observation of the ethical tradition, is now tested for his own worth. Goaded by desire and self-concern, he also fails in his role of father when he passes on the curse to his young son, Pooru, whom he professes to love the most. The idea of masculinity, as it comes through here, is of failed men. Devayani's father Shukracharya is, despite his learning and scholarship and his brahmin origins, guilty of both attachment and anger. Similarly, Yayati is guilty of self-centred desire indifferent to all else. The women come out no better and their pursuit of desire is equally single-minded. They do not hesitate to break vows, employ trickery and boldly set out to fulfil their sexuality. True, they also use the men in their lives as, for instance, Devayani who pushes her father to punish Sharmishta and curse Yayati. But their consciousness of their body and bold sexuality also announce a rejection of the 'docile' model perpetuated through the concept of dependency.

Another alternative to Yayati's masculinity is the one presented through Pooru who transcends his present to accept his father's burden. When, and if, his youth is returned to him, it can never be the same. The intervening experience would have stolen away impulse, spontaneity and the joy of innocent experience. But beyond this he also projects a softer side of human nature. This becomes very apparent in some contemporary rewritings of this episode, especially in Girish Karnad's play *Yayati*. Karnad wrote this play in 1960, at the age of 22, when he was going through a personal conflict whether to follow his own aspirations or those of his parents.[11] But it is now (in 2008) that an English translation by the author himself, in a slightly revised version, has come out.[12] Aparna Bhargava Dharwadker comments on the women characters as a 'quartet of sentient, articulate and embittered women, all of whom are subject in varying degrees to the whims of men but succeed in subverting the male world through an assertion of their own rights and privileges',[13] an observation which immediately provides one interpretative frame. Yayati is placed at the centre of action but the thwarting or the fulfilment of his desires is controlled by Devayani and Sharmishta, and later by Pooru's young bride, Chitralekha. If we treat Yayati's mind as the stage, we can immediately discern the pulls in contrary directions—Devayani, who almost holds his affection to ransom (because of her father's knowledge of the Sanjeevni mantra); Sharmishta, whose desire rises up to engulf him (and who again is motivated by the ulterior purpose of avenging her own humiliation at Devayani's hands): and Chitralekha, who confronts him with the fact of her own unfulfilled desire if Pooru's youth is transferred to Yayati. These contestatory positions are brought about by a set of circumstances outside the epicentre of sexual desire. The Devayani–Sharmishta relationship is crucial to whatever happens in this centre: the reversal in their earlier relationship, the slave's role to which Sharmishta is bound, her attempt to cast doubt on Devayani's self-worth—these are events that disturb the present love relationships. Chitralekha pushes Yayati into recognising his guilt and the importance of time present. The flow of time is linear and there is no way one can dip back into the river at the point where one has abandoned it earlier. Time is impermanent. If the metaphor of the river is employed to understand the flow of time, then the water is never going to be the same. The Yayati episode, both in the *Mahābhārata* and in Karnad's play, is a debate not only about the nature of sexuality but also about the nature of time and the simultaneity of different concepts.

Swarnalata, Devayani's maid, is portrayed as a widow unaware of her husband's death. Thus, she still dresses like a married woman. She forms the third circle. She acts like Devayani's subconscious and warns her against Sharmishta, and is the immediate cause of the slanging match between the two erstwhile friends. And she is also the bearer of the news of Pooru's sacrifice to Chitra (Karnad, *Yayati* 55). Chitra's response to this piece of news is in direct contrast both to her earlier view of her husband and to her later exchange with her father-in-law. This moment comes in the middle. The news suddenly raises her husband's esteem in her eyes. She had been tentative and apprehensive. He, himself, thinks poorly of his attributes (35), especially when the dynasty's valour and heroism are thrust upon him. Even the archery contest organised for the arranged *swayamvara* had to be cancelled as Pooru had none of these skills. He realises that 'deep down', his young bride is disenchanted. So the next best thing is to perform his duty, produce a son and accept the life of a worm (37). When he takes on his father's curse, it is also an attempt to compensate for his lack of military valour and to provide an alternative model of courage, related more to the mind than the body.

Chitralekha, who feels uplifted and privileged that her husband has demonstrated this rare virtue of rising above the claims of the body, screams when she actually has to face the reality (57). The young girl who had accepted with grace his lack of archery skills and rejoiced in the glory of his sacrifice now finally turns back to her own sexuality and firmly tells her father-in-law, 'I will not let my husband step back into my bedroom unless he returns a young man' (61). No amount of argument about family reputation and the duty of a Bharata queen are of any help. Instead, she turns back on him and tells him, 'You hold forth on my wifely duties. What about your duty to your son? Did you think twice before foisting your troubles on a pliant son?' (62). Ironically enough, her wedding gifts have all been of broken relationships, death wish and old age. Pooru takes on the curse of old age, Devayani flings away her marriage necklace that Swarnalata handed over to her and Sharmishta leaves behind the vial of poison (63). The promises of the future do not beckon her forth for within half an hour, 'half a century has driven across my bed and crushed the dreams on my pillows' (65). She challenges her father-in-law to step into her husband's role. Chitralekha revolves the mirror around him, compelling him to see his own pretensions, uncontrolled sexuality and his failures as a father from several perspectives so as to bring home to him the two different moralities he adheres to—one for himself, the other for others.

We get a glimpse of the kind of life Pooru and Chitralekha may have been able to build for themselves. He is appreciative of her intelligence and her practical attitude. She is able to laugh at the pretensions of her family and accepts Pooru with all his ordinariness (37). And Chitralekha considers herself 'immensely fortunate' in having found such a husband. 'The last fifteen days have been among the happiest in my life. He is warm, considerate, and loving. I have grown up amidst kshatriya arrogance. His gentleness is like a waft of cool breeze' (64).[14]

Swarnalata's life offers an insight into male behaviour and the manner in which it often, in order to pacify its own sense of guilt, attempts to mould others and interferes with their relationship with their own self. Her husband, himself a libertine, is unable and unwilling to accept the idea that she has had no relationship with another man. His own sense of insecurity manifests itself in his nightly torments and finally, to put his mind at rest, she makes a false confession and he leaves her. Unable to accept her innocence, he is also unable to live with the idea of infidelity.

Karnad's play takes up the events of the Yayati narrative and unravels the complexity of the human mind and the unaccountable causes which come together to result in any act. Even as the difference in gender codes is delineated, the cracks and the duplicity involved in the act of coding are also brought to light. Each woman, as she finally loses, fights her battle on her own terms and forces others to recognise her strengths. The multiplicity of gender roles within a family also reflects upon the impossibility of viewing any role—as father, mother, husband, wife—in any singular, self-contained manner.

In 1961, Adya Rangacharya also wrote on the same theme but the focus in his play was on the Sanjeevni. Rangacharya's play, titled *Sanjivani*, pays more attention to the Kaccha episode and elaborates upon the contest of power between the gods and the *asura*s, the meaning and

35

significance of Sanjeevni and the manner in which it impacts relationships. Why, he asks, do the gods need the secret of Sanjeevni? Being
immortal themselves, they have no need for it. In the opening dialogue
between the sutradhara and the actor, mortality vis-à-vis immortality are
under discussion—'there's a world of difference between immortal God
and a mortal dramatist' (195). The gods desired to know the art of Sanjeevni, so that they 'could come to earth and live, die and live again, rather than be immortal and go on in the same old way' (197). Throughout
this play, as in Karnad's *Yayati*, the doubt is aired whether Devayani is
loved for herself or because she is her father's daughter. Devayani's offer of love is rejected by Kaccha as sinful and incestuous (he has always
considered her a sister). The ensuing debate on the nature of 'a woman's
mind' deserves a detailed consideration. Devayani tells Kaccha that Sanjeevni itself is woman and when he laughs in response, she says:

> When you understand you can go on laughing forever. It's because you don't un-
> derstand that you came here to learn, didn't you? You come from the gods, you'll
> never die, how can you imagine the power of giving birth? Giving a stray seed a
> place in the womb, infusing the inanimate thing with the energy to grow and when
> it ripens and falls, creating fresh life even out of that—so it goes on eternally.
> What can you know of a woman's mind which makes a destructible seed immortal?
> (Rangacharya 205)

The knowledge of Sanjeevni does not promise the efficacy of
that knowledge. Potency, in itself, does not ensure the power to create. Devayani tells him, 'I am a woman. I am Sanjivani—I can create
many from one. I am Sanjivani—I can make even the old grow. I am
Sanjivani—I can fill the inanimate with vitality' (207). Devayani, in
this passage, has almost transcended her subjective desire in order to
define womanhood. 'Birthing' is an aspect of creativity, available only
to women.[15] The gods seek Sanjeevani so that they can also have this
experience.

The absolute quality associated with morality is also rejected. Kaccha differentiates between the morality of gods and the morality of the *asura*s but Devayani laughs at the idea and retorts, 'The Asura's morality has women marrying for love; it's not like the God's morality—women dancing to seduce men' (207).

The Yayati–Sharmishta and the Yayati–Pooru episodes also find a place in this play as they had done in V.S. Khandekar's novel titled *Yayati* in 1959. Apparently there was something in the air which inspired and motivated writers to choose myths for articulating contemporary issues. Dharamvir Bharati wrote *Andha Yug* (1953), literally meaning 'The Blind Age', critiquing Nehruvian India and Dhritrashtra, the blind Kaurava king's figure in the background which allowed Draupadi's *chirharan* (disrobing) to take place resulting in the 18-day war. It seems that just as Ram Rajya was the utopia that Gandhi looked back to and which underlay the freedom struggle, post-independence India turned towards the more realistic *Mahābhārata* for both its moral and political debates, with *The Bhagavad Gita* forming a link between the pre-1947 period and the present. Iravati Karve put together a collection of essays in 1969 (a work spread over several years) on the *Mahābhārata*, titled *Yuganta: The End of an Epoch*. These essays both explain and reinterpret the epic, focusing on some its characters and their moral struggles. The *Mahābhārata* war is usually referred to as *dharma-yudh*, where it is not only a question of right and wrong in moral terms but also the concept of justice which is at stake. The difference between moral values and justice is marginal yet significant. Morality concerns the conscience of the doer and his perception of right; justice means going across to look at it from the others' point of view.[16] Morality is a larger term and can accommodate the idea of justice. Both of them are observable (and judgeable) by society at large.

The *Mahābhārata* has several sections[17] marking major shifts in time or events. (For references to the full text of the *Mahābhārata,* the Gita Press edition of Ved Vyas's *Mahābhārata*, which is recognised as a standard text, is being used. All references to the narrative of the *Mahābhārata* are to this text.) The Yayati episode features in Adi Parv (The Origin); in the very next section, Sabha Parv (The Assembly), the listener-reader is present at a scene where Duryodhana and Yudhishtra are engaged in playing a game of dice, which to begin with has mal-intentions at the back of it where the Kauravas are concerned. Duryodhana is assisted here by Shakuni, his maternal uncle. Yudhishtra, known for his sagacity, has this one major weakness, gambling, and is foolish enough to go on playing a losing game. Finally, he is egged into staking first his brothers, one by one, then himself and finally their common wife, Draupadi. This contest marks the differences in the two camps, the difference in their moral values, relationships and in the motives of enticing the Pandavas to play the game. As Yudhishtra goes on losing, he is persuaded to stake some other possession until, having lost his property and his brothers, he also stakes Draupadi and loses her. The Kaurava camp is delighted and instructs a messenger to summon Draupadi to the assembly hall. Draupadi's arguments in Vyas's *Mahābhārata* are a clear indication both of the analytical and intellectual skills of Draupadi in particular and women in general. In direct contrast to the image of an obedient, docile body or a silent sufferer, she brings her own perception to the attention of the assembly. Vidur is the only one to advise Duryodhana to desist from his course; no one else intervenes.

When a messenger is sent to fetch Draupadi, she refuses to oblige and instead wants him to find out from the Elders as to the direction of her future action. But Duryodhana and his followers, determined to humiliate her, insist that she be brought to the assembly. Dushashana, who is entrusted with the task, refuses to listen alike to Draupadi's pleas or explanations and drags her to the assembly by her hair. Her anger is thoroughly roused and she curses Dushashana with retribution for this act, an act which has brought dishonour to the very idea of kshatriyahood. Karna is also one of Duryodhana's supporters and instigators. In fact, these are the acts which later form the basic cause of the *dharma-yudh*.

In themselves, they are only a representation of a greater malaise—the decline in moral values—and go beyond the individual to embrace larger concepts, ideals and deviations from those ideals.

Draupadi's concern is not only for herself but also for the embarrassment her presence will cause to Dhritrashtra, Bhishma, Vidur, Dronacharya and others. One can well visualise the whole scene with the Kauravas almost forming a group by themselves, the five husbands watching in suppressed rage, the Elders silent, tentative and uncertain. Why did they—the Elders—not intervene? On the other hand, in Vyas's *Mahābhārata* (the Gita Press edition), there is one sentence to the effect that Dhritrashtra was delighted at the initial victories. Repeatedly he would inquire, 'Have we won?' (164). The forces of right and wrong, good and evil are not confronting each other as Rāma and Rāvana (in the *Rāmāyana*), but here in the palace assembly hall, right and wrong happen to be kin to each other, existing side by side in the same human mind.

With the forces loaded against her, Draupadi now confronts the assembly directly. Her moral reasoning and analytical skills are in evidence when she asks whether Yudhishtra had staked her subsequent to having lost himself—the implication being did he or did he not have any moral right over her after becoming a slave? But no one responds—none of the mighty men assembled there. It finally falls upon Vikaran to voice his views. He questions Yudhishtra's right to stake her as she is the wife of all the five brothers—he alone cannot take sole possession of her. Secondly, he had already lost his own self and thus had also lost the right to stake her. Moreover, he was tricked into it and did not do it willingly. Vikaran's views draw a mixed response and one of his critics is Karna who dissuades him from intervening. The silence of the Elders is indication enough of their acceptance of the situation as a valid one in accordance with their interpretation of *dharma*. Why should he alone raise his voice against his own elder brother? Karna brings forth another argument on the basis of a monogamous marriage—Draupadi being already married to five men is in the position of a whore and as such her honour and dignity have ceased to be debatable issues.

As the act of disrobing begins, Draupadi closes her eyes to the outside world and prays to Lord Krishna and then, as the story goes, the one-piece of cloth that she had wrapped around herself[18] keeps on extending and multiplying itself in myriad ways. Where words and moral reasoning had fallen on deaf ears, this miracle finally restores the balance. Bhimsen now takes a vow in public that he will avenge this humiliation. With the assembly in turmoil, the Elders in the face of this miracle are now compelled to take note and respond to Draupadi's unanswered query.

At this point, Vidur comes forth to request a response to the question and comments on the situation as one to be judged by intention: what is the intention of the doer? Further, he points out that those who, out of fear of displeasure, do not come out in the open and remain passive observers are also guilty of wrongdoing. The person who presides over such a happening bears at least half the guilt, the doer a quarter and the silent onlookers the remaining quarter. When there is a public denouncement of wrongdoing, the whole burden lies with the doer. Even Vidur's position evokes no response from the senior-most people present—the bearers of both political and moral authority—and directions are given for Draupadi to be sent to the living quarters. Trembling with modesty, Draupadi now takes up a more personal position. First, she challenges the whole notion of the protection that husbands are supposed to provide, then the law of kinship which bestows rights on her as a daughter-in-law and finally questions the concept of *rajdharma*, the role and duty of a king. The Kauravas have attacked the very basis of *sanatandharma*. Being the wedded wife of Yudhishtra, she promises to obey the judgement of the present assembly but demands that a reply be provided in clear-cut terms to whether she has been won at the stakes or not.

Finally, Bhishma takes it upon himself to respond and enters into a discourse on the complexities and subtleties of the concept of *dharma*. It is extremely intricate and has multiple layers and contexts and the best of scholars, at times, fail to unravel its meaning. When *adharma* overpowers it, *dharma* is subdued. He tells Draupadi that her question is very subtle and has deep layers, and no one would be able to provide a definite answer. There is a long discourse but the outcome is that the responsibility is thrust upon Yudhishtra, who has the reputation of being a wise person, a *dharmaraj*. But it cannot be sorted out so easily. The responsibility of condemning Yudhishtra's action in staking Draupadi is then placed on his younger brothers—her other four husbands. But they, bound by loyalty to their brother and the *dharma* towards this bond, remain silent. Bhima is the only one to raise his voice, but that too to threaten total annihilation, not to lay the blame at his brother's door. On seeing the increasing chaos, Vidur intervenes and condemns that act of gambling if it has been undertaken with mala fide intentions. By summoning Draupadi to the hall, they have violated the sanctity of private space. Vidur pronounces that Yudhishtra had no right to stake Draupadi after having lost himself, because a slave has no rights. Finally, pushed by Gandhari, Dhritrashtra pronounces Duryodhana guilty and asks Draupadi to ask for a boon. She seeks the liberation of Yudhishtra. When another boon is granted, she requests the release of her other four husbands along with their dignity, honour and armour. A third boon is also granted to her, but this she refuses on the grounds that greed does not behove anyone. Her whole behaviour succeeds in winning even Karna's admiration. And with this, she wins over one of her most vocal critics (Vyas, 'Sabha Parv').[19]

This episode forms the thematic centre of the epic. All that happens before is a preparation for the convergence of these set of circumstances and all that follows can locate its source in this. The Kauravas' behaviour is opposed to all accepted notions of kinship, loyalty as well as the code of kshatriya behaviour. They violate the established norms of morality and respectability, erase the difference between public and private space and even the behavioural code of masculinity as it is perceived. The Pandavas, even as they uphold honour and loyalty, lose in the conflict between duty to their wife and duty to their brother. They too violate the code of masculine behaviour and the duty of protecting their womankind. The Elders all fail with the sole exception of Vidur. Bhishma's intervention can best be seen as an act of diplomacy. In this war between right and wrong, good and evil, the battle is fought single-handedly by a woman who with the weight of one question shakes the foundations of male supremacy and the superior reason flaunted as its base.

Right in the *Mahābhārata*, written so many hundreds of year ago, we have a woman's resistance based upon a query subtle and multipronged to defy all conventions. The code of feminine behaviour is not transgressed, but is opened out in several ways. She establishes her right to think for herself as well as her right to her body. Bringing into the public the debate about polyandry and a single husband, she compels both admiration and acceptance for the deviation from the norm and is praised as a daughter-in-law of the family. She is able to reach the conscience of Gandhari who, in the end, is the motivating factor behind Dhritrashtra's final pronouncement. True to her duties, Draupadi does not hesitate to address Krishna directly, bypassing her husbands, who, in any case, have failed to protect her. She redefines the concept of *pativrata*.

Draupadi is worshipped along with the other goddesses, yet 'no woman consciously would like to emulate Draupadi in real life' (Sundari 254). The rejected wife Sītā is accepted, but not Draupadi. Quoting from the ritual priest's blessings at a wedding, Usha Sundari points out that the blessing '*Jatha Nalasya Damayanti, Jatha Ravanasya Mandodari, Ramaysa Sītā*' does not include Draupadi's name (254). Is it because she is not an ideal but very real? I would imagine that the failure to include Draupadi is a linguistic and a numerical failure. The male mind has not been able to devise a way of referring to Draupadi and the five Pandavas as a couple. But we proceed with Usha Sundari's concerns, which are more specifically focused on the female mind, and explore why Draupadi is not accepted by Indian women as a full expression of femininity. Towards this end, she analyses Draupadi as a woman in psycho-social terms of the several questions she raises and discusses. Commenting upon her accomplishments, the auspiciousness associated with her and her polyandrous marriage, Usha Sundari comments in detail on her sexuality and spirituality. Unlike Sītā, she is not monodimensional and she is unwilling to compromise at a spiritual level: 'no passive acceptance, no psychic withdrawal, no tame surrender at the fact of defeat' (257). Perhaps the richness and multiplicity of her character cannot be cut down to the cardboard idea of feminine grace and duty. A couple of things which further need to be stressed, and have not been brought out in that measure in any analysis of Draupadi's character, are: her 'wifely' role is prioritised over her motherhood; she has the freedom and the independence to have an emotional relationship with Krishna—a relationship not sexual or physical, but falling in the definition of *sakha*, a friend. Brought up in a patriarchal structure, women become prisoners of their environs. But she has put forward the difficult combination of 'to obey and yet not to yield'. Her wifely duties also are not merely confined to the body. She is the confidante, trusted companion and equal of her husbands. Additionally, she enjoys a position of respect in her father's family and can depend upon them when in need—something that women are ordinarily dissuaded from doing (P. Ray).

In her novel *Yajnaseni* (1995), Pratibha Ray gives us a version of Draupadi's life in a first person narration where the emphasis is not only on the external events but also on her own emotional conflicts and unfulfilled desires. Half in love with Krishna, she is persuaded to marry Arjuna who, in obedience to his mother's wishes, has to share her with his four brothers. Once a code of conduct is established that no other brother should interrupt the personal space of the couple when they are together, even ordinary life is disrupted and it happens that Arjuna becomes a violator of this rule. Thus, he has to forego his year of life with her. Chance intervenes time and again, and Draupadi's love remains unfulfilled. If on one hand, there is this fragmented existence divided among the five husbands, on the other is the 'wholeness' with which she is to be absorbed

43

in the life of the one who is currently in residence. These are facts given in the *Mahābhārata* and prioritise the male approach. Pratibha Ray takes up these facts and explores the psychological depths of Draupadi's life.

The novel begins with the end and the very first sentence states a closure, 'Finis'. But does anything really end? The war is over. The *Dvapara-yuga* is about to end and the *Kali-yuga* to begin. And here is Draupadi, all alone, writing a letter to Krishna. And her story begins. A sad story with its tragic ending, mortal and human, despite the fact that Draupadi is born out of a sacrificial fire.

Draupadi's brother is also born out of the same fire. Right from birth, she is destined to avenge her father's insult; the *chirharan* becomes the climatic scene for this when the two forces of good and evil are aligned against each other and a scene in which Draupadi transforms her passive role into an active one through her open resistance to injustice and ignition of passions. Ray, in the initial chapters, concentrates on Draupadi's romantic interests and constant reminders to herself that she is not going to passively accept whatever is handed over, thinking:

> I was going to be the weapon for preserving dharma on this earth and destroying the wicked.... Should only woman be forced to be the medium for preserving dharma and annihilating evil throughout the ages? Is it the woman who is the cause of creation and destruction? Sītā had to become the medium for the destruction of Lanka and the establishment of Ram's rule. For this, she had to discard all the joys of her life and become a forest-dweller. Then, Ravan's lust imprisoned her in the Ashok forest, insulted her, tormented her. Finally, dharma was established on earth. The intention behind Lord Ram's birth was fulfilled. But ultimately what did Sītā get? The sentence of exile from Ram! Public test of her chastity! (8)

But even as she prays for strength to endure her destiny, she frets at the edges. All along she models herself after Sītā, but also resists the image as being one too far above her (36). She tries to imagine how Sītā would have acted in matters of choice:

44

What would *sati* Sītā have done if she had found herself in such a situation? Perhaps she would have sought refuge in Mother Earth saying, 'Mother Earth, Giving me shelter in your lap, remove my shame.' But I was not patient, all-suffering like Sītā. If necessary, I could rebel, I could even take revenge. (63)

And accepting five husbands instead of one is in itself a deviation from the norm, even as it is a compliance with Kunti's wishes and her own pre-ordained destiny. Draupadi, constantly allowing Sītā and her experience to be her own shadow existence, considers her own problem as a challenge to the entire race of women—a challenge to the purity of her character:

If a woman confined to the inner chambers, having no opportunity to see the face of a man other than her husband, was faithful, some possibility of her chastity being in doubt remained. But even after having married many men if she could remain faithful to them then she could be called *sati*. Perhaps that was why, despite having more than one husband, Tara and Mandodari were still *satis* who were saluted at every dawn. Urmila led the life of a prisoner for fourteen years in the inner apartments waiting for her husband. Yet, Ayodha city did not resound with shouts of praise hailing *sati* Urmila. (93)

Draupadi questions past examples and probes the mind of the common man. She lets her imagination run wild. Suppose there was a queen with a thousand kings who would keep on waiting for her to visit them! She thinks of topsy-turvy situations and asks, 'Why don't the scriptures speak of chaste men and unchaste men?.... [H]ave the scriptures prescribed lists of sins only for the women?' (94)

As she waits for the *swayamvara* to take place, two things happen. One, Karna is humiliated in public and forbidden from entering the contest. Two, the Pandavas, more specifically Arjuna, are nowhere in sight. They are supposed to have perished in a fire. Throughout this process, hoping against hope for Arjuna to appear, she mentally resists the idea of

45

marrying anyone else. She even asks her brother whether the proceedings can be stopped (33) and contemplates resistance. She is conscious of her romantic and sexual desire. Each of the five has different expectations from her and each one hinges onto a particular trait in her character. Homilies are delivered by both Yudhishtra and Bhim. Yudhishtra is more concerned with the difficulties of her role in view of the fact that husbands are possessive, and *Bhima* with his own self, his many hungers and his short temper and the great power of tolerance that women need to have (75).

In the assembly, when the game is lost and along with it Draupadi, Ray takes up in detail Draupadi's innermost reactions of anger and frustration. There is a sense of being vulnerable; will her husbands tolerate this? Is a woman a man's moveable or unmoveable property? (234–235) Shame, grief, fear and hatred jostle in her thoughts, but picking up courage she has the audacity to demand an explanation. For once a woman standing both inside and outside the masculine world frames it with all its limitations.

There are other reinterpretations of Draupadi's character but none more radical than Mahasweta Devi's short story, 'Draupadi', which takes up only the episode of *chirharan*, sees it for what it is—literally a rape—and shifts it to the contemporary context of police atrocities. The tribal woman Dopdi Mejhen is captured. She and her husband are santhal tribals and part of the Naxalite agitation for social and economic equality. Now widowed, she is captured while on one of her missions, gang-raped throughout the night and brought before the police officer. It is hoped she will now be more cooperative and reveal the names of her comrades. A number of other issues are present in the story but what concerns us here is her total reversal of the disrobing motif. She refuses to be robed and flaunts her naked body for men to be ashamed of themselves. Like Draupadi of the *Mahābhārata*, she uses her mind and body both as instruments of challenge and of critiquing the patriarchal, hegemonic system of values which manifests itself in many ways. Her resistance is through nakedness. 'Draupadi stands before him, naked. Thigh and pubic hair matted with dry blood. Two breasts two wounds.' She mocks him and shakes with an 'indomitable laughter'. Her lips bleed as she begins laughing, 'Draupadi wipes the blood on her palm and says in a voice that is as terrifying, sky splitting and sharp as her ululation. What's the use of clothes? You can strip me, but how can you clothe me again? Are you a man?' (M. Devi, 'Draupadi' 108–109).[20]

The other Indian epic is the *Rāmāyana*, the narrative of which is said to precede the events of the *Mahābhārata*, but the Valmiki version of which, believed to be the first scripted one, was written later than the *Mahābhārata*. Being less bold, less complex and less transgressive, it has been internalised in greater measure. Yet even within these normative boundaries, women succeed in voicing their questionings. Though both the epics have been retold (retelling is different from reinterpretation in the contemporary context), primarily to cater to regional, historical and religious demands, I'll move across Valmiki's, Tulsidas's, Kamban's and also the Jain *Rāmāyana*, which goes under the name of *Sri Padma Purana*, for purposes of illustration.

Mythology and myths have always been a good source for narratives—both fictional and filmic. It is very likely that more films have been made on the *Rāmāyana* and its main narrative of Rāma's life, his exile, the war with Lanka, Sītā's trial by fire and the twin sons challenging their father, than on any other subject. But, if we take the subnarratives, *Mahābhārata* has fared equally well with Yayati, Nal–Damayanti and Lord Krishna lending themselves to filmic productions. The annual region-wise and locality-wise stagings of the Ramlila have added another dimension as have Carnatic music and South Indian dance forms. Kathakali uses the *Mahābhārata* freely for its narratives. The history of performing arts is dotted with different representations either of the main or of the sub-narratives. The variations are regional as well as dependent on class and economic status. The magnitude of the infiltration of the epics into Indian culture, irrespective of religious beliefs and other questioning or alternative traditions like Buddhism, Jainism and Islam notwithstanding, becomes clear once we look at the history of Indian cinema. I consider it important because it is an evidence of the continuity of the oral tradition and accessible alike to the educated and the uneducated, literate and illiterate, young and old, rich and poor. For women, otherwise confined to orthodoxy, mythological cinema becomes a substitute for pilgrimage. Let me list a few titles related to the *Mahābhārata* along with the language in which the film was made: *Mahābhārata* in Sanskrit 1920, Hindi 1965, Tamil 1936 and Bengali 1994; TV Serial 1988–1990. *Nala–Damayanti*, based on a substory from the *Mahābhārata*—Bengali 1970 and 1993, Sanskrit 1920 and 1927, Oriya 1985, Tamil 1935 and 1957, Gujarati 1982, Kannada/Telugu 1957 and Hindi 1945. The story of *Yayati* was filmed in Sanskrit in 1923 and in Tamil in 1938.

The *Rāmāyana* list is much longer. *Ramrajya* was made in Sanskrit in 1926; and in Hindi in 1943 and again in 1967 and 1973. *Rāmāyana* was made in Hindi in 1933, in Sanskrit in 1922 and in Hindi again in 1934, Haryanvi 1985, Oriya and Bengali 1980, Gujarati 1981 and the TV serial came in 1987–1988. *Bharat Milap*, the narrative of the meeting of two brothers, was first made in 1942 in Hindi and again in 1965; *Luva Kuśa*, centrestaging the twin sons of Rāma and Sītā, was made in Sanskrit in 1919, Hindi 1951, 1967 and again in 1971, Bengali 1966, Gujarati 1978, Tamil 1934 and again in 1963. *Ram Navami*, celebrating the birth of Rāma, in 1956, *Sītā Shuddhi* (the purification of Sītā) in Sanskrit in 1925, *Ram Vanvas* (the exile of Ram) in Sanskrit in 1918 and *Ram Vivah* (Ram's marriage) in Hindi in 1949. Films have also been made on the monkey god Hanuman who brought his army to fight the war with Lanka and acted as a messenger to Sītā. *Rambhakt Hanuman* was made in 1969 and *Mahabali Hanuman* in 1980.[21] It should be noted that each of these films has been made by a different director and the narratives have individual variations, but they go on to establish both the widespread and the multilingual nature of the proliferation of these narratives and point towards the indispensability of considering them.

The oral tradition does simplify at times, and encourages intra/extrap-olation at others. In this epic of good versus evil, Sītā gets much more space than Draupadi does in the *Mahābhārata*, and character is much more important than incident. In the *Mahābhārata*, events compel the characters to remould themselves as desires clash with the compulsions of family and Mother Right. In contrast, the incidents in the *Rāmāyana* test the strength of the character. They do not necessarily mould it or re-shape it; the value is fully established: the question is will they or won't they come unscathed out of it. In the *Mahābhārata* the questions are: how will they react? Will they rebel or submit?

In Sītā's story, the events, which are of significance from a woman's perspective are Sītā's birth, which comes about not through any human agency but through a natural phenomenon of being born from a furrow in a field; her marriage based on a trial of strength of the suitor (or a super-natural power); her accompanying her husband into exile and thus defin-ing a woman's duty towards her husband along those lines; her abduc-tion; protection of her chastity during her captivity; the trial by fire; her banishment to the *ashrama*; birth of her twins; and finally her preference to die rather than unite with her husband. These events move from birth to death, through wifehood and motherhood, separation and estrange-ment. These events form the basis not only of her character but also of that of her husband. They are the hinges on which the narrative of the *Rāmāyana* turns itself. The different retellings, versions and question-ings also rest upon these as they are contextualised differently according to the demands and pressures of the changing social conditions.

In Valmiki's *Rāmāyana*, Rāma is not aware of his godhood and nobody treats him like an avatar. He is one amongst us. The whole narrative is thus about the moulding and strengthening of his character values: of adhering to his word and of being responsive to his father's dilemma and to the criti-cism of his people; in fact, his behaviour is governed by how others evalu-ate him. There is a constant struggle between desire and duty and as such there is a constant striving to underplay emotion and highlight the claims of duty. The contest is often between two sets of values, both equally justifiable, but each motivated by different concerns. When one comes to think of it, there is no category which has absolute value in itself: neither good nor evil, neither duty nor desire. They intermix and there is a vacillation from one to the other, defined by their immediate context.

In the different retellings, it is the perspective that matters: how are the main events of the narrative viewed, and the manner in which they are brought about. Every retelling arranges them differently and thus frames the events in line with the particular narrator's perspective. From this point of view, Kamban's *Rāmāyana* moves from the divinisation of Rāma, so evident in Valmiki's version, towards a humanisation of Rāma. It is obvious that the relationship between a man and a woman and the trials of a human being are bound to be different from the relationship between the divine and the human. Rāma's character, in its godhood, is definitely seen as deficient in a human relationship. Thus, as every event pulls him a little further into the human world, love, compassion and conflict find their place in his heart. Concepts like truth and duty move away from being seen as absolute categories and instead become uncertain, ambiguous and fluctuating ones. The Jain *Rāmāyana, Shri Padma Purana*, goes even further as it alters several relationships and goes on to introduce Jain priests, missionaries and saviours as agents of action, thus transforming both the nature of the major characters and the value structure projected in the epic.

Arshia Sattar in her 'Introduction' to the Valmiki *Rāmāyana* writes, 'The question that looms large over the *Rāmāyana* is that of the relationship between myth and history, i.e., is the *Rāmāyana* a "true" story?' She is of the view that one need not be trapped into considering it as 'history', but it is very likely to be based on a real happening, which has now outgrown

any meaningful dependence on the 'reality' that spawned it. What we have now is a remarkable tale that captures the imagination of all kinds of people, not just

because it is true, but because of the way it is told, because of the adventure and
magic it contains, because the way it takes a known and familiar reality and enlarges it to dimensions that are unknown and unfamiliar. (lvii–lviii)

Further, she adds that such an epic ought not to be literalised as 'The
Rāmāyana does not derive its meaning from a sacred geography or history: rather, it draws its significance from what it can tell us about ourselves, our decisions and the way we choose to live our lives' (lviii).[22]

In 1992, Paula Richman edited a collection of essays on the *Rāmāyana*,
titling the collection *Many Rāmāyanas: The Diversity of a Narrative
Tradition in South Asia*. The making of this volume began with A.K.
Ramanujan's essay, 'Three Hundred *Rāmāyanas*', which in Richman's
words challenges us to look at the *Rāmāyana* tradition in a new way
(xi).[23] Ramanujan places five different narratives side by side—classic
as well as folk—in order to demonstrate both the plurality of the narrative and the multiplicity of interpretations. In fact, all the retellings base
themselves on the same *katha* and work out its discourse in different
ways. Sexuality—expressed or repressed—is in itself an independent
discourse that determines both good and evil. What is virtue? Is purity—
'being untouched'—virtue, or is chastity, expressed through loyalty to
one's sexual partner, virtue? If loyalty is the test, then a modern mind
may well argue 'how come all the kings have so many wives? Not only
Daśaratha, but each one of the Pandavas and a host of other kings in the
subnarratives?' Does virtue then come to rest in the control of desire
vis-à-vis temptation? One would be led to take the argument further and
ask whether desire for the right partner is also virtuous or does it fall outside it? These are my questions, not Ramanujan's, but Ramanujan gives
two different passages to demonstrate the difference between Valmiki's
and Kamban's tellings. He chooses the Ahalya episode, an episode about
Indra's seduction of Ahalya while Gautama, her husband, was away. In
Valmiki's version, Ahalya is aware that it is Indra (though he has taken
on the likeness of Gautama), but she consents because of her curiosity to

51

know about the king of gods.[24] Returning, Gautama curses them both, emasculating one and condemning the other to deprivation to await Rāma's birth and arrival in order to restore her to purity.

Kamban, on the other hand, begins with Rāma's arrival in the abandoned ashram and inquiring about the origin of the black rock, when he is briefed about the Indra–Ahalya affair and their consequent punishment. By his very arrival, Ahalya is restored to her original form and beauty. In Kamban's version of the Ahalya story, Indra is the one tempted by his own desire and she learns about his identity only when he is ravishing her. The knowledge doesn't help her to halt the happenings at this point. The two tellings raise several questions which Ramanujan proceeds to discuss, but my question is not related to this specific instance but to an overall view of the nature of virtue, its relation to sexuality and the complex concept of *dharma* as it encroaches on every aspect of human behaviour and worldly desire. The overpowering presence of abstinence and deprivation constantly undermine desire. The 'self' is portrayed as an eminently controlled body.

The births of both Sītā and Draupadi are minus the human agency in the classical versions, and where it is not, it is still miraculous in some measure and sidelines the sexual process and the claims of paternity and maternity. Even Rāma's birth (and that of his three brothers), as well as the birth of the Kauravas and the Pandavas, (in the *Mahābhārata*) work outside the norms and concepts of normalcy. The infertility of Daśaratha's household is cured by a heavenly dose of divine *payasam* (rice and milk pudding) in Valmiki's version and a sweet *laddoo* in some others. The mass of flesh that Gandhari gives birth to dismembers itself into a hundred sons, while Kunti's sons are born as a result of a boon she has received and which she shares with her co-wife Madri. Sītā is born out of a furrow in a field and adopted by King Janaka; Draupadi is born out of fire *agni*, and is adopted by Draupad. Draupadi also has a twin brother. Sītā's birth is described in Valmiki's *Rāmāyana* through Janaka's narration,

52

Once when I was ploughing the sacrificial grounds in order to clean them up, the blade of my plough turned up a little girl.... I announced that since the child was not born from a human womb, she would be won in marriage only after a test of strength. (Valmiki 79)

Valmiki connects the two—her birth and her marriage—and thus weaves a web of destiny around her. But there are other accounts of Sītā's birth. Ramanujan refers to a South Indian folk *Rāmāyana* and in this particular version Sītā is Rāvana's daughter born out of him through a sneeze. Rāvana becomes pregnant when he cheats on his wife Mandodari and breaks his promise to a yogi. As a punishment, he becomes pregnant, in which one day is equivalent to a month and Sītā is born on the ninth day. He puts her in a box and leaves her in Janaka's field (Ramanujan, 'Three Hundred *Rāmāyanas*' 35–36). In some versions, there is the presence of the Oedipus myth; Sītā is given away because it has been predicted that Rāvana will be killed by his own daughter.[25]

The fact of birth through non-human agencies acquires significance on several counts. One, the human male is rendered dispensable and paternity is acquired through adopting a child or nurturing a child born of another. Two, as a consequence, as in the case of Kunti, motherhood is especially privileged.[26] Additionally, a superhuman intervention is also traceable in the cases of Sītā and Draupadi, bringing in the elements of nature: earth in one case and fire in the other as agencies of creation, a fact that would compel us at some later stage to debate the equation of woman with nature. In Sītā's case, it also draws our attention to the manner of the final termination of her mortal life by praying to Mother Earth to accept her back. The non-human births simultaneously achieve several things: the uncontrollable desire for progeny, the generosity and compassion with which another man or woman's child is adopted and nurtured and the manner in which relationships not of the blood can expand to become such. They also comment upon the nature of kinship and family, while sidestepping both 'purity' and lineage.

Valmiki does not romanticise Rāma's test of strength for winning Sītā's hand, but Kamban goes ahead to use it for romantic purposes (like Vyas does in the case of Draupadi). In Book I, dealing with childhood, Kamban describes the journey towards Mithila, and in a scene strongly reminiscent of Duhsanta's first sight of Śakuntalā in the *Mahābhārata* and subsequently in Kālidāsa's *Abhijnanasakuntalam*, he describes the scene: 'Her eyes met Rāma's and, stunned, they feasted upon each other. Their souls no longer in their possession became one' (Kamban 27). Sītā's beauty is described, followed by her reflections on the strangeness of her own behaviour. But it is Rāma's egoistic belief in his own steadfast virtue that is of importance. He thinks to himself, 'Since my mind can never tread a path that is not right, there is no need for further proof that the jeweled maiden, so ravishing, is a girl unwed' (Kamban 28). This self-confidence is strangely at odds with his later doubts regarding her behaviour.

It is important to ask the question: why are the courtship scenes romanticised in Kamban, and in Vyas's *Mahābhārata* and Kālidāsa's 'Abhijnānāśakuntalam'? It is equally important to understand the kind of spell romanticism casts on the woman, extracting willing surrender from her, prioritising desire over discrimination. Draupadi is nervous whether the brahmin young man (because Arjuna was disguised as a brahmin) would be considered an eligible suitor while Śakuntalā is placed within idyllic conditions for the law of attraction to work and Rāma's physical strength lays the basis of attraction.

Romance plays a dominant role in a majority of the subnarratives and forms the basis of subsequent marital devotion. It is obvious that physical attraction, love-making and sexual desire play an important role in husband–wife relationships. Philip Lutgendorf, in his article 'The Secret Life of Ramchandra of Ayodhya', elaborates upon this elements and points out that Ram *rasik*s (one who savours *ras*; *rasa* in itself defines aesthetic enjoyment in *Nātyaśastra*) selected some idyllic period in the hero's life and used it in a performative mode. Ram *rasik*s 'focused on a single phase of their Lord's story—the idyllic period when the newly married Rāma and Sītā…enjoyed each other's company amidst the palatial comforts of Ayodha.' Lutgendorf refers to the devotee's belief that the Lord had two *lilas*—one earthly and the other transcendental. Beyond the conventional events, there is a secret lila 'in which the quality of erotic attractiveness or *madhurja* predominates and in which Ram expresses his ultimate reality' (220).[27] Romance and eroticism are natural physical desires even as they help the patriarchal construction of power, control and supremacy, especially through the different kinds of morality being applied to men and women as well as to the public domain of the moral and immoral. The surfacing of self-interest and rationality shifts the romantic base.

The concept of *pativrata*—the duty-conscious wife devoted in mind and in body to her husband, one who follows a single-track thought procedure which requires a total subjugation of the self—is related both to this romantic ideal and its moral evaluation; it demands controlled desire channelised into one direction. Sītā's being a *pativrata* is first defined by her insistence upon following Rāma into his exile. Her *stree-dharma* (a wife's duty) is strangely in contrast with Urmila's, Lakshmana's wife, who is compelled to stay home as a caretaker of her mothers-in-law. The events that push Rāma into exile are also initiated by women, a fact that needs to be noted. Kaikeyi is advised by her hunchbacked maid Manthara to employ all her womanly wiles to push her son Bharata's claims forward for the kingship. In fact, the Daśaratha–Kaikeyi relationship is in direct contrast to the Rāma–Sītā relationship. Critics have not paid sufficient attention to this. Daśaratha's case is one in which there is a reversal of control. Kaikeyi has managed to guide the relationship and, at the moment, has an upper hand.

Valmiki's Daśaratha is not above using subterfuge. He tells his son,

> I have a strong feeling that I should install you as my heir while your brother Bharata is away from the city. He is an honourable and righteous man, devoted to his elders and slow to anger, but I know the human mind is fickle. (Valmiki 107)

Why does he do this? Premonition? Contrast between the son who is human and the possible godhood of his son Rāma? Why should Bharata object to Rāma? After all, he is the eldest. Manthara even dares to call Daśaratha a snake and a devious man (Valmiki 111). In fact, Kaikeyi defends her husband's choice of Rāma as the future king. She is initially not possessed by any sense of anger or dismay until Manthara, an external agency through which evil enters the mind, incites her to rebellion. She advises Kaikeyi to go into a darkened room, put on soiled clothes and refuse to speak to the king or even look at him (114).[28] I refer to this episode for several reasons: one, it shows Kaikeyi, as not having any objection in the beginning to Rāma being crowned king; two, the stratagem she follows has been absorbed in the idiom of many Indian languages and does not require any further explanation; three, it is the kind of attitude born out of a certain degree of helplessness and defines a weaker power based on an exploitative tendency centred on sexual desire; four, it contrasts with other forms of resistance which may be more open and transparent. Further, this qualifies as *triya jaal*, that is, womanly wiles. But its significance lies in the fact that 'protest' can take many forms. This is one kind. Gandhari's in the *Mahābhārata*, when she blindfolds her eyes on having been deceived into marrying a blind husband, is another. Instead of accepting her fate and being a helpmate to her husband, she blindfolds herself and shuts out the world. Her action has been interpreted conventionally as a wifely duty but, in fact it is a resentment against the deception underlying her marriage. Both these women pay a heavy price for their resistance. There are several other examples both in the *Mahābhārata* and *Rāmāyana*, when women are made to pay heavily for their acts of protest and questioning, for the audacity to think of themselves as human beings.[29]

But the Kaikeyi episode is important for another reason altogether. It highlights the mother–son relationship and a woman's concern for her progeny—a concern which recoils in most cases. Kaikeyi, by insisting on Bharata's right to kingship, manages only to alienate him and invite his wrath upon her head. She appears 'unwomanly'. Similarly, in the *Mahābhārata*, when King Santanu wishes to marry the fisherman's daughter, the one condition is that her son would inherit the kingdom. In order to fulfil this, Bhishma, the son of his union with Ganga, takes the vow of celibacy, so that he has no progeny and no counter claimants to his father's throne come into being. Satyawati also pays a heavy price and the line of inheritance is permanently flawed. The concern with progeny is also a strategy to gain power through proxy control. It further explains the disproportionate importance given to motherhood, primarily because it becomes a means to another end.[30]

To get back to Sītā's abduction, the incident cannot be isolated from all that has preceded it including Viradha's (a *raksasa*) holding on to Sītā and Rāma's words, 'I cannot bear the thought of Sītā being touched by another man. It upsets me more than the death of my father and the loss of my kingdom' (Valmiki 230). Sītā's discourse on *dharma* and the location of all action in reason is also important. She is able to view the Rāma–sage relationship in a larger perspective than her husband, and understands the violence of irrational persecution and the invasive power of thoughtless cruelty. In short, she is critical of her husband's stance. She points out to three major weaknesses related to desire and self-glory: lusting after another man's wife, telling lies and resorting to violence without any reason. Of these three weaknesses, Rāma, she can see, is heading towards the third (233–234). The third incident is Sūrpanakhā's wooing of first Rāma and later Lakshmana, and Lakshmana's thoughtless mutilation of her face by chopping off her ears and nose (245).

When the final abduction takes place, the couple has let down its guard. Sītā desires the golden deer and Rāma is keen to fulfil her desire. The warning note that Lakshmana strikes is ignored and Sītā accuses him of desiring her. Consequently, Sītā is left alone to be her own guardian and protector. The whole abduction scene—on both sides—is replete with accusations, subterfuge and action guided by impulse and desire. Rāvana has compelled Márica into taking part in a full-fledged conspiracy, very much against Márica's will and advice. Rāma has kept his sense of control and rationality aside; Sītā unfairly accuses Lakshmana to push him to follow Rāma. But despite all this there is no *lakshmana-rekha* actually drawn on the ground as it is mistakenly believed in common parlance. *Lakshmana-rekha* is part of most Indian languages, and is used to express the defining parameters of woman's freedom and space. It is based on the idea that when Sītā compels Lakshmana to follow Rāma, he draws a circle within which she will be protected, advising her not to cross its boundaries, but when Rāvana, disguised as a mendicant, comes to ask for alms, he insists that she step outside it and thus carries her away. The circle exists only in metaphorical terms both in Valmiki and Kamban, signifying the decorum of conduct (For details of this episode see Valmiki 269–275 and Kamban 136–146). In Valmiki's version, Lakshmana's reprimand is rather strongly worded:

> Shame on you for doubting me, when I am bound by my elder brother's instructions! But then, you have acted from the essentially corrupt nature that all women have.... May all be well with you and may the deities of the forest protect you, large-eyed lady! (274)

Sītā foolishly welcomes Rāvana into her hut, offers him hospitality and even responds to all his queries. He announces his intentions to her, tries to tempt her, tells her about his own history and all this happens before he carries her off (Valmiki 276–281).

Kamban's narration has other interventions. In his authorial voice he comments that Sītā did not realise that the deer was a trick; all this happened 'because Rāvana's days were numbered. It was time Dharma was reinstated'. Lakshmana's is the only voice of sanity (137). Rāma realises the trickery being played on him only during the pursuit (139). Lakshmana obeys her command to go to Rāma's help and leaves her to the protection of Dharma and the eagle chief (141). Rāvana describes himself in the third person and they have a debate on power, the destruction of

58

evil and Rāma's strength before he finally flies off in his chariot with the hut and all. Kamban also mentions the real reason for Sītā's remaining chaste. Rāvana was under a curse that if he ever touched an unwilling woman, he would die (142–145).

Tulsidas in *Ramcharitmanas* dwells extremely briefly on this episode, but he foregrounds it by long sermons on wifely duties and self-control. In fact patience, *dharma*, friend and wife all are tested only in times of crisis. He goes on to classify wifely devotion into four categories, but the highest among them is the one who does not have any thought of any man other than her husband and considers him the best. The next in order is the *pativrata* who considers all other men as brothers, fathers or sons. The third is the one who keeps herself in order because of the fear of *dharma* and her family's honour and the fourth and the lowest is the kind who remains good because she simply gets no opportunity of deviance. Not only does Tulsidas grade wifely devotion but his grad-ing locates it within (*a*) high esteem of the husband and blindness to all else, (*b*) placing men in non-sexual relationships, (*c*) goodness located in fear and (*d*) goodness located in compulsion (494–495).[31] Tulsidas, in his description of the last category, comes extremely close to Manu. At one point, Rāma tells Sītā that as long as he is engaged in battling with the *raksasa*s and putting an end to them, she should dwell in fire (515), apparently implying that the fire of her purity should keep seduc-ers and tempters at bay. Though Tulsidas does not describe any debates or reasoning and all is cloaked under the garb of a miracle, he also does not draw any *lakshmana-rekha*; Sītā is left to the care of the deities of the forest (599). It is obvious that the responsibility of protecting her-self is left to Sītā's own will and her temptation cannot be blamed on any other. Who fails—is it Sītā or is it Rāma's divine foreknowledge? Or it is a necessary fall, like that of Adam and Eve, in order to enable Rāvana's destruction? If so, why is a woman used as an agent? Again, the whole inheritance of the limits of womanly conduct has been based on the mythical *lakshmana-rekha*.

59

Sri Padma Purana radically departs from Valmiki and the other two versions, primarily by its need to place it within Jainism and the lineage of Tiranthkars. In the abduction episode, it is Lakshmana who proceeds into the forest and Rāma and Sītā stay behind. The plan is that Rāma will go to his brother's help—thus, Sītā's accusation that Lakshmana desires her is bypassed. Here, too, it is Jatayu who is left to guard her (Shri Ravisheshnacharya 284–285). In both Tulsidas and *Sri Padma Purana*, Sītā's debating and reasoning powers are ignored; she is rendered almost a passive follower while both Valmiki and Kamban delight in showing her the equal of the men in her debating and perceptive powers and the men are also human enough to feel tempted by thoughts of future glory.

Later, when Sītā is finally rescued and the war against Rāvana is both fought and won, Rāma needs a public declaration of her chastity. This episode, commonly known as *agnipariksha* (trial by fire), has come down to the present as a term identifiable with an ordeal, a severe test of a woman's chastity and fidelity. The manner in which it is depicted becomes important for any interpretative activity. Valmiki—whose Rāma is unaware of his divinity—is the most sympathetic. In fact, in the very first chapter of his account when a brief summary is provided, the account reads: 'Rāma took Sītā back but she was humiliated when he spoke to her harshly in front of all the people gathered there. Unable to bear the shame, that virtuous woman entered the fire' (Valmiki 8).

The actual episode takes place in the sixth book, titled *War* (Chapter 13). Rāma is reluctant to welcome her and on her arrival gives vent to his anger:

> I have killed the enemy, my dear, and I have won you back. In doing so, I have displayed the courage expected of me. I have avenged the insult and it no longer bothers me.... I have displayed my prowess and achieved my goals. I have kept my promises. Now I am free. (633)

There is a predominance of the 'I' in this passage and several more that follow. He justifies his conduct, the performance of his duty, the saving of his own and his noble family's honour and setting her free, says he is terribly suspicious of her character and conduct (633). Rāma's speech is at odds with his earlier conviction that he cannot be attracted towards the non-virtuous; it also sits oddly with his anxiety and anguish expressed in the fifth book, *Beauty*, when he weeps and longs for her with words like 'I cannot live for another second without my dark-eyed beloved' (506).

Sītā is not one to take it lying down, to be cast off as a rag doll, and accuses him of behaving like a low, common man and chides him for his narrow-mindedness, a man overcome by his anger and unable to see all action in a proper perspective (634–635). It is she who orders a funeral pyre to be built and treats this not as an ordeal to be undergone but as a final rejection of Rāma and justification of her own conviction that purity does not rest in the body. When everybody turns against him, it is then that his divinity is brought to his knowledge. Sītā is restored to Rāma and he defends his action on the ground that he needed a public vindication (635–639). But whether play-acting or vindication, the whole episode subtracts from Rāma's nobility. Sītā, however, succeeds in making the point that purity has nothing to do with the body. The notion of a public vindication brings the private into public space and expresses a wish to carry the opinion of others with him; it is an egoistic desire to declare himself above common emotions. Furthermore, the man has no hesitation in humiliating his wife in public. In Kālidāsa's 'Abhijnānāśakuntalam', once again Duhsanta is desirous of a public evidence that Śakuntalā is his wife for which a heavenly voice is required as testimony. The wife's dignity and the king's own word are all of no consequence where public justification is concerned. One wonders whether it is the royal seat which demands this kind of public certification or is it the male ego.

In Kamban's *Rāmāyana*, Rāma mourns the 'supposed' death of Lakshmana much more intensely than in Valmiki. In Valmiki's account he

61

has no further interest in Sītā (Valmiki 615), but in that of Kamban he is more self-critical and admits, 'My whole life is a catalogue of errors. Because I doted on Sītā, I let her coax me into a foolish act.' He realises that his past sins are catching up with him and his ego is somewhat humbled. He imagines the nature of public criticism—'all because this man of straw could not think beyond his wife' (Kamban 347). When Sītā is regained, Rāma's behaviour is as reprehensible in Kamban's version as in Valmiki's narrative. He puts all the blame on Sītā, is of the opinion that she is now bereft of all good and is of the view that she has done him immense harm.

> 'Solely because of the birth of one like you, womanhood, dignity, high birth, chastity, virtuous conduct, propriety and truth have all been destroyed, like the fame of a king without generosity.... Your behaviour has destroyed my peace of mind. Die. If you won't, go where you wish', said he. (Kamban 387)

And as a consequence of this, she herself gets the funeral pyre prepared, which is to become a trial of righteousness.

In *Sri Padma Purana,* the episode of the *agnipariksha* is missing. Instead, Rāma embraces her in gratitude that she is back with him (257). Though the second abandonment, of sending her into banishment, is also a part of this narrative. There too Lakshmana argues with his brother that public opinion alone cannot sully a person's reputation (277). Significantly, it is not Lakshmana who escorts her into exile, but Rāma's Commander-in-Chief (278–281), and Rāma's behaviour is critiqued as cruel and unworthy of him. There are several other changes in the Jain *Rāmāyana*, and one that is of significance is that she is taken care of by Prince Vrajjangh of Pundrikpur who considers her his elder sister. The irony remains in the fact that he too is another man not related to her by blood or kinship, and through this act a non-sexual relationship is recognised as acceptable (282).

David Shulman in his essay 'Fire and Flood: The Testing of Sītā in Kampan's *Iramavataram*', analyses the episode of *agnipariksha* both in Valmiki and Kamban. Shulman views it, and rightly so, as a justification of a woman's dignity, courage and superiority and announces that it is preferable to be a woman rather than a common man like Rāma (Shulman 92). Additionally, one needs to dwell on the narrative frame which is guided primarily by Rāma's destiny, and all the characters are performing pre-defined roles; where then is the agency? Shulman highlights a question that Sītā asks in Kamban's version, 'Can fortune give rise to lunacy?' (95). Sītā's anxiety and expectation are both high; she is prepared for the worst. Why? Is it that she has some intuitive knowledge of her husband's likely conduct? Sītā's counter-accusation of Rāma, as a heartless, low, common man, who has lowered his own dignity in thinking the worst of her and her public statement of her own purity as she goes on to question his *dharma* reflect on Rāma's limited vision. Even the fire of the pyre is burnt by the fire of her chastity (89–113). In this episode, Sītā, despite being caught up in the web of destiny, acquires an agency. If this is not protest or retaliation, what else is?

One more incident in this story, of sons (Luva and Kuśa) turning against their own father and compelling him to listen to his own life story told from their mother's perspective, a telling which acts like a mirror, has its own significance. Once again Rāma summons Sītā to prove her virtue, looking for a public display and approval (Valmiki 675–677). And then Sītā chooses not to return to Rāma but selects a way of proving her innocence which would be a termination of her earthly existence, 'If I have never thought about any other man but Rāma, let the goddess Mādhavi create a chasm for me!' (677), thus immediately establishing both her virtue and her superiority over Rāma. Not once does she bend before him or plead. During both the trials she recognises his oppositional role and treats him as a separate being—separate but equal—not superior or one in overall control.

William Buck's translation or retelling of the *Rāmāyana* has a strong aura of romanticisation, and as it focuses on the psychological territory it appeals to the modern imagination. The *Rāmāyana* has been retold, time and again, in different cultures, for different purposes and audiences. It has been pictorially presented through comic strips and currently through animation in TV programmes, and thus aims to capture a child's imagination. Harper Collins has recently brought out *The Rāmāyana: A Modern Translation* by Ramesh Menon. These retellings are different in nature from the spontaneous interpretations that seek to supply a multiplicity of perspectives. It is highly debatable whether we can call them translations or not, primarily because the nuances that go into the making of the meaning are reworked and the new writer's consciousness intervenes with the material before carrying it across into a different culture, language or period. Nevertheless, the continuity and the continued influence of the main events of the *Rāmāyana*, with all their religio-social burden, does not need any additional proof; the constant engagement with the main story, even as every teller turns it around and around to reshape and interpret it, is proof enough.

The retellings are variations, oppositions, questionings and resistance narratives. Often, the events are expanded to accommodate modern impulses and desires or those of the socially marginalised. The reader's attention is drawn to the two volumes edited by Paula Richman—*Many Rāmāyanas* and *Questioning Rāmāyanas*, which explore the various travels of the narratives and the different encounters that shape it.[32] A.K. Ramanujan's essay, 'Three Hundred *Rāmāyanas*', comments on the nature of difference in the perspective before turning to the mode. Oral narratives, in the main, have been either oppositional or additional. Ramanujan draws attention to a folk narrative, sung by an untouchable bard, which begins with Rāvana (called Ravula) and his queen Mandodari. The couple are childless and when Ravula, after due penance, receives a mango to be shared with his wife, he greedily eats the larger share and consequently himself becomes pregnant (35–36).

Ramanujan writes, 'In Kannada, The word *Sīta* means "he sneezed": he calls her Sītā because she is born from a sneeze.' Her name is given a Kannada folk etymology, as in the Sanskrit texts it has a Sanskrit one: there she is named Sītā because King Janaka finds her in a furrow (Sītā). At a later point, Ramanujan comments on this abnormal birth, which brings in a whole range of suggestions, 'the male envy of womb and childbirth, which is a frequent theme in Indian literature, and an Indian oedipal theme of fathers pursuing their daughters and, in this case, a daughter causing the death of her incestuous father' (37).

Oral themes acquire another dimension when they are narrated from the women's perspective as Velcheru Narayana Rao points out in 'A Ramayana of Their Own: Women's Oral Tradition in Telugu' (114–136). Women's songs are also a departure from Valmiki's version. There is, in addition, an inner division across caste lines as upper-class brahmin women and lower-caste women have employed different strategies even as they both seek to subvert mainstream ideology. Kept out of Sanskrit studies, women use this exclusion to their advantage in order to subvert authority. The Andhra brahmin women, Narayana Rao states, do not treat Valmiki as an authoritative or a correct version. These songs are normally sung in women's gatherings, in their backyards and while performing household chores (115). In the conservative brahmin society, women are segregated and female sexuality is 'severely repressed'.[33] The social conditions provide enough cause for protest and resistance and what can be better than doing this through subverting ideology and questioning role models? Songs have a double advantage; they help articulation and communication and when they are associated with religion, there is no way they can be censored. Additionally, they also create alternative role models for man–woman relationships, project a woman's perspective on rejection, build on sisterhood and give vent to their resentment of any imposition. Some of the song sequences go back to Kausalya's pregnancy and morning sickness and go on to depict Rāma's babyhood. Several others focus on Sītā's puberty and the games Rāma and Sītā play in the early phase of their marriage (118). It is interesting that one of the songs provides a reason for the trial of the prospective suitor:

> In her childhood Sītā had casually lifted Śiva's bow which was lying in her father's house. Janaka was amazed at her strength and decided that only a man who could string that bow would be eligible to marry her. Only a hero can be match for a hero.[34]

Here the emphasis is placed on an equal marriage.

Non-brahmin women's songs are brief, incomplete fragments. Perhaps, as Narayana Rao points out, there is a rejection of Rāma as hero and an obvious pleasure drawn from depicting the gods as slaves subject to control (131–133). Whether or not there is any consciousness in the continuity and repetitiveness of these songs is an entirely different matter, but there is no disputing the fact that their point of origin lies in a subversive questioning.

Feminist critics have gone a step further in focusing on the subversive quality in women's perspectives on the *Rāmāyaṇa*. I draw attention to Usha Nilsson's essay, 'Grinding Millet but Singing of Sītā: Power and Domination in Awadhi and Bhojpuri Women's Songs', and Madhu Kishwar's 'Yes to Sītā, No to Ram: The Continuing Hold of Sītā on Popular Imagination in India', both included in *Questioning Rāmāyaṇas* (Richman). In fact, the title of the collection itself makes a statement that the versions of the *Rāmāyaṇa*, critiqued and elaborated upon and referred to are those which question classical/epic/traditional versions either in their selection of events, shifting of emphasis or additions, interpretations and perspectives. Ironically, these deviations or alternative interpretations may form the target of fundamentalists.[35]

Paula Richman points out that though the oppositional tellings do not have a 'pan-Indian status', their multiplicity is astonishing:

One has to step back, however, and look at oppositional tellings as a whole, in order to realise the magnitude of their collective presence within the *Rāmāyana* tradition. By looking at them as a category, we can best see the influence they wield in people's everyday lives. (*Questioning Rāmāyanas* 11–12)

To get back to Usha Nilsson's essay, 'Grinding Millet But Singing of Sītā', she observes that long before Indian feminists protested Tulsidas's tirade against women, 'women singers have resisted and subverted authority in their songs' (Nilsson 137). Focusing on Bhojpuri-speaking areas, she goes on to comment on both: their united opposition to the dominant male discourse and the surfacing of differences amongst them. These songs often express sexuality, the desire for one who is forbidden—like Sakshwana's for Sītā. Women tend to emphasise the human aspects of the main characters and do not hesitate to talk about conjugal harmony as well as disharmony. At times, their accounts substitute accepted versions of male role with versions that shift the credit to women, empowering them and bestowing on them an agency (142–143). This is directly in contrast to both the Valmiki and Tulsidas versions. Sītā, in these songs, behaves like any other young woman going off into tantrums, enticing and resisting at the same time and openly showing her resentment against having been neglected (143–145). She is as much capable of sexual desire as any other human being. Subjects like dowry also surface over and over again. Jealousy, fear of the beloved being attracted by some other man and deception, all such emotions and fears come into play. One of the songs is about Rāma's sister who persuades Sītā to draw Rāvana's picture and sneaks about this to her brother (148–149). Thus, betrayal by a woman of the trust of another woman also finds a place in these narratives. Again, it is not Valmiki but ascetic women who come to Sītā's help. These songs go on to imagine the many ways in which women relate to one another—at times positively, displaying solidarity, at others negatively, violating the trust vested in them. Like the non-brahmin Telugu women's song-versions of the *Rāmāyana* story, these Bhojpuri women's songs also reflect a caste difference—upper caste privilege is resented and questioned but in the main the songs of both the upper caste and the lower caste women prioritize women's roles, elaborate upon relationships, foreground women's perspectives and join 'together in contesting dominant patriarchal traditions' (158).[36]

Madhu Kishwar analyses the concept of *pativrata* in the context of the *maryada purshottam* (epitome of propriety) male. Kishwar, working with interviews across a cross-section of society, observes that women are critical of Sītā's passive acceptance of the *agnipariksha* as well as of Tulsidas's underplaying of the injustice done to Sītā. Rāma does not meet their standard of an ideal husband ('Yes to Sita', 286–288). Motivated by a sense of his personal perfection, he fails in his relationship to his wife. Women are inclined to interpret her appeal to Mother Earth to take her back as a statement of protest, 'It amounted to saying: "No more of this shit"' (289).

Kishwar has a specific reference to Mithila—the region associated with Sītā's parental home. She refers to the travels that Sacchidanand Vatsyayan (Agyeya) organised in the early 1980s to journey through the area. The writers who joined this group collected songs, talked to people and wrote about them.[37] The people of Mithila still grieve for their wronged daughter. Women tell their husbands (through their songs) to go to Sītā's help, and a host of superstitious beliefs have come into practice in order to prevent other daughters from suffering Sītā's fate. Rāma's presence is often erased, his name omitted from marriage songs. Another writer of this group, Shankar Dayal Singh, observes that the people of this region have taken 'a strange revenge in a silent way' by naming all their temples devoted to Sītā and Rāma as Shri Janaki Mandirs (Kishwar 297).

It is important to pay attention to these emotions, songs and voiced or silently expressed resentments and critiquings of normative role models on several counts. First and foremost, because they move across regions; again, they cut across class, caste and gender (very often men think on the same lines). And when they do not, the feminine viewpoint is further heightened. As most songs belong to the oral tradition, the level of education is irrelevant; instead, it is the collective critiquing subtly expressed or strongly framed which is of importance. When a majority of women prefer Śiva to Rāma as an ideal husband, as many of Kishwar's interviewees do, it is primarily because of Śiva's devotion to his wife and 'the fact that he allowed his spouse an important role in influencing his decisions' ('Yes to Sita', 305). Kishwar observes that Sītā's offer of *agnipariksha* is viewed as an 'act of defiance that challenges her husband's aspersions, a means of showing him to be so flawed in his judgement that the gods have to come to show up Rāma for his foolishness' (306). Her refusal to give a second *agnipariksha* is a public rejection of Rāma as a husband, which brings her initial acceptance of him to a full circle and which even as it shows her initial judgement to be mistaken, bestows on her the right both to choose and to reject.

Resistance and protest are often subtly expressed through questionings, attitudes and narrative strategies. There is a great deal beneath the surface. The co-relation between the past and the present, in the form of a constant dialogue, is a constant re-evaluation of masculinity, patriarchy and the position that it so reluctantly concedes to women. Sally Goldman, commenting on Sītā's voice in Sundarakānda, 'how wretched to be under the power of another', sees it as an expression 'defiant of the patriarchy that controls her life' (223). Sītā's withdrawal of her sexuality during her captivity and her advice to Rāvana to turn his thoughts away from her do not represent any weakness but a control of the highest order. Suppose for a moment that Sītā had reduced Rāvana to ashes through her own power, what would the world have thought of Rāma? No matter how she behaves—protects herself through her own agency or quietly waits for her husband to rescue her—Rāma is unlikely to come out of the whole episode as unflawed.

The engagement with Rāma's story in Indian culture is reflected in contemporary writing. There are many spaces that have the possibility of being filled up, reversed or reinterpreted. In Kusum Ansal's novel, *Uski Panchvati*, exile is turned around first as walking-out of an unhappy marriage and then as a space to accommodate adulterous desire. It creates a certain legitimacy for desire over sanctioned relationships. Panchvati, being the place where Rāma, Sītā and Lakshmana had made their abode in the forest, as the title of the novel sends a cultural signal to the reader. It is a story of a woman who marries the younger brother, mainly because she is attracted by the elder brother. She is artistic by temperament and a painter. Her husband is insensitive to her talents and emotions; he wants to confine her to domesticity and the unhappy woman leaves her marital home. Then follows a relationship across forbidden boundaries; a child is born, the lover dies and the husband now adopts his elder brother's child born of his own wife.[38]

Nabaneeta Dev Sen, a reputed writer, has reinterpreted Rāma's story in a series of short stories. I draw attention to one of her short stories, 'The Immortality Trap'. The story centres on Sītā's abduction and the war with Lanka. Rāma blames Sītā for Lakshmana's death and expresses the feeling that though a wife can be replaced, a younger brother cannot be replaced (9–12). Trijata, the demoness, who is with Sītā, wonders whether Sītā would like to return to that loveless marriage. But Sītā refuses to believe all that she sees and hears. She sees it as a trap and refuses to listen to Trijata's advice. While Sītā is preparing for the funeral pyre, Rāma and Lakshmana are restored to life. And the final comment comes from Valmiki:

> Truly, how inscrutable is the character of woman! Terribly complicated.' Narad smiled 'Why do you say complicated? Even after knowing that her life is joyless and hollow, she is lured into the trap of immortality. A woman too deludes herself, just like a man does, may be even more. Even after knowing that Rāma does not love her, poor Sītā could not resist the temptation of the first great epic of India. She's willing to pay the price of terrible suffering in life in order to acquire immortality in art. (N. Sen 19–20)

It is only through suffering that cultural role models are made, but they move simultaneously between illusion and reality, appearance and truth, leaving enough space for alternatives, conjectures and remouldings.

I recall another beautifully framed story about Sītā and Śurpanakhā being brought together through the agency of Luva and Kuśa and getting together to analyse the contradictory impulses in Rāma's behaviour. The coming together of women who have both suffered at the hands of Rāma establishes a reaching out across the male presence. It is, in fact, a dividing of gender lines. This story by Volga, titled 'Confluence', is set in the *ashrama* where Sītā lives with her two sons—Luva and Kuśa. One evening as she anxiously waits for her sons to return from their day in the forest, they arrive with a bunch of colourful, fragrant flowers for the evening prayer. On further inquiry, they reveal that the flowers are from a beautiful garden owned by a very ugly woman with a fearful face, a woman without a nose or ears. Through the boys' comments, it dawns upon Sītā that the woman is perhaps none other than Śurpanakhā, a woman disfigured by Lakshmana. Her heart goes out in sympathy for the lonely woman; her thoughts go back to her own life during the exile. She had been happy then—but now she has been abandoned by her husband, the man she loved. And Śurpanakhā has not been able to get the man she loved. Both are in a similar position. Next day, she decides to go in search of the garden. The two women meet and friendship springs among them as the true meanings of love, goodness and beauty come to light. Their experience has unveiled hidden realities to them.

'Confluence' works in two different directions: one, the solidarity and friendship that is born of true understanding between women who have suffered at the hands of the same man, and two, Sītā's decision that she'd return to Mother Earth rather than return to Rāma. If the women reject the man, the sense of abandonment automatically becomes irrelevant. It becomes a question of will and perspective. Volga's story belongs to the twenty-first century and absorbs contemporary feminist thought.

At the beginning of this section, I had pointed out to the filmic representations which persist in endlessly renewing the collective memory. But the film, an expensive medium, is in the hands of experts. Drama, on the other hand, has both the categories—the sophisticated and the popular. The latter is often in the hands of ordinary untrained people who engage with it due to faith, fun and passion. Philip Lutgendorf makes a distinction between popular and oral; all oral literature was not necessarily open to women and shudras (*The Life of a Text* 56). Tulsidas's *Ramcharitmanas* by having been written in Hindi (khadi boli) lends itself more easily to recitation and performance across social divisions. Different regions have developed their own style of the Ramlila performances, such as the Ramnagar, the Chhattisgarh and Chitrakut schools. In addition, almost every locality in a big city sets up its own amateur performance in the months of October–November coinciding with Dussehra and Diwali, festivals which celebrate first the victory of Rāma over Rāvana and then his return to Ayodha. If on the one hand there are village variants (248–249), on the other, sophisticated ballet performances and experimental forms existing parallely in an attempt to challenge existing structures.[39]

The all-pervasive influence of the *Rāmāyana* in the different regions and languages may vary, but its dissemination through performance, films and electronic media keeps it alive and facilitates its getting under the skin of the Indians as role models; writers, readers and viewers are increasingly beginning to open them out to questionings and reinterpretations. The story with its stress on fidelity, *dharma*, obedience, sibling relationship, valour and morality touches on almost all aspects of human life. It lends itself to parody, fragmentation, deconstruction and fixation alike—hence the need to constantly debate the issues of sexuality, desire and relationship.[40]

III

Working through Space: Patriarchy and Resistance

છ૭

In 1914, Tagore published a short story, 'Stree Ka Patra' (A woman's letter),[1] addressed by a wife to her husband. The narrative consists of just one letter, without any other external frames, and covers a period of 15 years through retrospective capturing of experience, emotion and reflection. After the usual—or perhaps not so usual—beginnings, for never before have the couple had any need to correspond, there is a short paragraph of four sentences. Every sentence makes a definite statement. It begins, 'Your family's middle daughter-in-law had come to Jaganathpuri on a pilgrimage' (note the past tense and third person), moves in the second to the first person announcing a stepping outside the 'daughter-in-law' persona. Then, she explains the source of the courage to find her voice: it is this stepping outside. And in the final sentence, disassociates herself from the daughter-in-law's role. This paragraph problematises space of every kind—physical, social, familial, emotional and intellectual. It problematises the use of space in a power relationship. Agency vis-à-vis passivity, access to religious space (pilgrimage) as opposed to the controlled environment of family space and the confining roles of wife and daughter-in-law all come to the fore.

Then follows an account from the initial bride-viewing, the marriage ceremony, a brief motherhood, appreciation on account of her beauty, criticism on account of her intelligence bringing the narrative to the

73

present moment of separation, which has been brought about by her dissatisfaction with her inability to help a fellow human being. Her sister-in-law's orphaned younger sister, Bindu, is reluctantly sheltered and forced into marriage with a semi-lunatic. When Bindu finds herself bereft of all help, she sets herself aflame—simultaneously reversing the image of Sati and frustrating any further help. Mrinal, the writer of the letter, can no longer accept the inhuman brutality of the system and hence the letter announcing an end of her dependency and a rejection of her marital home, thus closing all possibilities of return.

This short story beautifully and through a few brief strokes depicts a picture of patriarchal control, oppression and the unequal relationships that are established through the act of imposing restrictions. Almost all cultures define taboos through space. There are sufficient examples in myths, legends and fairytales. The notion of 'exile' is also linked with space, as are Sītā's abduction, Draupadi's disrobing or Eve's eating the forbidden fruit. Each of these women is dislocated. While Sītā and Eve literally go into exile, Draupadi's disrobing is located in a public space and violates her sense of privacy. Her questioning further goes ahead to shrink male space. Purity and pollution also rest themselves on space. It defines both order and chaos. But more than all else, gender roles (and inequality) are defined by it. Partha Chatterjee is oft-quoted for drawing attention to the distinction between home and the world as enacted in the nineteenth-century colonial cultural politics (*The Nation and Its Fragments*), but it is a construct widely used for placing women within domesticity. Additionally, they are considered 'custodians' of tradition/ culture/family honour and the accompanying baggage. Custodianship implies marginal glory and a heavy responsibility, but in reality has neither power nor agency. Domesticity is believed to consist of its own rewards.

Two ancient texts, written/composed almost contemporaneously, which define and place women in oppositional spaces are *The Laws of Manu* and *Nātyaśastra*. *Manusmriti* or *Manavadharma sastra* lays down the behavioural code for different roles, castes, classes and stages of life. It goes into detail about the degrees of recognition different kinds of marriage ceremonies possess and validity or otherwise of inter-caste marriages, so much so as to rating the category of the caste into which a man marries. It classifies men into different *varnas* and lays down laws of inheritance, rights of the progeny and claims of the male child; in fact, it is least concerned with the individual, but is overtly concerned with relationships across generations, lineages and continuities. In this the brahmin male has a priority over all else. Manu is viewed as a generic term for *manava*, human being, and thus the authorship, so far, is believed to be a composite one. It is believed to have been written around first century BCE.[2]

Bharata Muni's *Nātyaśastra*, believed to have been composed at about the same time,[3] lays down the aesthetic principles of performing arts on the basis of a wide range of knowledge of anatomy, motor and sensory systems, principles of mathematics, the relationship between the senses, body and mind and goes on to build a theory of aesthetics. The author announces it as the fifth Veda, and proceeds to use Prakrit—the people's language—as opposed to Sanskrit, the language of the brahmins. It was inclusive in its concept of audience, all *varna*s were included. And it adopted its main features from the four earlier Vedas, 'namely, the Recitation from the Rgveda, the song from Sāmaveda, the Abhinayas (the historionics) from the Yajurveda and the Rasas (sentiments) from the Atharvaveda' (Tarlekar 2). This is also a classificatory *sastra*, but in a sense which is inclusive rather than divisionary. Here too, the woman takes centre stage, but in a theatrical space and performative enactment, not domesticity.

Manu's *The Laws of Manu* uses space for control and hierarchical distances; *Nātyaśastra* uses space for creating a community of artists, performers, musicians and audiences. Women feature in both—in one within domesticity, in the other the theatre. Somehow, together they do achieve a demarcation through the notion of respectability and the difficulty of crossing over from one space to another. In this chapter, these

75

two texts, their value structures, gender positions and representations will be taken up for consideration.

Defining Moral Norms

The Laws of Manu is in the main a work about moral principles and hence it has a philosophical import; but as these laws proximate a legality in the degree of punishments and inheritance laws, this aspect acquired a greater prominence during the colonial period. A *dharmasastra*, defining moral good, it ventures into *karma*, the code for worldly action. Despite its discriminatory stance against women, it needs to be examined in some detail in order to assess its impact on women's position and its daily encroachments on the lives of the marginalised, whether on the basis of caste, gender or marital status. Wendy Doniger considers it a 'pivotal text of the dominant form of Hinduism as it emerged historically' and comments: 'No modern study of Hindu family life, psychology, concepts of the body, sex, relationships between humans and animals, attitudes to money and material possessions, politics, law, caste, purification and pollution, ritual, social practice and ideals, and world renunciation and worldly goals can ignore Manu' (xvii).

The work was first translated into English in 1794 by William Jones and later into German in 1797 by J. Chr. Hüttner. It is at this time that the title 'Laws' caught on in preference to other meanings of *smriti*, *sastra* or *dharmasastra*, giving it a quasi-legal authority over and above the moral, religious or social authority. Doniger's 'Introduction' to *The Laws of Manu*, which she has translated along with Brian K. Smith, sums up the main arguments, provides a brief account of the work's historical journey and traces the political inferences of its prominence. She comments on the use of the word 'Laws' as one which 'skews it towards what the British hoped to make of it: a tool with which to rule the Hindoo' (Doniger xvii–xviii).

Located in its original context, *Manusmriti* has been viewed as a response to the challenges offered by the growing strength of Buddhists and Jains—both religious movements were forms of resistance in themselves—and as such is 'pivotal in the priestly response to the crisis of traditional Aryan culture' (Doniger xxxv). Thus, its categorisation tends to be authoritative, fixed and without any concessions. Of its 12 chapters or sections, the first is concerned with duties, pre-eminently of the priestly class, and defines the four *varna*s; in the second chapter the focus shifts from religion and society to the individual, and to desire as a motivating force, and rituals with both their performative and transformative details—naming, initiation, *brahmacharya*, brahminhood, marriage and sacrifice. Even the respect due to certain degrees of relationship and towards guests is specified. In the third chapter, moving outside *brahmacharya*, marriage and matrimonial alliances that are disapproved are listed; caste and class are to be matched before the householder life can be undertaken. The Hindu male is expected to pass through four *ashramas*—*brahmacharya*: studentship and celibacy; *grahastha*, the life of the householder: family and worldly life; *vanaprastha*: forest dweller and the fourth of *sanyasa*: the period of renunciation.

Manusmriti goes into great details, degrees and grading about the types of food to be eaten or shunned, vegetarianism, non-vegetarianism, purity and pollution. One can see how these very things, in some way or the other, are also discussed in the epics—only forest-dwelling as exile upsets the right order as it comes before that of the householder. Again, in the *Mahābhārata*, polyandry transgresses several of the principles advocated by Manu. Violence is present both in sacrifice and war, but the nature of the violence in each case is different. While the priest has full control over the sacrificial religious ritual, the kshatriya fights war and has no control over the actions of the enemy. Privileging sacrifice over war, Manu places the brahmin at the top of the social scale.

Chapter 8 is concerned with several legal issues, arbitration of disputes, fines and punishment, sales, thefts, adultery and a host of other crimes. But it is the 9th chapter which deals with the status of women, which I propose to discuss in detail at the end of this summary. The 10th and the 11th chapters are largely concerned with rank, status and livelihood, grounds on which one can lose caste. The concluding chapter works through knowledge constructs, action, rewards and punishment in terms of Hell and Salvation. It is the idea of the 'self' that interests me here, and the interconnections which Manu establishes between the mind-and-heart and the body's action. There is a recognition of an internal consciousness.

A self works, functions and develops at multiple levels—physical, the elemental and the living soul. The living soul comes into being through meditation. He describes it in the following manner: 'The recitation of the Veda, inner heat, knowledge, purification, suppression of sensory powers, the rites of duty and meditation on the soul are the mark of the quality of goodness' (Manu 281–282).

This is repeated on several occasions in a number of different ways and stresses the connection between *tapas* (asceticism), energy and goodness (see 286, 288 and 289). But significantly, it does not appear that this notion of 'self' includes the categories of women, the untouchables or any of those categories which have not been prescribed the four *ashrama*s (stages) of life, and focuses primarily on the priest and the brahmin.

To return to Chapter 9, this is a chapter that very systematically argues that women are dependent, 'not fit for independence', and need to be guarded right from birth to death, guarded against addictions, temptations, seductions, in fact against all that is worldly and worth desiring. A wife needs to be guarded for the legitimacy of the progeny, particularly a male child. One of the ways a man can keep a woman away from temptation is by amassing wealth and creating enough work to keep her energies engaged. Except for the marginal praise Manu bestows on women who 'guard themselves by themselves' (198), he considers them to be untrustworthy and unfaithful. Furthermore, a wife's life is submerged into her husband's; sale or rejection does not free her. But he does list certain causes that can make annulment possible. Further, bride price is considered reprehensible.

The inheritance laws favour the male line; a daughter inherits only her mother's property, and whatever she inherits from her father is through her male child. Begetting a child for a dead brother is sanctioned for the male; the adoption of a child born of the wife's union—a premarital relationship—by the lawful husband is also sanctioned. In all this, a woman is equated with land. Widow remarriage is permitted in some cases.

It is evident, even from this brief account, that several of these practices—observing strict rules of purity, untouchability, brahminical power, constructing women's dependence—are prevalent in some measure or the other, in some pocket or the other even now, but it is mostly a question of strategy (keeping women engaged), power hierarchy and ritualistic practice, but not necessarily of legality. In fact, certain practices, both in the past and the present, expressly go against it. As for instance, it is the sages who were tempted and their meditation disrupted by the *apsara*s; it is men who have sought to constrain women, shun them, move into *ashrama*s or forests in order to practice *tapas*, develop asceticism and consolidate energy. They have avoided life 'in the world' to gain ascendancy over it. Injustice, covetousness, bride price—nothing has disappeared despite Manu.

The 'laws' have over the years become handy weapons of persecution: they do not represent a realistically practical way of living; instead, they lay down the route to an ideal and desirable state so that hierarchies are not disturbed.[4] Wendy Doniger is of the view that

> Hindus themselves have always taken Manu seriously *in theory*. In the realm of the ideal, Manu is the cornerstone of the priestly vision of what human life should be, a vision to which Hindus have always paid lip-service and to which in many ways they still genuinely aspire. Like all textbooks (*sāstras*), it influenced expectations, tastes, and judgments, beneath the level of direct application of given cases.... Even today, Manu remains the pre-eminent symbol—now a negative symbol—of

the repressive caste system: it is Manu, more than any other text, that untouchables burn in their protests. (lix)

But the codification Manu's laws received during the colonial period when the British adopted it as 'personal law' (supplementing general law) contributed to its semi-legal status and made religious affiliation the basis of law. The British privileged Manu for entirely administrative reasons and perhaps a little also because they were unable to comprehend the multiplicity and variations of the Hindu caste and religious practices. The book was significant for 'practical reasons' (Doniger ix). It was not important to them whether it was actually practiced or adhered to or not. It also did not matter that it would harden religious and caste divisions and gender roles, but it was handy as a base for law. Wendy Doniger asks: 'Were the British right to privilege Manu? Did they do it to advance their own interests, or because they found that this text was really in use?' (lxi). But whether in use or not, she argues, 'As an *applied* legal text, Manu does not deserve the status that the British accorded it' (lxi). Several other alternatives were available and they went ahead to make use also of the commentaries (lx–lxi). As Janaki Nair has pointed out in *Women and Law in Colonial India: A Social History*, the Orientalist understanding laid the foundations of modern legal structures in India. For their purpose they depended on the *sruti*s, *smriti*s, *dharmasastra*s and a variety of commentaries. But unwillingly and unknowingly they hypostatised the process of evolution and change and completely bypassed the margins of society. They also 'overlooked the historical specification of the text's application' (Nair 20–21).

The fixity and the legal authority which the use by the British imparted to it, and the manner in which the whole civilisational discourse used it to mark the differences and distinctions between the two cultures led to an unrealistic adherence to Manu's code and a hardening of the existing social divisions. The Indian social system with its divisions and practices became the site on which both sides began to play the game of reform. The 'woman' question was centre stage throughout the nineteenth century. Questioning of Manu's views and resistance to it surfaced from several quarters and on account of different reasons. Fictional accounts and male spokesmen like Raja Ram Mohan Roy and Vidyasagar apart, women too jumped into the fray. Right from the birth of a girl child, child marriage, age of consent, privileging of the brahmin to sati, widow remarriage and property rights all became issues for which social debates and movements were organized at several levels. The restrictions on food and inhibitions surrounding caste were issues that rose to the surface fairly early in the nineteenth century, in the heyday of Hindu College in the 1830s. At this stage—from 1830s to 1860s—a fair amount of conversion was from amongst the brahmins.[5] One may as well ask why a privileged category needed to convert. There could be several speculative answers, one of them being simply to get away from fixities and in search of newness and greater space for human action.

Without going into details, one needs to recognise that various reform movements varying in degree and inclination competed with each other. These were attempts to get out of the quagmire, which apparently was pulling people in—Brahmo Samaj, Prarthna Samaj, Arya Samaj happened to be only some of these. One could further debate the relationship between the development of these movements and the national struggle as well as the nation's need to define its position vis-à-vis the West. Were the reform movements in themselves, initiated by the Indians, or the dependence on British initiatives in the matter of religious reform, a misguided move, is a larger question for history to decide. But they did divide the society across communities and religious sects, and apparently brought the Bhakti Movement to an end. But all reform movements had a mixed response and a mixed measure of flexibility and fixity. Religious reform, initiated by the Indians themselves, was often a defensive move and guided by the need to appear rational and to address the main charge made against Hinduism.

Towards the end of the nineteenth century, in the 1980s and 1990s, and in the early decades of the twentieth century, there are several fictional representations dealing with the oppressive social practices against women, including child marriage, polygamy, unconsummated marriages, early widowhood, sexual repression and deprivation, and social ostracism, excesses further enhanced because of poverty or absence of property rights. One can imagine how difficult it must have been to struggle against the resurrected ghost of Manu in the form of law. It is necessary to point out that the preceding centuries had witnessed a spurt of other resistance movements, one of which was the Bhakti Movement, spread over several centuries and different parts of the country, across class and caste, and language. This too addressed the 'woman' question, including a woman's relationship to her god; in some measure it also addressed domesticity, its confines and sexual claims. But this will come up for discussion in the next chapter. For the moment I would like to focus on some of the writings and social cases of the 1880s.

In 1888, Pandita Ramabai, a learned Hindu woman, wrote *The High Caste Hindu Woman* for her Philadelphia host group. This is a work in which she directly addresses Manu's prescribed code of behaviour. In 1882, in northern India, an anonymous book *Simantni Updesh*, apparently written by an educated woman in Persianised Hindi had already appeared. From the years 1884–1887 the well-known Rukhmabai case was the subject of legal and public debate. This too questioned child marriage, absence of a woman's agency, marriage and inheritance laws and compatibility reopening the gap between the code and behavioural realities, as well as compelling society to face the personhood of women. Tarabai Shinde, in *Stree-Purush Tulana* (Comparison between women and men), wrote a fiery outburst in defence of equal laws of morality and hit out at reform, which was limited to debate and the moral guardians who ignored the whole question of sexuality. Shinde's work was written in Marathi. At about the time when *The High Caste Hindu Woman* was being written, Krupabai Satthianandan had already written her autobiographical

82

novel *Saguna: A Story of Native Christian Life* which was serialised in *Madras Christian College Magazine*, 1887–1888.

Protest took various forms and adopted different channels—political forums, reform societies, educational reform, opening schools and institutions for women (providing social support) and a host of other things. It is impossible to go into all of them here. Suffice it to say that there was a great deal of male support, especially when men encouraged (and at times insisted) that their child wives be educated,[6] when they opened the doors of higher education for them,[7] and when they supported their self-efforts from outside. But women themselves were also anxious to create space for themselves, especially if parental support had provided them with education as in the case of Pandita Ramabai. There were others who educated themselves against odds as Rassundari Devi describes in her autobiography, *My Life* (written originally in Bengali in 1868, published in 1876).

Ramabai did not begin as a feminist, despite the fact that as a young girl she had had access to learning, and in her own personal life she had struggled on several counts—the loss of her entire family at the hands of successive death, her scholarship and then her inter-caste marriage. Meera Kosambi in the 'Preface' to the *Selected Works* writes, 'The genesis of this book was my shocked discovery in late 1995 of Ramabai's anti-feminist and seemingly even anti-women ideological stance in *Stri Dharma Niti…*' (vii), which indicates another aspect of the women's silent struggle against patriarchal guardianship. It is so difficult to unlearn what has been thrust down one's throat and consequently internalised. In such conditions only deep resentment, anger and hardship, or great learning and questioning can push one to rebel. A combination of knowledge and morality alone could lead to a conscious moral action. Thus, she took upon herself the responsibility of negotiating the gap between knowledge and action for her less privileged sisters (Kosambi 37).

Ramabai, on several occasions, referred to Harriet Martineau's account of the American people, their families and women. This obviously impressed her; thus, when she was in Philadelphia to attend Anandibai Joshi's graduation from the medical school, she almost simultaneously undertook two tasks: the first, to give the American people a picture of Indian women's condition; and second, to write for her sisters at home a corresponding account of the American women. In each case, the chosen audience and the chosen language are different. And despite her critiquing of Manu, and realisation of the wrongs being done to women, Ramabai is limited both by her caste and her approach. An excess of scholarship and a homage to reason clearly also acted as deterrents to empathy and going across fully to the women's cause.[8]

Rachel Bodley's introduction to the 1888 edition gives a sympathetic account of both Anandibai Joshi's struggles and Ramabai's visit.[9] Bodley begins with the sentence, 'The silence of a thousand years has been broken' (i). True, the silence had been broken and expressed through, and meant for, a foreign audience; it was in itself an act of remarkable courage. But silences had been broken earlier too—some known and some unknown to history. This work—Ramabai's—is in actuality a bringing of the two cultures face to face. From one perspective, one needs to examine very closely the forces of patronisation while critiquing writings addressed to the West, those written with the aim of cultural communication, and those engaged in nation construction or an appeal for help. Writing is greatly influenced by its objective, audience and context. Whatever be the context, the clarity with which Ramabai sets about her task and proceeds systematically through Manu's code as applicable to different stages of a woman's life is remarkable.

The points she selects to highlight are all drawn from the overarching hold of religious beliefs and values on Hindu social life, going into details about all that is taboo and all that is permitted. Then follow the preference for the male heir and the superstitious beliefs surrounding them. As a consequence of this preference, men grow up to be egoistic, self-centred and anti-women: 'Brothers...too begin by and by to despise girls and women...Subjected to such humiliation, most girls become sullen, morbid and dull.' But 'there are some fiery natures' (Kosambi 138). A girl literally has no childhood, though she is always treated as a child and not an adult. Early in life, they are roped into household chores and begin preparing for their future life in the husband's house. Ramabai comments on the strict restrictions of the caste system in the case of marriage alliances; choices are limited and parents, for whatever reason—poverty, large size of family, social reputation, fear of god's wrath—are unable to keep a daughter at home if no suitable match is found (Ramabai 143). Thus, Manu's advice, though sound, is not always easy to follow. But this does not mean that marriages are never happy, or that childhood is always a time of neglect. Throughout the work, Ramabai interlaces her description of the life and practices of the brahmin community with anecdotes from her personal experiences as well as with citations from Manu, constantly pointing to the gap between social practices and the prescribed code and thus stressing the social pressures that are often at play.

It is the chapter on widowhood that brings out the discriminatory practices against widows (as compared to widowers), not only in matters of remarriage but also disfigurement, deprivation, near starvation (one meal a day of restricted food), dependence and exploitation. Often there is a continuous stream of fasts. Ramabai's plea is for setting up educational institutions, enabling women to protect their rights and rehabilitating widows. The comparison between East and West is stressed with the purpose of winning support:

Will you not, all of you who read this book think of these, my countrywomen, and rise, moved by a common impulse, to free them from lifelong slavery and infernal misery? I beg you, friends and benefactors, educators and philanthropists, all who have any interest in or compassion for your fellow-creatures, let the cry of India's daughters feeble though it be, reach your ears and stir your hearts. In the name of humanity, in the name of your sacred responsibilities as workers in the cause of humanity, and, above all, in the most holy name of God, I summon you, true women and men of America, to bestow your help quickly, regardless of nation, caste or creed. (179)

The High Caste Hindu Woman was part of Ramabai's fund-raising efforts, hence the impassioned plea, which in retrospect appears to be more in the line of missionary work than a direct protest. But one must also remember that the Indian male was not only conservative but often resistant to women self-help groups working for consciousness raising (Kosambi 8). Men felt threatened by female initiatives. Also, by now (1883), Ramabai had already converted to Christianity and an additional bond of religion had been formed. Conversion in itself remained a contentious issue for women, whether they did it on their own or followed their husbands into the new religion as Lakshmibai Tilak[10] and Krupabai Satthianandan mother did.[11]

Conversion was not always a permanent bridge; the gap between the convertees and others persisted, which persists even to this day. The 'natives' had been framed as primitive for too long. Kosambi comments that 'the suddenness of Ramabai's conversion continues to remain a mystery...' (14). Similarly, the sudden change in the Radha–Harichandra relationship in *Saguna* following their conversion is surprising, and even if one concedes some ground to the change in social environment, it remains slightly propagandist. Gauri Viswanathan, participating in a larger debate, admits of the 'worldly' function of conversion and asks:

> Why, for instance, does history throw up so many instances of conversion movements accompanying the fight against racism, sexism and colonialism? What might be the link between the struggle for basic rights and the adoption of religions typically characterised as minority religions? What limitations of secular ideologies in ensuring these rights do acts of conversion reveal? Does that act of exposure align conversion more closely with cultural criticism? And finally, what possibilities for alternative politics of identity might be offered by conversion as a gesture

86

that crosses fixed boundaries between communities and identities? (Viswanathan, 'Preface' xvi–xvii)

Devoting a whole chapter, 'Silencing Heresy', to Ramabai's conversion, Viswanathan proceeds to examine the connection between feminist struggle and religious dissent. In this case, the involvement in a social cause had already led to a move outside the limited view of religion as performance of duty, ritual and a move towards personal salvation. Her critiquing of the social customs was in itself enough to alienate her from the religion she was born into. Her own scholarly training also intervened in any unquestioning acceptance of another faith. She continued to question and make fine distinctions of meaning. In fact, the spiritual struggle for her was a ceaseless one (*Outside the Fold*, 122–123). Viswanathan is of the view that she 'ruptured the Orientalist celebration of Eastern philosophy as a repository of sublime mysteries' (147). This view cannot be accepted in its totality. True, she may have been one of the very few convertees to carry on the process of questioning within the new religion, but Western glorification of Eastern philosophy as Wendy Doniger's 'Introduction' to *The Laws of Manu*, especially when she expounds on Nietzsche's views and admiration of Manu, served a larger purpose. The debate has never been a matter of simple polarities; it is much more than that with colonial resistance, cultural defence and nation construction all thrown in. Ramabai's life, her evolution through the different phases of experience, her ongoing questioning and her ability to persist despite criticism, do establish her right to be recognised as an individual voice of dissent. Religion was in itself a patriarchal construct, and each religion worked with its own hierarchies.

Pandita Ramabai makes a reference to Rukhmabai's case in *The High Caste Hindu Woman* (Kosambi 156–158). Rukhmabai was contesting a case filed by her husband for restitution of conjugal rights. The case was complicated by property rights, inheritance laws, marriage ceremony, the act of consummation and whether the question of 'restitution' in the case of an unconsummated marriage was possible or not. Even the right of Rukhma's mother to inherit to the property of her first husband came in for dispute. More than anything else the intentions of the mother (why did she pass on the property to her daughter on her own remarriage?), those of her mother's second husband (why did he choose a worthless relative as a husband for his step-daughter?) and a woman's right to choice in the case of child marriage became matters of consideration by the court.

Sudhir Chandra has given a detailed account of this case in *Enslaved Daughters*, pointing out the complexity of the responses. There were several aspects to the whole issue: the orthodox Hindu community, the reformists, the British and the religious communities other than the Hindu. The debate that surrounded the case brought into visibility the tentativeness of the reformists and the various interpretations of ancient law and tradition. Chandra observes that her supporters, by invoking an uncorrupted tradition, went on to invoke a reason 'from which flowed universal principles, such as those of inalienable human rights.... Rather than face the difficulties involved in the exercise, they took recourse to exegetics that almost always discovered a convergence between "tradition" and "reason",' while her opponents' stand reflected 'deeper fears which colonialism had inspired', ranging from individual sexuality to disruption of domestic control (Chandra 116–118). The case evokes admiration on several counts: the firmness and clarity on part of Rukhmabai, her continued persistence at considerable cost to herself, her willingness even to submit to a prison sentence rather than go back to her husband and the ability to recognise both her right to choose and the nature of compatibility. Man–woman relationships, secondary in orthodox Hindu homes and often confined to the *antahpura*, were now in the open. Compatibility also was hardly a consideration at a time when women were treated as passive beings. Equally surprising is the fact that leaders who were engaged in the struggle for nationalist freedom betrayed their own instincts towards fundamentalism as in the case of Tilak, who clearly considered Rukhma's stand untenable.[12]

Enslaved Daughters: Colonialism, Law and Women's Rights traces the history and the complex set of issues that kept on cropping up. Rukhmabai's stand questioned the parental right to dispose of a daughter in marriage by raising the question of consent, acceptance and choice. She, as a child of 11, had no say in the matter and as such had not given her consent. Chandra refers to her act as 'an inspired gesture of defiance', which was an assertion of her right over her person (Chandra 1). Many a woman before her had been forced into an unwilling marriage but few had shown the courage to resist. At one level, it was a direct challenge to the traditional notion of *pativrata*, the devoted wife, who unquestioningly accepted her fate. The colonial law, as it unveiled itself, was as limited as the religiously propagated moral law. None of the two had the scope to be context-sensitive. It was not merely a matter of polarities of the ruler and the ruled, but it brought to the fore the whole question of reform, the agency of reform, the force of tradition and the accountability or otherwise of colonial law. Did the British have the right to shape colonial law in accordance with religious affiliations? Did they have the right to apply British norms or British laws pertaining to marriage and inheritance to the Indian scene?[13] Was the idea of 'justice' culture-based?

Rukhmabai's case in itself was not an unusual one. Many a woman, married as a girl, had outstepped her husband in beauty and intelligence but had continued to live in an unequal marriage. Pandita Ramabai gives the example of her own elder sister,[14] where the sister's husband was inferior to her in every sense. Very likely, at times, mediocre men were chosen in order to be able to keep the daughters at home and have the son-in-law live in the in-laws' house. But the whole question of compatibility compels one to look more closely at its romantic, physical and intellectual components and no law is capable of dealing with that. Rukhmabai's non-compliance came to rest on the issue of consent, which implied the necessary maturity, the right of choice and the agency to be able to be a willing party. Thus, her stand was of a much wider import than a question of like or dislike.

Was she privileged in terms of access to education or not? Pandita Ramabai was instructed by her own mother, other women with the support of their husbands or fathers, but Rukhmabai educated herself through self-effort (Chandra 16–18). Later, after the case was behind her, she went on to qualify as a doctor and worked as a doctor in Surat (Chandra 202–203). This trait of determination was also behind her decision to contest her husband Dadaji's claim (for restitution of conjugal rights), a decision which her mother did not support. The social import of her decision went much beyond a personal matter: it attacked child marriage, parental control and the whole notion of marriage as sacred. It looked upon it as a contract between the two parties—the man and the woman—and brushed aside the father's right to give away his daughter as *kanyadan*.[15] Mr Justice Pinhey's judgement in September 1885 in favour of Rukhmabai roused the fears of the orthodox community and lines were now more sharply drawn as forces both opposing Rukhma and supporting her started planning their attack and defence strategies. Conscience, moral justice and values got thickly embroiled with issues of maintenance, validity of infant marriages and sacredness of tradition. The case, like a pebble in still waters, had sent ripples all over, ripples as sharp as splinters. This was rooted in the Indian socio-political situation.

Dadaji went in for an appeal and the case came up for another hearing. The press gave a wide coverage and entered the debate actively. Behramji Malabari, a Parsi and a social reformer, had constantly been commenting on the case. There was a lot of concern and sympathy for Rukhmabai among the sensitive. And even as legends and myths were quoted, their applicability was questioned. It may have been possible for Damayanti (of the Nala–Damayanti story) to accept her situation, but every Hindu girl cannot be expected 'to be a Damayanti in this Kaliyuga' (Chandra 66). Sudhir Chandra refers to the positive comment of an orthodox Hindu, Dewan Bahadur Raghunath Rao, made on the case. The Dewan drew attention to the fact that 'the spouses' consent and consummation were essential for a Hindu marriage to be valid' (Chandra 67). Evidently, the divisions marking the orthodox and the liberal were not so sharply defined that there could be no crossing from one to the other.

For Rukhma, the battle continued for another two years. She was asked to return to her husband or else go to prison. Adamant, she was willing to go to prison, rather than accept life with a man she was averse to. Thus the 'personal' was first made into a legal issue, then a political one and finally a public issue. Her defiance brought forth another aspect of the whole case. In India, where individual will and privacy were always marginalised, and where the nationalists had irrationally considered a division into the domestic and the worldly possible, everything had boomeranged as the impending prison sentence aroused public passions. Chandra writes, 'Even the stolid colonial bureaucracy was shaken by the embarrassing prospect of the young rebel's imprisonment' (Chandra 111). The human-ethical considerations were ranged against the socio-legal. Rukhma was not asking for the right to remarry, only the permission not to cohabit. No decent man would take a woman by force. Criticism and mockery were also levied at her. The whole situation was frightening, the public gaze all-enveloping—one can only imagine the strength of the determination that sustained the young girl as she challenged 'both colonial law and indigenous authority'. The authorities realised the public agitation and scandal that would follow in the wake of her being actually sent to prison. The case finally ended through a compromise. Dadaji accepted two thousand rupees in satisfaction of all costs and agreed not to execute the decree against her (Chandra 160–162). The legal solution had not worked—the first judgement and the second both had failed to adequately meet the requirements of the case. The organised orthodoxy felt shaken (and threatened) by the spectre of her martyrdom, and thus inevitably and inadvertently came to her rescue.

91

The Rukhmabai case marks another stage in the battle for 'right to the body', a battle the beginnings of which are visible in Draupadi's case. Additionally, it also marks a resistance to women's subordination to discriminatory cultural constructs. The long-drawn-out legal suit and the public debates that surrounded it also critiqued the institution of marriage and blurred the boundaries between public and private space. Increasingly, it demonstrated the need for women's agency to come forth as full-fledged members of society.

The anonymous *Simantni Updesh*, like the Rukhmabai case, deserves a detailed attention for several reasons. For one, it is totally indigenous; two, it addresses Indian women and in an Indian language; three, it is much more critical and forthright in its perceptions than Pandita Ramabai's *The High Caste Hindu Woman*. Moreover, it was written as early as 1882. From the literary aspect, it uses several different strategies—proverbs, colloquialisms, myths, storytelling, satire and mockery. Finally, and more important than all else, it pushes the women to take the initiative in getting rid of old oppressive practices and transforming their own mindsets, reminding one of a song, currently very popular with women activists—'*Tu khud ko badal, tab hi to zamana badle ga*' (Transform yourself, only then will the world change). *Simantni Updesh* is characterised by a rare boldness of style and language, at times verging on an aggressive tone. The anonymity of the text raises further questions. Is it a lapse on part of the first publisher? Or will further research yield more information about its origins?[16] Or does it follow the Indian tradition of oral literature when anonymity often veiled either a long oral tradition, collectivity, or a downplaying of the ego? One could also venture that anonymity is also a shield for boldness.

Gender, not caste or region forms the base of this text. Though most of the experiences and customs that are described are restricted to North India (Punjab and Uttar Pradesh), for once the cultural barrier between Hindus and Muslims is crossed. Many of the practices, the stress on jewellery, the material base (constructed by society) of a woman's life, and the double standards of morality are common to both. The issues which the writer targets are everyday practices, observation of fasts, hierarchy in family life, confinement to domesticity, the wrong values which have been internalised by women, woman to woman relationships, the strife, division and jealousy over men—sons and husbands—all come in for heavy criticism. Instead, rationality, comfort (in matters of dress and ornaments), education and freedom are projected as positive values. The reference point is not necessarily Vedic or Sastric; it is predominantly the way men and women live. There is every evidence that the writer is an educated and aware woman, well-placed in life with a fair amount of social experience and freedom, gifted with keen powers of observation, analysis and reasoning.

The text opens with a poem, an invocation addressed to the Supreme Power, and is followed by another, which is a prayer on behalf of all women, the main idea of which is 'how long can we live this life of imprisonment? With none else to guide us, God you need to come to our help' (*Simantni Updesh* 22). There is a gradual moving from verse to prose, from a general prayer to a collective prayer on behalf of all women, expressing helplessness, praying for help, freedom and compassion. It goes on to state that even actual prisoners are better off than women, for at least their sentence has a term. At one point, the authoress mentions Munshi Kanhailal Alakhdhari as a just and a fair man. He is respected for his pro-woman attitude. Others who also favour the cause for women's equality and freedom are Pandit Shiv Narayan Agnihotri, the editor of a journal; Rai Navin Chand, another staunch supporter of women's education; and Swami Dayanand Saraswati, leader of the Arya Samaj and a well-known educationist.

The first few chapters are in the nature of a prologue. Finally, it is acknowledged that the real initiative has to come from women themselves (28). The details of the flow of thought are interesting, because they demonstrate an inner structure in the writer's thought. There is then a very interesting dialogue between two women about jewellery, the heavy ornaments they extract from their menfolk on various pretexts, such as by pretending to sulk or going without food. The similes are full of satire and mockery—a woman's anklets are based on the design of the chain used for tying elephants. Most of the ornaments have been paid for by enduring physical beatings, abuses and near starvation (31). Gifts of jewellery are commonly viewed as the sign of prosperity and love. Often the burden may break one's back, drag the pierced ear, make walking difficult, leave bruises on the body, but it is still worn and shown off and used to signify social, marital and emotional status.[17]

A sufficiently long section is devoted to jewellery because it is one great hindrance to self-respect, a great material bargaining counter, a dividing line between rich and poor, a married woman and a widowed one as also between men and women. If one could transcend these petty compensations, there would be time and energy to be directed towards other ends. Often these heavily decorated women move barefoot. Many a proverb places woman at the feet of man and one idiom that expresses her lowly status is '*paon ki juti*' (the shoe on my feet). Dress comes in for another long discussion, where the body is centre staged—its exposure or veiling, its colour or lack of colour. Comfort is often given the go-by. Behind this criticism is the idea that women give more importance to appearances—to externals—rather than to learning and self-improvement.

Simantni Updesh, even as it begins by focusing on the externals, soon zeroes down on the body, sexuality and morality. Once again it is the self, governed and controlled by moral strength, which is considered important. Endowed with the same kind of sensual awareness and sexual desire that a man is, a woman is subjected either to deprivation, at times a lifelong deprivation, or compelled into secret alliances, which are never likely to lead to happiness. The authoress is responding to Manu's charge of women being easily seducible. Widowhood, motherhood, childlessness are all discussed and the merits and demerits of each discussed as far as emotional strengths and conditions of happiness are

94

concerned. They are alternative states of being and are relative in degree to each other.

There is also a chapter on the *dharma* of a wife, that is, *pativrata dharma*. None of the scriptures lays down any other prayer, ritual or practice for women other than *pativrata*. There are tales of rewards for the devotion to the husband, miraculous cures, return from death and the like. Most gender discriminations, including initiation rites, rise principally from the belief that a woman is considered subordinate to man. This chapter—Chapter 22—is a bold critique of the principle of *pativrata*. There is no rationality behind this belief which is purely motivated by selfish male interest (91–93).

Simantni Updesh is realistic in its approach and offers practical solutions as it aspires to bring about a change in the attitudes and the way women think; in short, it seeks to transform the self-image of women and in the process alter value structures substituting real strength for all that is superficial, decorative and material. The writer is not interested in pushing women into spiritual or religious frames of mind as the Bhakti Movement or refuge in ashrams have advocated from time to time. Her focus is on improving the quality of domestic and social life and to reduce the suspicion, distrust and manipulation that pervade relationships. One may turn around and ask, is it not too ambitious or idealistic? Perhaps not. Her criticism of patriarchal domination is aimed at unveiling its degenerative influences on human character and life.

A work which belongs to 1876 is the Bengali autobiography of Rassundari Devi, an amazing record of the determination of an average woman caught up in the daily grind of household chores. This personal text is also a social text. Rassundari Devi was born in 1809, married at the age of 12 and from the ages of 18 to 41 gave birth to 11 children. At age 59, when she was widowed, she wrote her autobiography, *Amar Jiban* (My Life), which was published in 1876. Later on at age 88 she dictated a second part, which was then printed in the new enlarged edition in 1897. Why is the autobiography important for us? Perhaps because it gives a first hand account of the frustrations that beset a girl child, right from her childhood under the oppressive burden of custom. Rassundari, herself a cared-for child, suffers from loneliness at her dislocation from her maternal home, a feeling which persists well into her marriage despite a caring mother-in-law. Throughout her life, the repeated conceptions and childbirths failed to bring her any closer to her husband, who in his own way was a good man in all respects. The emotional understanding never developed. Perhaps it never had a chance to develop. The laws of purity virtually confined her to the household; although there were eight maidservants in the house, none of them was permitted into the kitchen. Thus, with the large number of people to feed, children to be looked after and guests to be attended to, she very often did not get the time to eat her food the whole day long. There is a total absence of choice and/or of authority.

This long list is only peripheral. The real refrain of the autobiography is her desire to be educated, to be able to read and write, a desire which she strove all her life to fulfil. There is the childhood experience of going briefly to a Bengali school (24), but this soon came to an end. Thereafter, there is a constant lament that education was not open to girls (40, 42, 44, 51–52, 54–56, 64). But then there is another strand of continuity, when she begins to recognise the letters, tries to learn writing, practices from the pictorial elements, observes her children being taught, learns to read and does this in secret and in the afternoons with the maid servants, and is mortally afraid of her reading ability being discovered and yet she persists. There is a longing for the poetic and the unattainable: 'Has anyone ever been able to hold the moon in his hands? No, never. It was a futile wish' (63). The autobiography, repetitive and simple, is honest, transparent and reflective. Rassundari Devi examines her own experiences and feelings as closely as possible, without trying to praise her own courage. Also, there is no blame apportioned to anyone. It is the spirit of the age, which circumscribed the lives of both men and women, and women, as they were subordinated, suffered even more. Her life is an example of an individual evolving ways and means of reconstructing the world around her. All along, her love for Chaitanya, her devotion and her poetic compositions interrupt and create a parallel narrative.[18]

Each of these women resisted patriarchy in some way or the other, but none of them defied the norms of dress or the code of social behaviour. They got busy with what they wished to do, such as to learn reading, to self-educate themselves, go in for higher studies, practice as doctors, teachers or social workers, but they conformed to the 'womanly' behaviour. Ramabai lived life as a widow; Rukhmabai donned the widow's garb on the death of the husband she had rejected; Rassundari Devi brought up her children and mourned her dead. They spent their energies on extending their boundaries.[19]

Outside the Confines

Domesticity nurtured its hierarchies through confines, an unequal moral law and a different *dharma* for the woman wrapped up in the concept of *pativrata*. Patriarchy worked through exclusions and power. A contrast to this is the public space of the devadasi, the courtesan, the public woman, who while she had access to learning, music and dance, was kept out of family life.[20] They had relatively more freedom, but they had their own struggles against exploitation, deprivation and social castigation. These women, with a few exceptions, were mostly from the low-caste, non-brahmin families or were slaves. In rare cases were women from the upper caste donated to or offered at the temples.

Bharata's *Nāṭyaśāstra* is one of the earliest treatises on the performing arts, contemporaneous in time to *Manusmriti*, and it is also a compendium of how the human body can use its *mudra*s (hands, finger and body movements) to communicate and evoke the necessary emotional response. G.H. Tarlekar, commenting upon the social status of the actors, traces the meaning of the word *Nata* (through its synonyms *Sailūsa* and

Jayajiva) as indicating one who makes his livelihood through his wife (Tarlekar 223). He goes on to mention that Manu prohibited brahmins from becoming actors. Kusilavas (bard, connected with music) have lower legal status, and their testimony has no validity. Food sharing with actors is also taboo. Tarlekar further refers to *Visnusmriti* (Tarlekar xvi, 3–8) as assigning the profession of actors to the illegal progeny born of a Sudra man and a Vaisya's daughter. In short, the acting profession was not considered respectable. This applied equally to the female members of a troupe—actresses were considered as women of loose morals, easily available, courtesans and prostitutes. But he adds, 'the art was great' (212). Herein lies the irony. The beautiful, the aesthetic, the emotionally enriching was out of bounds for the respectable. Women were the greater losers as they were traditionally barred from learning. Just as pilgrimages became an escape route, devotional music and worship of God became a vacuum-filler.

Various dance forms had all male performers, with men dressing up as women. In some others, following the principle of segregation, the cast was all female. In some dramatic performances there were, and increasingly are, mixed casts. Classical Indian theatre concentrates less on plot and more on movements and evocation of emotional response in adherence to the *rasa* theory. The emphasis is on representation and the whole range of emotions. Bharata makes a distinction between *bhava* and *rasa*. There are 49 *bhava*s. *Bhava* mean a 'mental state'. They are responsible for the initiation of sentiments, leading to their expression either through facial muscles, eyes or through gesticulation and posture. *Rasa*s are outwardly related to the other party, the spectator, viewer or reader who participates in the *bhava* through the agency of the *rasa*. Tarlekar identifies the primary purpose of *natya* as to give *paranirvrti*, the highest bliss. But he insists that the secondary purpose of imparting instruction is equally important (66).

When Tarlekar describes in an Appendix (Appendix D, 317–323) the costumes that were in use in ancient India, it is obvious that the female body has a centrality on the stage with its contours and curves, fully exploited for the purpose of evocation. It automatically leads to the questions: did women form part of the audience. It is extremely doubtful, given the gender roles and difference of spatial ordering. Kapila Vatsyayan views Bharata's view of theatre as an organic one, closely related to philosophy and conceptualised on the basis of Upanisdic thought (Vatsyayan 54).[21] The world is a 'configuration of the five primary elements of earth, water, fire, air and space'. Man is distinctive because of his capacity of reflection. Bharata uses the idea of the cosmic man as *purusa*. But even as he prioritises the connection of the body and the mind, woman is further objectified in the theatre as her body and beauty are first perceived, sung or talked about by the other characters in the play and then transmitted through movement and words to the audience. Would it be legitimate then to consider the *Nātyaśāstra* also a patriarchal imaging of women? A related question is what did the classical dramatists make of it and how were their women characters shaped and presented.

An important play is Kālidāsa's 'Abhijnānāśakuntalam' (hereafter referred to as 'Śakuntalā'). Kālidāsa is one of three classical dramatists whose plays are among the extant works of that time. The period to which Kālidāsa belonged cannot be identified by any certainty, but scholars place him between first century BCE to fourth or fifth century CE.[22] The story of 'Śakuntalā' is borrowed from the *Mahābhārata* and given a dramatic form. The full title means 'the recognition of Śakuntalā' (or the 'knowing' of Śakuntalā), resting the whole play on the recognition by the man who had married her in her father's absence, taken full responsibility for the act and then conveniently forgotten it due to loss of memory/a curse/or in order to await divine approval and get public sanction.[23]

Śakuntalā is a child of nature and, like the deer, is the object of male pursuit, dwelling in the forest *ashrama* of her foster father. Śakuntalā is the daughter of the *apsara* Menaka and Kaushik and is thus partly of a different world. The play has a seven-act division, titled the Chase, Concealment of the Telling, Love's Fruition, Śakuntalā's Departure, The

Repudiation of Śakuntalā, Separation from Śakuntalā and Śakuntalā's Prosperity. Working through the play, it is the king who is first seen engaged in the pursuit of a deer belonging to the hermitage when an ascetic intervenes, pleading for the deer's life. This prepares the way for the king and his companion to approach the hermitage, and on citing Śakuntalā with her companion Priyamvada, he hides himself in order to observe her. He is also a silent commentator (his remarks are meant for the audience) on the friends' conversation, as he stands on 'forbidden ground' (in the sense of not coming out in the open), and listens to what is not meant for his ears. The girls continue to talk of being 'wedded', 'marriage of vine and tree', 'budding youth', 'ready for enjoyment' (Rajan 177), terms romantically, metaphorically and erotically laden and creating a scene of two circles of observers within the play—the girls watching and admiring nature, the men admiring the girls and the admiration and enjoyment being further relayed to the audience. The subject of union and of the king's protection is also introduced, and the king, with his intentions quite clear in his own mind, discloses his presence but not his identity. The meeting soon develops into a full-fledged romance.

The second act is centred on the king and his men. The third brings us back to the hermitage and to Śakuntalā and her friends. The king's courtship is progressing well, but Śakuntalā is reluctant to commit herself. Repeatedly, the subject of remembering and forgetting comes up as does the subject of 'knowing'. At one stage, Śakuntalā tells the king, 'Even though your wishes remain unfulfilled and you *know me* only through conversation, do not forget me' (209, emphasis added). Śakuntalā's oneness with nature is also emphasised. Despite the romantic attraction, the young girl is not entirely bewitched. There is a slight feeling of distrust towards the king's overtures.

The next act is again located in the hermitage. Duhsanta, the king, and Śakuntalā have gone through a *gandharva* ceremony, bypassing the *kanyadaan* ritual during the sage Kanva's absence, and the king returns to his palace. Śakuntalā's companions once again talk about the remembering and forgetting. Śakuntalā neglects the laws of hospitality and the great sage Durvasa curses her that her beloved one will fail to remember her (215). Śakuntalā is then sent to her husband's home. The fifth act is located in the palace; Śakuntalā arrives but the king has no recollection of the marriage (237), and the ring, a token of remembrance, is also conveniently lost. There is a total reversal in the king's behaviour. Now he perceives her as a cunning woman. Finally, Śakuntalā is enraged:

> Ignoble man! You who are like a well-covered grass…you judge every one by the measure of your own heart…who would stoop to imitate your conduct…practising falseness while putting on a mantle of virtue? (239)

The king does remember; he is feigning forgetfulness, for at this point he thinks to himself, 'The lady's anger is real—the spontaneous outburst of one who lives in the green world…' and then:

> When I cruelly denied our secret love
> Then did she dart flaming glances on me…. (239)

Śakuntalā doesn't plead any more; instead, she tells him what she thinks of him: 'A man whose mouth is honey, but whose heart is stone.' The king's character, which is worldly, and Śakuntalā's character, which has always been free of deception, are the ones that are being weighed in the scale. Śakuntalā, abandoned as a baby, is now once again abandoned as a wife.

There is no possibility of return to the hermitage. This act, the fifth, one of confrontation and conflict, of moral judgement and creative tension between forces of right and wrong, forgetting and remembering, control and indulgence, forms the dramatic centre of the play. No longer is Śakuntalā the young romantic girl deluded by love, enamoured by the king's lavish praise, inexperienced and innocent, but a woman, on the verge of motherhood, confronted by the reality when she is being rejected (by her husband) and abandoned (by her father). Knowing his own nature well, the king is afraid of losing his virtue and of being tempted. He asks Śakuntalā's escort: 'Am I deluded, or, is she false?'

The decision of the case now is left to the birth of Śakuntalā's child, and the birth signs the child may have. But Śakuntalā is rescued by her mother, not fit for mortal homes, flawed as they are. The king who is outwardly relieved is inwardly perturbed, and the audience is once again thrown into uncertainty—does he or does he not remember?

Act six is about the recovery of the king's ring, which Śakuntalā had inadvertently lost. It is recovered from a fisherman who had found it in a fish he had caught. We then return to a full spring-laden garden, but the palace is as if in mourning. The union does not take place; there is no joyful return by Śakuntalā. In the seventh and the final act, the king is once again in a hermitage, this time a celestial one, where a young boy is being held back by hermit women. The child wants to count the teeth of a lion's cub. The child is not scared, and the king marvels at his strength and boldness. The king feels drawn towards the child and experiences a strange sense of pleasure. The women notice the resemblance between the king and the boy. Śakuntalā, however, does not recognise him. The play ends conveniently in clearing the king of all blame with the problems being traced to Durvasa's curse. His wife and son are restored to him. Patriarchy values its own power.

From beginning to end, it is the king's desire, his lineage and the continuity of his reign that hold the plot together; except for the fifth act, Śakuntalā is helped by other agencies at every step—birth, rescue from rejection and restoration. She is all along compared with nature and is placed in positions of subordination to events, fate and destiny. Chandra Rajan, comparing the play to the story as narrated in the *Mahābhārata*, considers the play a blend of 'romance and fairytale'. Śakuntalā is never really placed in the 'gilded' world of the palace. She is and still remains a child of nature. In the *Mahābhārata* story she is portrayed as a fiery and spirited girl who fights tenaciously for her son's rights. She literally reads the Law to the king when she finds him obdurate, gives him such a tongue lashing that we practically see him squirming on his jeweled throne.... Kālidāsa has drastically changed his sources to convey his own vision of life and his view of certain problems.... (Rajan, 'Introduction' 94)

One wonders whether the play does justice to Śakuntalā or more to male whims and desire—for it is she who suffers and is subjected to single parenthood. But referring to Kālidāsa's version, Chandra Rajan asks, what is 'knowing' and how does one know? First, Duhsanta knows her only carnally; his pursuit of helpless animals seems to be his main royal occupation. It is only when she is not available to him that he regrets having let her go. True, at the end he realises her true worth as Rajan points out, but to my mind it is more through the fact of his own fatherhood and Śakuntalā fulfilling the role of a virtuous wife than because of any genuine realisation of her true worth as a person.

Avadhesh Kumar Singh uses Kālidāsa's play in order to construct an Indian theory of postcolonialism (40–58). He too agrees with Chandra Rajan that the story in the *Mahābhārata* is more fair to Śakuntalā and shows her as a fiery young woman conscious alike of her birth, status, identity and rights, located in the spirit of matriarchal society (47–48), while Kālidāsa's heroine is timid and obedient. Women are clearly subordinate (48–49). But the binary opposition Kālidāsa uses throughout between the court and the hermitage, the earthly and the celestial, the natural and human, nature and culture, creates a power relationship based on control, invasion, pursuit and aggression. Śakuntalā obviously, like the deer, is a captive, surrenders to the king's persuasion, ends up paying a heavy price for it and is finally rescued through divine intervention. Singh's theory takes up the control of 'a distant territory' as a colonial construct, resulting in the loss of innocence, and identifies forgiveness as a distinctive quality in the Indian theory of postcolonialism (55). One is compelled to ask why did Kālidāsa transform the main woman character's stand or tone it down? Was it the growing patriarchy that led him to this conservatism and an insistence on the ideals of *Manusmriti*? Or was it the compulsions of the dramatic art and the concentration on the *rasa* theory that brought about the elaborate portrayal of nature and beauty?

The story of Śakuntalā has also been the subject of many films in several Indian languages. To list a few, two different versions were made in 1920, with many more to follow in 1929, 1931, 1941, 1943, 1961, 1966 and a TV serial in 1986.[24] These indicate the continued interest of the people in the tale. Romila Thapar begins her essay 'Śakuntalā: Histories of a Narrative',[25] with the comment, 'The manner in which we construct the past is now acknowledged as an important process in the writing of history. This involves appropriating the past, an act in which the concerns of the present are apparent' (1). She goes on to point out that the different variants highlight the gender perspective (4). In the *Mahābhārata* story, Śakuntalā is the 'reverse of the *pativrata*, the ideal wife' (Thapar, 'Śakuntalā' 7). Kālidāsa's play shifts to a consideration of royal power and Śakuntalā is made to 'conform to the *pativrata* ideal' (Thapar, 'Śakuntalā' 12). Referring to the remark that *gandharva* marriage is a form of seduction, Thapar asks whether this is a 'resentment against a woman's transgression of patriarchy and her taking an independent decision, for he insists that she must suffer the consequences of such a decision' (12). It is ironical that a woman who in a bardic version (that of the *Mahābhārata*) began as a questioning, independent woman, capable of taking a stand, is transformed through retellings and translations, as Thapar points out, and is depicted as a child of nature, pliant and malleable. This image appealed to the Western imagination and fell in comfortably with the idea of India as an effeminate culture, representing a 'natural' world awaiting a civilising discipline. Thapar states that 'a touch of racism entered the idyllic picture of closeness to nature' ('Śakuntalā' 17). Tracing the progress of the story through James Mill's criticism with his charge of a self-indulgent culture, and even through Tagore's view of Śakuntalā's as the 'fall of Śakuntalā' (Thapar, 'Śakuntalā' 18–21), Śakuntalā is transformed from a passionate and independent woman into one who is a moral transgressor whose sins account for her suffering.

Getting back to the narrative in the *Mahābhārata*, the narrative of Duhsanta and Śakuntalā carries within it remnants of earlier stories. Marriage is entered into subject to a contractual understanding that the son born of this union will be crowned king during the lifetime of his father. Like the births of Sītā and Draupadi, Śakuntalā also has a divine origin, though in this case it is the union of the sage Visvamitra and the *apsara* Menaka. Agency of the woman is stressed and is evident much more than in the case of Sītā, Draupadi and Satyavati. In their cases their fathers were instrumental in arranging their marriages, but in Śakuntalā's case, her foster father was away. She negotiates the marriage terms herself. When the king advocates *gandharva vivah* he tells her that she can give herself away, thereby bypassing the father's role of giving her away (that is the ceremony of *kanyadaan*). Śakuntalā responded to his request by saying that if this was way accepted by religion, and she had the right to give herself away, she had a condition.

In the *Mahābhārata* story, Śakuntalā's pregnancy lasts three years, her son is of unusual prowess and grows up to be brave and courageous. Śakuntalā makes the trip to the palace only when her son has left his babyhood behind. But the king feigns ignorance. The *Mahābhārata* text effectively states that he did so as he wanted a public affirmation of the legitimacy of the child's lineage. Śakuntalā's response to the king is full of anger as she tells him to consult his conscience; his actions have reduced his stature and dignity. Then follows a lengthy discourse on the importance of a wife in a man's life. But even as this is pronounced, the superiority of the paternal right over maternal nurture is proclaimed by the sage. The story precedes the main narrative of the Kauravas and Pandavas, and it sends out a mixed message where gender equality is concerned. It primarily becomes a story of nation construction, of holding people together. Over and above these, it does recognise the agency of women, the association of female virtue with birthing and continuity, the proxy nature of power that women acquire through motherhood and the contractual nature of marriage, which places it firmly within reciprocity rather than hierarchy. Kālidāsa's revisionary rewriting retains only some elements of Śakuntalā's fiery independence, but he compensates by giving Śakuntalā a degree of freedom when she opts out of the marriage; unfortunately, both these versions highlight romance and procreative relationships but downplay her sexuality. Rewritings work through selective representations and attempt to fit in with the prevailing social and moral code.

The open space that the performative art made available was also categorised by restrictions and discriminations. I propose to discuss some autobiographies of actresses in order to bring out their struggles, loneliness, sense of deprivation and the courage to survive.[26] The first of these is Binodini Dasi's *My Story and My Life as an Actress*, originally written in Bengali, the first ('My Story') in 1912 and the second ('My Life as an Actress') in 1924–1925. Binodini was one of the first generation of women to join Bengali theatre as a professional actress in 1874. Women actresses or women in public were treated as the 'symbols' of culture, while women in domesticity as custodians of culture. This was the beginning of middle-class Bengali theatre. Many actresses were recruited from the prostitutes' quarters and thus from houses of disrepute, the other side of the border of respectability.

Theatrical activity, curiously, was a part and an extension of the reformist movement, and revival of classic Indian culture and tradition was one of its concerns. Rimli Bhattacharya observes that professional actors were beginning to write their autobiographies, discuss theatre histories and in general beginning to show an awareness of their professional needs and environment. She goes on to observe that an 'overwhelming number of features would suggest that Binodini Dasi's writings fall clearly into the stereotypes of the "feminine"—the personal, the confessional, the lament and so on,' but due to its transformation, first from a commissioned article to a privately published, rewritten and re-scripted book and the history of her relationships, the book stands apart (R. Bhattacharya, 'Introduction' 24–25). Writing, in her case, was almost a trespassing into another class, that of the *bhadramahila*, the respectable woman, and after her exit from the theatre, a substitute medium of expression. It is like talking to her own self, going over her memories, communicating with the other, a counting of her losses and keeping her dead alive. One of her chosen addressees is her guru, Girish Ghosh.

Binodini Dasi also published two collections of poems and a few articles in newspapers and theatre journals spread over a period of about 30 years, from 1885 to 1915 (R. Bhattacharya, 'Introduction' 18). But it is the autobiography, which with its concern for creativity, theatre art and personal emotions stands apart. She refers to herself as one born to suffer (*janamdukhini*) and her life as a narrative of pain (*bedona katha*). Absolutely alone, viewing herself as a fallen woman, she desperately needs a listener (B. Dasi, 'Preface' 49). The story is dedicated to her guru and protector; this is also an offering to him in her bereavement. There is a reference to an earlier preface written by Girish Ghosh, which the actress did not like as it glossed over certain facts. She prefers to write the naked, undecorated truth, even if it be unsavoury and bitter (54). The first section consists of letters, part of a correspondence with Girish Ghosh, but represents only her own responses.

Binodini Dasi's autobiography falls into two parts, or one can say they are two different first person accounts dealing with different aspects of her life. When she writes about her life, she begins from childhood; acting and her association with the stage come into it, but the focus is not on them; it is on the events of her life, the emotional currents, the relationships, the losses. The men she had a relationship with are not named; they remain cloaked in the word 'protector'. She admits to having sexual relationships and a brief period of motherhood, which came to an abrupt end with the death of her daughter.

There is a strong sense of community and kinship. Poor people are quicker to come to each other's help than the well-to-do. Her childhood is one of poverty with neighbours often coming to their help. Marriages are solemnised, her brother is married off at age five and his infant wife's ornaments support the household's expense. He died a couple of years later and except for a brief mention, no further mention is made of the sister-in-law. Binodini's child marriage has also been lost midway with an aunt-in-law taking her husband away and ceasing all contact with them. The writer does not spend too much time on these events; they are peripheral to her emotional life. But their inclusion in the narrative indicates both a social normalcy of ties being formed and a class difference, especially as not much fuss is made about broken marriages or widowhood, events which would have been reprehensible in the so-called respectable classes/society.

One of the most powerful and full of knowledgeable admiration for Binodini is the essay 'Srimati Binodini and the Bengali Stage' by Girishchandra Ghosh, which is included in Rimli Bhattacharya's 'Afterword' (210–220). Ghosh's essay is also part self-revelation: 'I will be obliged to speak of my own life. This is no ordinary obstacle: of all the difficult things in this world, the most difficult task is to speak about oneself' (R. Bhattacharya, 'Afterword' 210). He shows no hesitation of speaking about her as a fallen woman; she herself, in her own account, uses this term to describe her own condition. The self-image, thus, is not based on any illusion; it is stark and over-realistic, it is how the world sees her. Binodini's self-image is a sad reflection on the laws of social morality and respectability which use such strong dividing lines. Ghosh also perceives in her writing 'a bitter critique of society' (212).

An actress's life is emotionally very demanding, requiring rigorous practice, control over voice and body and the ability to transform the personality through dress, make-up and expression. They are the vehicle of *bhava*, and every different *bhava* possesses the actor in a different way. Girishchandra Ghosh, who often acted as the male lead in her plays, was a close friend and guru, and was in more than one way her connection with the world of the educated and the Western theatre. He was her source of inspiration. Ghosh is controlled, fairly objective in his description of her roles, revealing the real actress behind the roles that won her public applause.

Binodini Dasi's account of 'My Life as an Actress' is written at the end of an acting career and in retrospect. The theatre was an addiction for her when she was engrossed in acting, and the theatre is an addiction even at the time of writing. Memory and forgetfulness, vivid and hazy frames, move before the screen of her mind. She recounts how they were instructed to shut off the audience, to concentrate on the stage. This helped to create an enclosed world within which role-playing became natural.

'My Story' is far more personal; it is the story of her anguish, her *bedona katha*, a tale of comparisons with women who had homes and husbands. The prologue consisting of four letters of her correspondence with Ghosh (dated Sraban, 1316, i.e. 1909), is one such cry of agony. She asks: 'Whatever it is that I have done throughout my life: has that been work for God? Such low acts: could they have been for God?' 'My restless heart asks time and again, "What is my work in this world?"' (56). There is not much satisfaction in giving pleasure to the audience: 'did the members of the audience ever see my inner self?' (57).

There were phases of depression, of a sense of loss as when her rich young protector pushed off to his village and got married. There was a sudden realisation that there were boundaries which could never be crossed. A world outside her reach, which would always lie on the other side. In one such mood of self-reflection, Binodini Dasi writes:

Utterly despicable and degraded is our status in society, but let them not read it who will despise or ridicule this insignificant bit of writing. Let them refrain from sprinkling salt to further irritate the deepest wounds in a woman's life.... How many are the unfulfilled longings, the wounds burning with pain that are alight in her heart: has anyone ever seen any of this? They become prostitutes forced by

circumstances, lacking shelter, lacking a space; but they too, first come into this
world with the heart of a woman.... None but a fellow sufferer will understand how
painful and tortured this life is. (104–105)

Who is responsible for this state of affairs? Men who may take advantage of them? Caste, poverty, social discrimination? Who bears the final
responsibility and guilt? Companionship of men, some kind of intellectual communication, a tapping of talent or access to music, dance and
higher education may be possible, but the doors of family life are closed.
The choice is between two alternatives, both of which are necessary and
desirable. And the choice to have both is just not given. Moreover, the
right to exercise any particular choice is also not one's own. Morality, and
with it the notion of respectability, act as exclusionary strategies where
performing artists are concerned. Minoti Chatterjee, in her essay titled
'Creatures of the Sub-world: Nineteenth Century Actresses of Bengali
Stage', points out that the talent of these women was immaterial, 'the
woman actress could never supersede the fact that she lived a public life
and consented to be hired for amusement by any one who could command the price' (338), she goes on to ask whether it would be appropriate
to talk of an 'emerging feminine consciousness'—not activism, but varying perceptions of how women perceive and experience the world (351).

Sudhavna Deshpande, writing about the early twentieth-century Marathi theatre, also discusses the question of respectability. A factor that
contributed to an introduction of the element of respectability was when,
with increased commercialisation, the middle classes began to participate
in the enterprise. This was more so when films opened out other avenues.
Many actresses wrote their life accounts, gave interviews to magazines
or dictated their life stories. And many of them have similar stories to
repeat in the nineteenth and the first half of the twentieth century. Hansa
Wadkar is one such actress. Towards the end of her life, during one of her
illnesses, she was interviewed and the work published as *Sangyte Aika*
(in Marathi) in 1966 in *Manush*. The interviews and recordings were

completed by Arun Sadhu. Rajhans Publishers later published it in book form.[27] Shyam Benegal went on to make a film based on it, a film titled *Bhumika*, literally translated as The Role.

Hansa's mother was a devadasi's daughter (thus traditionally outside family life). Right from childhood, Hansa was trained in singing by her grandmother and was pursued as a future wife by a neighbour Jagannath Bandarkar, who extracted a promise from her early that she would marry him. He did so at a time when she did not even grasp the meaning of marriage. As she narrates her life story, the reader realises that her future husband used unfair pressure to have her, that the father incapable of providing for the family, played a passive role. Economic needs pushed Hansa into films at an early age, terminating her studies and putting an end to all her dreams of higher education.

In the main, it is the story of her growing up, the different skills she had to acquire like learning the *tamasha* style of performance, singing, riding and other such accomplishments. The reader also gets a glimpse of the lighter moments on the sets, the occasional romantic complications and friendships or disagreements with co-workers. But despite the fact that these details trace her growth as a star and the story of her popularity and decline, the strand of personal narration is the one which is significant. There is first the pressure applied on her to go frequently to Jagannath's house, in a way literally pushing her into his arms, then the compulsion to go to work to support the household, in order to enable her brother to continue his studies and her father to drink to his pleasure; later comes the marriage to Jagannath Bandarkar, which is also an exploitative one, then her miscarriages, the decline into alcoholism, being suspected of having a relationship with her leading man and getting literally trapped into another relationship that effectively ended both her marriage and her career. Hansa Wadkar's life story is a representation of the in-between world that actresses, especially those who came from the *devadasi* clan or other marginal castes, lived in. Even when marriage and family life became accessible to them, the relationships were often exploitative. They had little control over their choices or their earnings; the men—father, brother, husband, lover—all equally exploited them. Almost like a refrain, the narrator voices her unfulfilled desire for a peaceful family life, for the right to domesticity and the time to look after her children. She had expected that marriage would free her from work, but this had not happened. Hansa describes the first major quarrel with her husband, when he lashed her with a leather belt, on the basis of some rumour he had heard against her, and sternly asked her to take an oath of good behaviour:

> My mind rebelled. I had not done anything. Why did people fabricate such reports! And why should he believe these rumours! Anger rose within me. My eyes flared with rage. 'I have not done anything wrong, why should I take an oath?' Again, he hit me hard. I was on fire. My husband doubts me, fine. God's picture was before me. I stood before it. I ground my teeth in anger and silently took an oath—I have not committed any sin so far in my life—but I take an oath in Duttaji's name, from now on I will not care about anybody. I was completely transformed. In a moment I changed. (Chapter 2)[28]

She turned to drink, and feelings of revenge, of hitting back, took possession of her. On another occasion, it is a set of gold bangles that her husband takes away, which become the obvious cause. But the truth is the feeling of distrust and of betrayal that now defined their relationship. Again and again she asked herself: 'Is this a home? Is this family life? I was discontented from both sides. My whole being was agonized' (Chapter 8).

In many ways, she perhaps had more freedom than a housewife. She travelled, laughed and sang, had some resources to care for her parents, conversed with men, attended public functions and developed other interests like driving and riding. But she experienced no real freedom either in an unhappy marriage where she and Jagannath were constantly pulling in opposite directions or in the supposedly more conventional set up of Joshi's house (Joshi was the man with whom she lived for three years). Joshi had two other wives. She was literally a servant in that household, cooking and slaving for the whole family. In sheer desperation, she contacted Bandarkar to come and rescue her. He did come to her help—but that was about all. There was no way of getting back to the uneven keel of their early years.

Hansa Wadkar finally landed up in a third relationship, which gave her some kind of a family life. There is a constant struggle between her own desire for a life of normalcy with some degree of freedom thrown in, an equal, reciprocal and caring relationship on one side and the barrier her exploitable body created for her on the other. Everyone—her family, her husband, her lovers, the magistrate who was to sign the papers when Bandarkar rescued her from Joshi's house—all of them had not a moment's hesitation in exploiting her.

Is women's desire for domesticity a purely romantic wish? The prison-like domesticity of Joshi's house is also extremely confining and offers no hope of equality. The autobiography leaves one with a great feeling of sadness and unfulfilment. A woman's life seems to be divided into different sections—body or mind; may be there is the third category consisting of desire—desire for the other, for love, for freedom, for equality, for a host of unrealisable things. One is left with the unanswered query: what is freedom? Any speculation of any other kind of life would also be futile. The battle goes much deeper. It is one between creativity and domesticity, between creativity and freedom and between the right to the body and the right to the mind. Women, like men, clamour for the freedom to live in both worlds—not divided or fragmented ones. The notion of respectability divides these worlds. One is compelled to ask: is there an inherent, irreconcilable opposition between a woman's need for artistic creativity and her need for romantic/sexual fulfilment? Does she have to transcend her body to exist as an individual?

The relationship between women: Hansa's with her mother, mother-in-law and grandmother, with her co-actors, the girls she formed friendships with, with Marybai, the woman who looked after her through her pregnancy, and with the more senior women actors who advised and protected her—all these create a parallel world of relationships where the sexual body does not interfere. The struggles are many, but at some point respectability, freedom and creativity do come together—at least in some cases. Regrettably, one has to admit that it is often caste and class that play an important role and education is a third category.

Contrasted with Hansa Wadkar's life is Zohra Segal's who had the advantage both of class and education. Her life, despite its transgressive acts, took a different course. Not only are respectability, freedom, creativity and domesticity combined, but the usual conventions and stereotypes are fully subverted. Born in a Pathan aristocratic family and educated in reputed institutions, she went on to a dance school in Germany, joined Uday Shankar's dance troupe and then acted in Prithvi Theatre. Zohra married a Hindu, thus crossing another boundary. Her autobiography *Stages* is subtitled *The Art and Adventures of Zohra Segal*. And the subtitle is an indicator of both sides of her life as she moved from one phase to another, taking charge of her life, finding her way from one art form to another, moving from dance to acting, from stage to films and from India to England and back again, signifying a convergence of personal and performative worlds.

There is one chapter that reveals both her fear and her sense of achievement: 'Family Matters'. The opening paragraph reads:

Happiness for an artist is knowing that your closest family members—father (my mother died when I was eight), sisters and brothers—don't look down on you. Naturally, my sisters admired me, and although my father never actually said he appreciated my work, he came to the Uday Shankar shows and in his own way was proud of me as a dancer.... The greatest surprise and blessing was my mother-in-law who, after seeing me in the role of a vamp in *Deewar*—with low-cut dresses and make-up, smoking a cigarette and flirting with the younger of two brothers—told me she knew my innermost being was pure, even in that outrageous role. (215)

Zohra Segal still continues to perform, and some years ago, both Zohra and Uzra acted in the play *Ek Thi Nani*, where the two real life sisters acted as sisters across the border and the two cultures—of India and Pakistan—as their different gender biases and histories were enacted.[29]

Zohra looks at herself as 'the vanguard of modern Indian women, someone who broke the barriers but only by chance. Frankly, I took up a career because I was afraid of getting married....' (215). But there was no deliberate design behind it. Travel, the need to take her decisions and manage her own money, exposure to different cultures—all helped to mould her native spirit of independence.

In direct contrast to Zohra Segal is the life of Malka Pukhraj, who like Zohra, also came from a Pathan family. But there were differences of class, circumstances and the levels of education of the two sets of parents; differences were also there in the levels of sophistication, social environment and opportunity. But Malka Pukhraj's autobiography titled *Song Sung True: A Memoir* is written by her, originally in Urdu and translated by Saleem Kidwai; thus, it carries within it the whole ambience of her surroundings, the large kinship network, description of her times and sketches of the people she came across. There is a strong sense of independence, perhaps inherited from her mother. She goes back in narration to the time when she was born, based on what she must have been told, but as the young child was growing up she observed the tension between her parents. Her mother lived with her parents, but when she began to feel anxious about the young child's education, she reconciled with her husband, so that her ambitions to see Malka famous could materialize (11). In retrospect, Malka reviews her parents' relationship, and one can sense a feeling of regret that she had been indifferent to her father as a child. He was a man capable of great generosity even though careless of his personal needs (17).

Malka's early education began with the learning of Urdu and Persian. She was later apprenticed to Ali Baksh, a well-known singer. This was the traditional education available to women of her community. The

115

young Malka was mischievous, bossy and unsparing in her dealings with others, displaying early the sense of self-protection so essential for her survival in a man's world.

There are short chapters on specific subjects—such as 'My Father, My Education, My Aunt'—and thus she works through her experiences. Very rarely do we find the emotional self surfacing. But it is her mind that acts like a sieve and selects her memories. I found her recollections of her father objective and neutral, but at one level fair. She took note of the masculine dilemma when her mother was persistently indifferent to him. He was caught between his many responsibilities—his elder daughter, neglected and ill-treated, his younger daughter who shared her mother's contempt for him and a fatherhood with all the duties but no rights—and yet the man did not allow himself to be bitter or vindictive. Instead, he willingly gave away all he had and allowed his young daughter Malka to go on extracting money from him like an experienced moneylender in return for a small loan.

The memoir depicts the life of a family, of a community and the travels of this group. The territory is mostly North Indian, from Kashmir to Lahore to Delhi. Like Zohra Segal, Malka Pukhraj also briefly worked in films, but for the most part she was a singer and her associations were mostly with royalty—Maharaja Hari Singh, her patron, other royal dignitaries who visited him like the Maharani of Cooch Behar or the Maharaja of Patiala, aristocratic people, artists and professionals and of course a host of admirers.

Two episodes/relationships deserve to be mentioned. One is when she went with her mother and accompanists to participate in a festive event at Patiala with the celebrations lasting one month. When the Maharaja—who had a reputation as a philander, a polygamist and an exploiter—made unreasonable advances, she stood her ground and, along with her mother, ran the distance of 12 miles to the nearest railway station in order to get to safety. This is a remarkable display of spirit, courage and quickness of reaction, very much in line with her childhood behaviour, and there is none of the false coyness or womanly yielding or helpless-ness. She comes through as an amazingly strong person. The second is the long drawn-out courtship of her admirer Shabbir. She kept him wait-ing for years, extending the date of marriage by a year or two every time. Why? One wonders whether it was a sense of power she experienced, or of insecurity? Or is it that she valued her independence and freedom to an extent that made her oblivious of desire? Or was it only one-sided love? Again, the likelihood that marriage would curb her other associa-tions—did that act as a barrier? Just as she mercilessly went on extract-ing money from her father in return for a petty loan he had once taken. Once when they, Malka and Shabbir, were talking to each other, Malka's mother entered the room:

> I did not notice anything till my wretched mother actually entered the hut. The two of us fell silent as if we were confronted with a venomous cobra about to strike. It seemed as if we had been caught red-handed committing some huge crime and for no reason we felt we should be ashamed and repentant. Neither of us said a word to mother. (264)

Following this episode, her mother became Shabbir's 'implacable foe'. Why? Though the narrative has a great deal of history—social his-tory, description of royal lifestyles, of the social life around her—neither the community life nor her personal life emerges. The discretion is exces-sive. Apparently, one reason for her mother's disapproval is the fact that the daughter's marriage would result in a loss of income to the mother. The Mirasi community, to which they belonged, is a community which sustains itself through performance. The reader can connect her mother's anxiety for her education—the kind necessary for her profession, dance, music and language—to this fact. The strong sense of self-preservation in both the mother and daughter, the marginality of her father to her and her mother's existence and the absence of any restriction on her grow-ing relationship (does one use the word intimacy?) with Maharaja Hari

117

Singh—all form the subtext of the memoir. It is simply not possible that emotional or familial conflict did not take place, but the narrative maintains silence over this. There are hints, but no emotional outbursts ever take place.

Her mother's hostility achieved directly the opposite of what she had desired—it sent Malka into Shabbir's arms and their love affair blossomed. They conversed in languages she couldn't comprehend fully. So far she had just valued him as a friend, but now she began to like him as a suitor. Her whole being rose in rebellion against her mother's constant watch, and she began to ask herself the same questions over and over again:

> Why should anyone watch over me? Did anyone have the right to do so? Did they consider me their slave that I could meet the people they wanted me to and not the ones I wanted? I was angry at the way they were behaving. (268)

This episode made her aware of the manner in which she was being used and in which her family controlled her movements, her friendships and her associations. Shabbir was a persistent lover and wooed her, borrowed money to meet her many demands, wrote to her regularly and visited her almost every weekend, sometimes absenting himself from work without leave. She had other visitors, not suitors but men who came to meet her and were willing to oblige her no end. Finally, when she married him, it was because she had learnt to respect him, because Shabbir's mother welcomed the idea and because Shabbir was fast sliding down at work pining for her love. But the matter came to a head when her mother, uncle and grandfather got her to Jammu under a false pretext in order to prevent her from marrying Shabbir.

The only episode she records with all its conflict and agony is when it is discovered that she has been receiving Shabbir's letters at someone else's address and an uncle reports that she still meets him. When she did not admit to these accusations, her mother took off her slipper and beat her. This led to her final rebellion. Malka began to ask herself, 'For what crime am I being punished? I have kept them in comfort and wealth since the age of nine' (275).

And a few months later she refused to sing anymore. 'I will not sing at all. You already have enough to live comfortably…. Damn this situation when a two-bit person can walk into the house…. Damn the car, the horse carriage, the jewellery the clothes and the money. Damn everything!' (279). Then one night she arranged to leave with Shabbir for Sialkot and get married. Malka had found the courage to take the final step. Apparently, women of the community were not encouraged to marry while they were young and beautiful, and a clinical distancing from customers was encouraged. Their socialisation process took care of that. Even after the *nikah* ceremony had been performed, efforts were made to get her back, not even hesitating to use force (291–293).

Marriage was a totally different experience; new relationships were developed and the financial ups and downs began to take their toll. Then a brief film career and a much more visible singing career with recordings in the studio and broadcasts over the radio. In this phase both the notion of freedom and of dependence are defined differently. Family life, husband and children, a wider audience, freedom from the spatial royal palaces—life is more real and perhaps less fragmented, but as years passed equally exciting, uncertain and adventurous until finally it comes to an end with the death of her husband. It is only after his death that a full realisation came to her of the beautiful life they had shared. The escape from the clutches of her family, from a superficial sense of freedom to domesticity, which even if it made claims on her, also gave her personal space and freedom to pursue her interests. In one way, it is a journey from a convention-ridden life to a relationship that brought about a change in her social circle. Domesticity did not succeed in cloistering her—it had never aimed to do so.

One can trace a history of rebellion and transgression through myths, personal narratives, histories and life stories of women in different kinds of space—both open and closed. Zohra Segal and other women like her rescue the women on the stage from a strict separation. Today's film and stage worlds support this, but the negotiation from the body to a shared visibility of the strength of mind, from a distant and alien notion of respectability, for an idea of respectability that is vested in personal morality and not the empty, social, gender-discriminatory, caste-driven notion of respectability, has been made possible by education, strength of character and family support, which together help cross barriers. We have other life stories of this journey from across one world to another, accounts that speak of defiance, courage and determination, such as Durga Khote's and Begum Khurshid Mirza's. Khurshid Mirza came from a respectable Muslim family and her entry in films was not appreciated by her community. For a couple of years, she was not permitted by her parents to visit them. But as she was already a married woman, the whole responsibility was thrust on her husband.[30] Similarly, Durga Khote came from an aristocratic family, and was well-educated. In her autobiography *I, Durga Khote: An Autobiography*, Durga Khote devotes the first chapter to describing the land, home and their lifestyle with a horse carriage and horses and trainers coming from Australia. She writes,

> ... we all learned to dance and sing. We played games like tennis.... We knew our Shakespeare, Tennyson, and Wordsworth by heart, but we were also made to memorize slokas from the Gita and Saint Ramdas, and hymns to Lord Vyankatesh and Lord Shiva.... (Khote 13–14)

There was an early exposure to theatre as her father nurtured a passion for the theatre. Whenever Gandharva Theatre Company was in Bombay, she accompanied her father to watch the plays as frequently as thrice a week.

With the advantage of this background, she grew up with a mind of her own and wanted to join politics. (This was the period of 1919–1920, when Gandhi was back in India from South Africa.) But she continued her education and got married into an equally well-to-do family. Her autobiography reads very differently from Hansa Wadkar's, though in their acting life they worked together and were supportive of each other. Her entry into films was due to a strange turn of events. Her husband's family lost its money, and Durga Khote in search of job turned to giving tuitions, until one day she got an offer for a short ten-minute take. She accepted. She writes, 'I was a woman in need. This was like a straw to a drowning man. So I assented.... I was terrified. I had no clue what I'd got myself into. I literally did not know I had done' (33). Not that the transition was easy. Except for her parents, everyone else was against her decision, and behaved as if they literally wanted to kill her (35). Equations and relationships altered; tensions had to be lived with and the financial responsibilities passed on to her with the family's failing re-sources. Khote also separated from her husband at about this time. How does one live with it all? Bharata in the *Nātyaśāstra* counts amongst the qualities of a good actress not only beauty, passion and feeling but also knowledge and skills, and one who is 'capable of using reasoning' (Ira-vati 63). The ability to make choices is perhaps an essential ingredient of human existence, and one that can render the division between closed or open spaces irrelevant. But social structures exercise a great authority, always difficult to rebel against. Thus, small, petty ways of revenge that often lead to self-destruction and anguish or large, transgressive steps that sweep opinion before one become the two possible routes.

IV

Getting Back at Men through God

In the bhakti movements, women take on the qualities that men traditionally have. They break the rules of Manu that forbid them to do so. A respectable woman is not, for instance, allowed to live by herself or outdoors, or refuse sex to her husband—but women saints wander and travel alone, give up husband, children and family.

—A.K. Ramanujan ('Talking to God' 11)

* * *

Ranjha-Ranjha kardi hun mein aape Ranjha hoiee
Sado mainu dhidho Ranjha, Heer na aakho koiee.
(Chanting Ranjha's name, I myself have become Ranjha.
Call me Dhidho Ranjha, refer not as Heer).

—Bulle Shah (192)

The above two quotations, so different from each other, comment on the complexity and the multiplicity of strands in the Bhakti Movement as it moved from region to region, century to century, language to language and across boundaries of gender, role models, castes and rituals of worship. In fact, the Bhakti Movement is not one, but many. It also overflows from the precincts of temples and mosques and carries with it a socialist–egalitarian agenda clamouring for a dismantling of oppressive and discriminatory structures. Right from the sixth century BCE, from the rise of Buddhism to the present dalit movements, this parallel social consciousness, constantly fretting at the brahminical supremacy and the power hold of the upper castes, has manifested itself through a chain of resistance movements that have questioned the monopoly of knowledge projected through Sanskrit learning, scriptures and their exclusionary practices, idol worship and temples that confined god and kept human beings out on the basis of caste, purity and pollution, privileging the priest, and the laws of the household that tied women to their homes and subordinated them to male control.

True, all these movements were not identical; true also that all of them are not perceived as the Bhakti Movement, but equally true is the fact that resistance of some kind or the other, a resistance that seeks equality and the recognition of human beings as *human* irrespective of caste, gender and social power, is a common strand in all of them indicating the connection between religion and social life.

K.S. Srinivasan in *The Ethos of Indian Literature* suffixes two maps, one of them tracing the 'Ancient Trade and Cultural Routes: Exchange Across the Vindhyas', which connects the whole country with three movements: Trika Saivism, Siddha Cult and Bhakti poetry, moving from South to North and then East and moving from East to North East and southwards. Of these, the Bhakti Movement is the one most widespread. These socio-religious movements, aimed at liberating both god and man (inclusive of woman) from their bondage to brahmanical power monopoly, are evidently a power struggle. Braj Ranjan Mani places them all in the context of a 'debrahmanising' process (Mani). He observes that resistance to the caste ideology, in sharp contrast to the brahmanical presentation of the past, actually began as soon as it came into existence (Mani, 'Introduction' 17). And both Buddha and Mahavir (Buddhism and Jainism) lead the anti-Vedic religious movements focusing on the human being and defining a more compassionate god. Morality rather than ritualistic practice were centrally placed in the behavioural code, emphasising deeds and as such action in contrast to the caste of birth.

The anti-brahmanic movements differed in nature from region to region. One of the many causes of this was the brahmin–kshatriya stronghold in the North as contrasted to the strong brahmin–shudra divide in the South. In the North, this implied that martial castes like the rajputs not only supported brahmin power, they also connived with it, while in the South purity and pollution became overriding concerns. Both Buddha and Mahavir descended from kshatriya families, as did Nanak (in the fifteenth century). Thus, they were moving outside their castes. The Bhakti Movement of which Nanak (the founder of the Sikh religion) was a part had a few brahmins rebelling against their own castes, but by and large the *bhakta*s came from castes that were oppressed, like the shudras: leather workers, weavers, blacksmiths, tillers of soil, gardeners, potters and the like.

It is important to look at the Bhakti Movement, its major causes, trends, and it main principles before zeroing in on the gender question. Mani refers to its various strands as 'movements from below' which are a watershed in Indian history in both religio-literary terms and the broader socio-cultural contexts (134). God was transferred from being a transcendental presence to being housed in the individual; salvation was no longer to be worked for through mantras and rituals, or asceticism, but included dignity of labour and life-in-the-world (inclusive of marriage, a householder's duties and responsibilities). Most *bhakta*s chose their own gurus, who often happened to be people of a lower caste. Mira, a royal princess, took Ravidas as a guru. If the temples closed their doors on them, they, freeing their god from closed doors, carried him in their hearts; they either discouraged idol worship and worshipped a *nirguna* (formless) god or substituted him as one of them, who could dwell in humble abodes.

One main feature that strikes one is the quality of total surrender or merger in the loved one, who, in this case, happened to be god. The romantic impulse in a woman's life often works negatively. The concept of *pativrata*, love and sacrifice for the other, has not only been internalised over a period of time as a befitting role model for women, but has also formed part of the female models of heroism as manifested in the practice of sati or *jauhar*. The romantic impulse subdues women, extracts limitless devotion from them and the very body which is the medium of attraction and seduction is transcended when pain and suffering are embraced. One can see how, in almost all cultures, romance has acted as an enticing principle for female subordination. The striking image that Coleridge strikes in 'Kubla Khan',[1] with a line such as 'woman waiting for her demon lover', capturing the woeful need for the lover, is matched at the other end by Katherine Mansfield's subdued narration of a whole household and three generations of women revolving around a single man—son, husband and father—in her short novel, *The Aloe*. Women since ages have enslaved themselves to the idea of love. Feminist desire for personal space has to negotiate the idea of romantic love also in different terms and perhaps that is one of the reasons that the separation between sex and romance is also placed in different perspectives. Earlier, whores, prostitutes and courtesans used their bodies, but sooner or later, as was inevitable, it led to a romantic involvement, hurt and disappointment. The separation was forced by a society which distinguished between the good woman and the bad woman on that basis. But now with a greater awareness and control over the body, sexuality as a power in itself, separable from the idea of romance or any lifelong relationship, is an acceptable way of negotiating the difference.[2]

But 'romance' is the accompanying surrender of the will, erasure of a separateness, a total appropriation of or by another, a relationship of roles that can change from that of lovers to that of mother or son, or child and mother, with god being the lover, a mother, or a child and as such totally absorbed in by the devotee. The Bhakti Movement thus subverts the function of romance from a means of possession, subordination and seduction to one of merger, total oneness and an equal reciprocal relationship. Sufi poets, like Bulle Shah and others from the North Indian tradition, form a parallel movement and influence. Not seen as part of the Bhakti Movement, it is inspired by a similar impulse as it moves outside holy places, scriptures, priests and an authoritarian godhood that demands total obedience to a more open, non-scriptural system which looks for god in the human being. God is not confined to the written word or the number of times one prays or in pilgrim centres, but in the heart of men. Sufi saints also sought to give a human face to religion, a more liberal in-the-world face. Both Bhakti Movement and Sufism also have their aesthetic dimensions, a liberating of languages used and an inclination towards music.

Bulle Shah, when he sings of the mad frenzy of worship and admits that he is Heer who is now submerged in Ranjha, first crosses over to the woman's role and then places the relationship in one of the most well-known love legends of Punjab, Heer–Ranjha. Sufi saints and *bhakta*s (men and women both) often take on female roles and god is the lover. Narsi Mehta, the Gujarati saint poet of the fifteenth century, writes:

> *Many women colour their eyes with collyrium,*
> *My case is different from all of theirs.*
> *I have thrown off all my ornaments and aids to beauty*
> *Until my lover once more calls me near.* (Mehta 62)

It is the playfulness of Krsna (Lord Krishna) with his *gopi*s that is talked about and becomes the reference point. Love play, attraction, passion all become permissible emotions:

> *Someone sang the fifth raga*
> *Near my house.*
> *Suddenly my love rushed in*
> *And grabbed me by the hand....*
> *His passion grew as he looked on me.*
> *To raise my passion to his own,*

He played his flute for me ... .
Then he came into my house
And there he enjoyed me. (55)

Suddenly the puritanical attitude, the prohibitions on gender equality and lovemaking, the distance from god, all disappear, and the terms of romance, love legends, passion, fervour of desire, and *virah* (separation), come into full play. For the *bhakta*s, feelings are more important than learning or power; in fact, men have to cast off their sense of power, ego and centrality. This, in part, accounts for the longing to submit themselves as women. A.K. Ramanujan commenting on this writes, 'One of the last things they overcome, in these traditions, is maleness itself' ('Talking to God' 10). We find a similar trend in Mira's devotional songs when she dissolves herself in Giridhar and sings and dances for him in an adulterous passion. (I propose to discuss Mira at length at a later stage in this chapter.) But she happened to be a woman. The point is that Bulle Shah, Narsi Mehta, Kabir, Chokhamela—men from different religions, regions, castes and backgrounds—freely use the romantic idiom to express their religious feelings and ideas, thus breaking down the division between the intellect and the heart. Looking at the devotional hymns of men is of importance in order to comprehend the impact and significance of this movement which was subversive of a great deal of elitist, codified value structure and which sought to place god–man relationships on a different footing altogether. It was a native upsurgence addressing its own social concerns frontally.

It is necessary to discern the shifts here in order to also comprehend the gender differences in the Bhakti Movement itself, for women had to negotiate not only the Vedas and Upanisads but also *Manusmriti*, with its confining role models and the overall notion of respectability that divided public and private space. The question which is relevant to both men and women of the Bhakti Movement is, 'how, in the face of a system bearing down on one, can one experience love?'[3] Ramanathan in her

127

'Foreword' to *Songs of Chokhamela* asks, how does one believe? What does one believe in? 'In such a case how is faith to be comprehended? Faith in what?' Further, when you have nothing to give up, what do you give up? There is literally nothing to be given up for the poor and the oppressed, or for all those living on the peripheries of existence (vii).

Chokhamela was a fourteenth-century untouchable saint poet and an ardent devotee of Vithoba and belonged to the Varkari cult.[4] One of Chokhamela's compositions goes as follows:

> *Five elements compound the body impure; all things mix*
> *Thrive in the world.*
> *Then who is pure and who impure?*
> *The body is rooted in impurity.*
> *From the beginning to the end,*
> *endless impurities*
> *heap themselves.*
> *Who is it can be made pure?*
> *Says Chokha,*
> *I am struck with wonder,*
> *can there be any such*
> *beyond pollution?* (Chokhamela 57)

There is a consciousness of self and a resentment at the social exclusion:

> *How far*
> *How long now*
> *Hari, should I hold back from you?*
> *I wait*
> *guarding your door.*
> *I see you and you*
> *throw me out. This*
> *conduct isn't very good.*

Perhaps it suits your greatness.
What, says Chokha,
can I tell? Waiting,
I waste myself. (15)

The imagery of most of the Bhakti poets is romantic, earthly and physical, apparently in a move to reduce the 'divinization' of worship and to bring it closer to human emotions. Kabir, who was greatly admired by Nanak and whose *doha*s are also included in the Sikh holy scripture, *Sri Guru Granth Sahib*, wrote several very sensuous poems; they reflect Sufi thought as well and are secularist in spirit. Very often, god is comprehended as an earthly lover:

My eyes are heavy with sleep my love,
Come, let us go to bed.
Lovelorn, my body quivers and quakes. (Kabir 86)

G.N. Das in his Introduction to the translations, expresses the view that Kabir considered love (devotion) the most vital part in the union of the soul and the Supreme Soul; that the Sufi view of the attraction between *jivathama* and *paramathama* is based upon this love. Kabir carried this forward by projecting the view that *jivathama*, which 'has to be the prime mover must represent the feminine element', hence the submergence into a female voice (14). It is thus that the feminine is privileged, and the sensuous and the physical recognised as ways of 'knowing' the ultimate reality.

The Bhakti Movement, despite its humility and general spirit of peace-keeping, was constantly resisted by the power holders and wielders. Girish Karnad in his play *Talé-Danda*, based on the religious movement of Virashaiva socialism in Karnataka led by Basava, a brahmin by birth, traces the history of the violence that infiltrated the movement primarily because it challenged political authority and divided the people and also

129

because it happened to be radical in both concept as well as demonstration. Basava refused to undergo the sacred thread ceremony and thus he 'de-casted' himself. Braj Ranjan Mani observes that their egalitarian ideals implied a new morality. The apparent cause of the violence was when Basava's followers decided to solemnise the marriage of a brahmin girl with a boy of the cobbler caste. This was in direct violation of the laws laid down by the *dharmasastra*s (Mani, *Debrahmanising History* 162–164). This incident led to revolution, bloodshed and the movement's end, so vividly captured in *Talé-Danda*. The meaning of true religion implied a crossing over, which was held in abhorrence by the conservatists.[5]

The dominant shifts which the Bhakti Movement initiated were in the idea of devotion, feminisation of the devotee, introduction of an intimate relation between god and devotee and the transformation of worship into a personal act of devotion without any need of priest or husband. It simultaneously facilitated the crossing of barriers, and enlarged the notion of freedom, radically transforming the self-image of the oppressed women and the lower castes. It moved into colloquial idiom and the spoken languages of the people, including non-verbal arts like music. Sound and chanting were important parts of these mass movements, movements that evoked the strength of feeling. The whole of *Sri Guru Granth Sahib*, a direct development of the Bhakti Movement, is entirely based on classical ragas. The Bhakti Movement was a travelling movement in more senses than one—it moved from one place to another over the centuries, roughly sixth to the mid-eighteenth; its followers travelled from place to place; they went on pilgrimages, which were a community activity; their leaders like Namdev and Nanak travelled widely, spreading their message and rejecting fixities of all kinds; even their gods travelled with them and were not, in most cases, confined to temples. And more than all else, ideas travelled as the subversive elements revealed the hollowness of life-denying structures. It is natural to ask, how and in what manner did women respond to these movements? What place does it have in the resistance tradition of feminism?

Women in the Bhakti Movement

It is quite obvious from the patterns of history that no major social or political revolution has ever carried the women's cause along with it. Neither the French Revolution, nor the Russian, nor the Indian freedom struggle was able to do that. Women may benefit marginally, but that is about all. In this respect, the Bhakti Movement is a kind of an exception on several counts. One, women had to contend with an entirely different set of restrictions as far as the *dharmasastra*s and the role models were concerned; they had to not only contend with the superiority of the god-like husband figure, but also to bypass him; they also had to define their choices clearly because the choices were related to marrying or staying single, coping with sexual desire, negotiating the body and its involuntary processes, and giving up or adhering to motherhood roles. Men could be *bhakta*s as well as householders; how were women to reconcile these two roles? In fact, they had to attempt a new definition not only of morality but also of freedom and 'legitimate' desire. And what about economic independence? How were they to earn a living?

Tharu and Lalita go as far back as the sixth century BCE to the songs of the Buddhist nuns, written in Pali. Mutta, the daughter of a poor brahmin, obtained the consent of her hunchbacked husband in order to pursue her own devotion to god. Mutta sung of her unique sense of freedom:

So free am I, so gloriously free,
Free from three petty things—
From mortar, from pestle and my twisted lord,
Freed from rebirth and death I am,
And all that has held me down
Is hurled away. (Tharu and Lalita Vol. 1, 68)[6]

Sumanglamata also sings in the same tone: 'A woman well set free!.... How wonderfully free, from kitchen drudgery.... Free too of that unscrupulous man' (69). Early women nuns are celebrating their freedom from kitchen drudgery and unwanted, undesired sex.

The women saint poets of south India, Tamil Nadu (the Sangam poets), Karnataka and Maharashtra have been researched on and written about in fair amount of detail. Bhakti Movement was late in developing in North India; the sufi poets were more dominant, but there is a bridging through influences. Nanak was influenced as much by Shaikh Farid as by Kabir. In Kashmir also, the Bhakti Movement had its women devotees. But it is evident that more work needs to be done on the whole northern region as both literary histories and folk traditions have not really recorded a strong female presence. There could be several other, and often conflicting, reasons: constant state of unrest, invasions, war or fear of war, presence of invaders, shifting power structures, border areas and also the greater gender equality which Sikhism offered (this however was post-sixteenth century).

A.K. Ramanujan, in his essay, 'Talking to God in the Mother Tongue', has done an amazingly wonderful summing up of the trends in the Bhakti Movement in Karnataka. He has also, through a flow chart, narrated the various ways in which some of these women coped with sexuality and household confines. Husbands, mothers-in-law, children—all had to be dealt with. Mahadeviakka, a Kannada Virashaiva saint poet, according to the legend, was married to a chieftain. She told him not to touch her, and if he did so against her will, she would leave him. This came to happen. She walked out on him and wandered in search of fellow *bhakta*s. Men are placed by her only in asexual relationships such as father and brother. The idea of cuckolding her husband through a relationship with God, the lover, is acceptable to her. In one of her songs, she plans to give the slip to her sister-in-law and 'go cuckold my husband with Hara, my Lord.'[7] In another poem she voices her conflict:

Husband inside,

Lover outside,

I can't manage them both.
This world
and that other,
cannot manage them both.
O Lord white as jasmine
I cannot hold in one hand
both the round nut
and the long bow. (Mahadeviakka 16)

From among the women in Virashaivism, several were married, the marital status of several others is not known and nothing can be said about them with any certainty. A few also remained single. Akka Nagamma and Akka Mahadevi are believed to have been married; Akkamma, Bonta Devi and Goggavve remained single and many others lived in matrimony, such as Ayidakki (wife of Marayya, both husband and wife were agricultural labourers); Gangambika, married to Basavanna, a brahmin and Guddavve, Kalaveya, Kalaveyya, Ketaka Devi, Lingamma, mostly shudra women, were all married.[8] Besides their roles of wives and mothers, other roles like working in the fields or other paid occupation also had to be negotiated. Worship or devotion, even when a whole-time concentration, was not and could not be a whole-time occupation. Most of the people in the Virashaivism Movement were workers. Vijaya Ramaswamy, commenting on the inferior status of women even within this protest movement, refers to a *vachana* of Basavanna, wherein woman, in all her roles, is seen as *maya'*, illusion, a mirage that attracts and allures:

To give me birth, Maya bore me—as mother.
To delight me, Maya was born—as my daughter.
To embrace me, Maya shared my bed—as wife.
So many different ways she has,
Maya, to worry and trouble me;

Not in my power to unhinge this Maya;
And you are amused, O lord of the Meeting Rivers![9]

Debating the point about woman as the dangerous 'Other', Vijaya Ramaswamy concedes that the majority of the verses of the male saint poets do not lend themselves to the self-other polarities; 'Basava often refers to himself as a woman whether as a loving bride or an adulterous wife' (Ramaswamy, *Walking Naked* 150). Proceeding to quote from his *vachana*s, she refers to one where the poet says:

Let the whole world know: I have got a mate.
I'm a married woman. (Ramaswamy, *Walking Naked* 150)[10]

There is another reference where the image is that of a prostitute:

Will our lord of the Meeting Rivers
love me for empty words—
even as a sinful prostitute
who takes her nightly fee? (Ramaswamy, *Walking Naked* 150)[11]

Perhaps the devotee is struggling with his own desire, and for whom 'any contact with the other gender would be a distraction' (Ramaswamy 151). It is evident from the name of the movement that it is directed towards devotion to Śiva, as opposed to the cult of devotion to Krishna—as in Mirabai's verse—and as such it also involves a worship of the *linga*, the phallic symbol, and looks upon Śiva as the eternal bridegroom. (A large number of Hindu women worship the *linga*, observe a fast on Mondays, Śiva's day, to pray for a good husband and happiness in marriage.) He is both the creator and the destroyer, and is known for his *tandav-nritya*, the dance of destruction. Feminine protest within Virashaivism does not try to displace or replace the *linga* with any other symbol; instead, both men and women look upon Śiva as the eternal husband, submitting themselves to him and shifting the burden of lordship from earthly contexts to divine ones. *Linga-dharma* also came to replace the brahmin initiation rights. Vijaya Ramaswamy describes these initiation ceremonies:

> The birth rituals in Vedic Brahmanism called *jata karma* and *nama karma* are replaced in Virasaivism by *linga-dharma*. The bestowing of this sacred *linga* by a Guru is done for both male and female babies by tying the *linga* around their neck. The Guru utters the *Panchakshari mantra* called *Namah Sivaya* into the ear of the child irrespective of the class/caste or gender. It is interesting to note here that in orthodox Hinduism it is only Brahmins who are entitled to this kind of initiation by their spiritual teacher. It is moreover only the privilege of the Brahmin male to receive the initiation into *Śiva Panchakshari* although Brahmin women can be initiated into '*Shakti Panchakshari*'. Thus the bestowal of *linga* and the initiation of children, irrespective of their gender or caste, reflects the revolutionary content of Virasaivism. (153)

Gender equality was a rare achievement even within the Bhakti Movement. In the monastic orders and even in a resistance movement like Buddhism, which questioned caste hierarchies, gender hierarchies persisted, and it was quite common to keep women confined to inferior roles and exclude them from the possibility of right to asceticism or salvation. The nakedness of the female body has always appeared to be a threat to men, irrespective of the fact whether they are *sadhu*s or ascetics. In direct violation of these taboos imposed by orthodox religion, women *bhakta*s ask whether spirituality has a gender.[12] But whether one recognises it or not, or is reluctant to acknowledge it, gender is a complicating factor and social prejudices persist. Even under these conditions, when the women *bhakta* dared to step outside the home, defy norms and restrictions, one is compelled to acknowledge their courage and the strength of their faith. Women have been targeted, labelled whores, confined within their houses and punished in other ways for daring to step outside male defined space.

How did women expand their space? And how did they transcend the body? Was it by rising above it, ignoring it, or refusing to acknowledge it? Or through finding alternative modes of existence and sublimating desire. A.K. Ramanujan's flowchart lists some of the strategies women saints adopted. These can be listed as such: refusing marriage to a mortal; becoming a courtesan; miraculously skipping youth, through sheer willpower and faith and during their youthful period by using their beauty and sexuality; walking out of marriage; even becoming male or an old ugly woman; refusing widowhood norms; refusing motherhood; marrying god; walking naked; or breaking caste barriers. These are examples he cites from the lives of the women saints. Male devotees did not confront any of these problems and did not have to resort to any such strategies of bypassing gender.

Mahadeviyakka, in one of her poems already cited, expresses the difficulty of holding on to both the worlds (Ramanujan, 'Talking to God' 16). She walks out of her marriage, and in the process discards her clothes and goes around with her long hair covering her nakedness (12).[13] Lal Ded from Kashmir behaved in a similar fashion. Lal Ded lived in the fourteenth century and is among the earliest Kashmiri women mystic poets. Neerja Mattoo observes:

> When we look at her work, we find many of our notions and stereotypes thrown to the winds. Though a victim herself, she never revels in victimhood.... Through her mystic verses she brought the most subtle concepts of the highly complex Kashmiri Shaiva philosophy out of the closets of Brahminism and made its practices accessible to the poor and illiterate, in their own language and idiom instead of Sanskrit. (333)

Lal Ded refused to stay confined to domestic tyranny and its power hierarchy. She left home and pursued her search for god. Her mystic verse captures both her anguish and questioning of the brahminical code:

Your idol is stone, the temple a stone too—
All a stone bound together from top to toe!

What is it you worship, you dense Brahmin?
Bind but the vital air of the heart to the mind. (Mattoo 334)

Dissatisfied with her male Guru, she also gave up her slavish dependence on him and struck a note of independence in her own individual pursuit of the true God:

A thousand times I asked my Guru
Pray how name Him who has no name?
I asked in vain, exhausted and sunk.
Till out of nothing, something emerged. (334)

Most Bhakti poets, even as they worship a Hindu god, Krishna or Śiva, express a secular emotion where other religions are concerned. Because they outstep the ritualistic confines of religion and have the courage to question patriarchy, they also erase religious differences. Lal Ded writes:

Śiva is everywhere—know Him as the Sun.
Know not the Hindu different to the Muslim.
If wise, know yourself as a ray of His,
That alone is the way to know the Lord. (Mattoo 335)

There is, as Mattoo points out, a natural use of domestic imagery when the devotee feels, 'In love's mortar pounded and ground my heart—/.../ Roasted and burnt and consumed it myself, / Yet know not whether I live or die?' (336)

This is one way of both centre staging domesticity and relocating it to an entirely different context, adding experiential levels to philosophical thought. One is compelled to pause and ask oneself the question: was this not a reformulation of the philosophical debate and mystical experience, and did it not compel society to look at itself afresh? It is evident that any critiquing or violation of the patriarchal norms must have come after a

137

great deal of internal conflict and must have also required a tremendous amount of courage and an intense personal conviction to be able to put their rebellion effectively into practice. Mahadeviakka (also known as Akka Mahadevi), commenting on her own nakedness, writes:

People,

male and female,

blush when a cloth covering their shame

comes loose.

When the lord of lives

lives drowned without a face

in the world, how can you be modest?

When all the world is the eye of the

                                    lord,

onlooking everywhere, what can you

cover and conceal?   (Mahadeviakka 15)

It was on the basis of nakedness that the two Jain sects defined themselves—the Digambars and the Svetambars—and it was on this very basis again that the female body was discriminated against, because the nakedness of a woman was seen as different from a man's. Mahadeviakka extended it to women by actually practising it and becoming unconscious of and indifferent to her own physicality, thus transcending the body in its totality.

One of the earliest women saints is Avvaiyar, who lived during the Sangam period of Indian history. The legend surrounding the birth of the poetess recounts that she was one of seven siblings, all of whom were discarded at the time of their birth on their father's orders as they were born of a marriage between a low-caste girl and a brahmin boy. Each of the siblings grew up to be talented and precociously wise, and each one of them questioned the brahminical code in different ways. Amongst them, Avvaiyar, the eldest of the siblings, was horrified when a marriage proposal came for her. How could she serve a husband when engrossed in the worship of God? She posed this problem to her God:

Should I marry and experience family life?
Why did you give me this charm and beauty?

Her prayer was responded to; she was transformed into an old woman, thus bypassing youth, its desires and claims (Chakravarty, 'The World of the Bhaktin'). Her poetry criticises a wide range of institutions. She wrote extensively, even on subjects like ethics and medicine and spent her life as a wandering teacher. In almost every other respect, in social and intellectual discourse, she lived a full life. Except for this choice where it was either marriage or her devotion to her chosen god, Avvaiyar was not excluded and did not exclude herself from other spheres of life. The householder's life was not looked down upon, except that it was easier for men to live in both the worlds and order them to their liking.

Today, one may look sceptically at the miraculous acts the *bhakta*s have been credited with, but religious literature is replete with accounts of such happenings, and as one travels through India, there is tangible proof of several of these things actually having taken place, as Guru Nanak's travels and the miracles associated with them in Ladakh, North East and other places go on to prove.[14] One has to concede that faith and devotion can achieve miracles.

The divide between domestic life and the one of renunciation, theoretically, is rejected by the *bhakta*. In the case of women, there were a few exceptions, primarily because of the patriarchal notion of control; in other cases, perhaps a natural abhorrence to the sexual act, and *bhakti* enabled them to choose an alternative course. There are two other interesting aspects of the resistance by women saint poets, and one needs to pay some attention to them. One, that religion was not necessarily a confining aspect

139

of life, or one that denied fullness. Avvaiyar or Avvai, as she is more popu-
larly referred to, participated in secular political life (Chakravarty, 'The
World of the Bhaktin' 25). Two, for married women, even the concept of
cuckolding the husband by an intense emotional relationship became acceptable. There is the case of Mirabai, to which we will return later.

Karaikalammaiyar, another South Indian saint poet, transformed
her sexuality by acquiring an 'awesome power which terrified the men
around her'. Uma Chakravarty observes, 'In her new form which denies
her sexuality, she is inviolate—no man will come anywhere near her—
she is now the feminine ascetic par excellence.' Chakravarty connects it
with creative energy and comments, 'Karaikalammaiyar is cast in a Kali-
like mould. She inhabits the world of the *pretas* in the cremation ground.
Ultimately her salvation lies at the feet of Śiva' (25).[15] The relationship
between protest, Kali and creative energy needs to be explored in greater
detail. For the moment, it is the nature of sexual desire that needs to be
explored. Were women able to conquer their sexuality and sexual desire,
sublimate it and channelise it differently or transcend their bodily needs
in their entirety? Their poetry does not allow us to accept these explanations. Andal is conscious of physical desire and expresses it:

> *Only if he will come*
> *to stay with me for one day*
> *if he will enter me*
> *so as to leave*
> *the mark of saffron paste*
> *upon my breasts.* (Chakravarty, 'The World of the Bhaktin' 25)[16]

Mirabai's *bhajan*s express extreme devotion and desire for total submergence, to become one with Krishna. The 1979 film version (*Mirabai*)
has a scene where Mira is experiencing a sexual experience in front of
the Krishna idol. Romance and romantic images of union are but only
a prelude to the sexual desire. Protest, staying outside marriage, does

140

therefore necessitates a sublimation, and whatever fulfilment they seek is in the wished for and desired adulterous relationship.

Krishna *bhakti*, which allows greater space for playfulness, also had a foothold in the South. Andal, believed to have lived in the ninth century, died young, but her songs express an intense devotion for Krishna. Her conviction that she could not marry a mortal as she was already married to Krishna anticipates Mira's stand (which came much later, in the sixteenth century). At age sixteen, she went to meet her lord at the Srirangam temple and the legend believes that she was finally absorbed into the stone image of Vishnu.[17] The emotions expressed in the poems addressed to Krishna deal with desire, disappointment, frustration and a strange intimacy. They also underline the attraction she feels for his handsomeness, his 'glowing face, his dark-hued form'; he arouses an emotional (and physical) response in her (Dahejia 38).

In Maharashtra, the spread of the Bhakti Movement took place between the thirteenth and the seventeenth centuries. It drew its followers from all castes and communities, though the majority were from the oppressed and disadvantaged groups. Again, it had among its followers people of both Shaiva and Vaishnav affiliations but the god they worshipped was Vithoba, everyman's God, the God who dwelt in their cottages, and the significant practice was the annual pilgrimage to Pandarpur. Vidyut Bhagwat describes Vithoba as

the God who was more or less like any one from the toiling class, man or woman. Vithoba was seen as a common Marathi peasant, free from excesses of miracles. He did not expect any kind of sacrifice, in animal or other forms, and was a friend, a mother figure. ('Heritage of Bhakti' 168)

The Varkari Movement threw up several poet saints like Namdev and Tukaram, whose verses were sung everywhere and became part of everyday speech, just as Kabir's *doha*s did. Of the women poets also, there are several like Janabai, Bahinabai, Muktabai and Venabai. Poetry, it appears, was the most natural expression for the intensity of devotion. A great part of this verse was in folk idiom. These women poets, like the South Indian women poets, also had to negotiate their body, family life and patriarchy. Of these, Muktabai is perhaps the earliest, belonging to the first two decades of the thirteenth century. Janabai is believed to belong to the thirteenth and fourteenth centuries, Bahinabai to the sixteenth and Nenabai to the seventeenth century.[18]

Janabai came from a shudra family and at the age of seven was handed over to the saint Namdev's family, where she grew up and lived the rest of her life. Namdev's household was one which followed the Varkari *sampradaya*, but Janabai's poems leave on record a sense of gender discrimination:

Let me not be sad because I am born a woman
In this world; many saints suffer in this way. (Tharu and Lalita Vol.1, 82)

Tharu and Lalita observe:

In Janabai's poetry we find a response that gives a sense of how women translated the concerns of a dominant ethos as they pressed it into service.... Her sensitive poetry, which is popular even today, illuminates the everyday life of ordinary women and addresses its joys and strains.... It is in the love she has for God that Janabai can imagine and reach out toward a freedom and a power her life could hardly have provided her. (Vol.1, 82)

Total surrender and an accompanying indifference to public opinion, to womanly modesty and to a consciousness of her body are expressed in the following poem:

Cast off all shame
and sell yourself
in the marketplace
then alone

can you hope
to reach the Lord.

Cymbals in hand,
a veena upon my shoulder,
I go about;
who dares to stop me?

The pallav of my sari
falls away (A scandal!);
yet will I enter
the crowded marketplace
without a thought.

Jani says, My Lord,
I have become a slut
to reach Your home. (Translated by Vilas Sarang. Tharu and Lalita Vol. 1, 83)

The Hindi term for such a condition would be *besudh*, not to be aware of one's self and one's surroundings. God as 'Other' is central to her consciousness, as to that of many a woman *bhakta*. Perhaps that is the only way to break through the cordon of patriarchy.

There is another remarkable poem by a Kannada woman poet, Sule Sankavva (twelfth century), which goes even further than Janabai's image of crossing the constrains of modesty. Sule Sankavva was a prostitute and she uses the imagery of her trade:

In my harlot's trade
having taken one man's money
I daren't accept a second man's, Sir.
And if I do,
They'll stand me naked and
kill me, Sir. (Translated by Susan Daniel. Tharu and Lalita Vol. 1, 81)

Ruth Vanita comments on the subservient location of several of these women *bhakta*s, their allegiance to a guru and ordinarily being listed in history as an appendage to their gurus:

> The presence of these exceptional women as *sant*s did not substantially change the image of women in *sant* teachings and traditions; indeed, the women *sant*s themselves sometimes endorse this image. Also, most of them remain subordinate to a male *Guru* who is often a relative and refer to themselves in terms of their familial relation to him.(49)

The subordination of women to men—whether social or willed—subtracts from their sense of independence, but not from their bold-ness, courage or resistance. In fact, Vidyut Bhagwat (with whom I am in agreement) considers the Bhakti Movement as one which 'paved the way for India's early modernity' ('Heritage of Bhakti' 166). It involved the peasant classes and allowed 'ordinary people to dream of freedom of self-determination' (166). In another essay, Bhagwat writes with refer-ence to Janabai:

> She was a maid-servant of Saint Namdeo. But what a giant leap she could take! She challenged the elite leaders of the society, the whole community, even God, all alike with pointed questions. She dared to move about in the open marketplace taking off her *sari pallav* from the head down to her shoulder, a thing never done by a woman before. Was this not a trumpet call to all women to defy the shackles of meaningless customs and assert their freedom? ('Man–Woman Relations' 224)

Bhagwat also refers to the thirteenth-century heretic movement, *Mahanubhava*, which was designed primarily for the *sanyasi*. It dif-fered from the Bhakti Movement as it did not attempt to build a com-munity life; it also did away with any identified object of worship. This protest movement was radical in several ways. It also imposed a ban on the 'ritual isolation of menstruating women, a common feature

144

of Brahminism'. And it has left behind a great line of women writers such as Mahadamba, Kamalaisa, Hiraisa and Nagaisa (Bhagwat, 'Man–Woman Relations' 224).

Protest also needs to be contextually devised. One important aspect is the social reality it is struggling against; and the second, the issue of equality which is important in its manifestation whether through rejection, defiance, indifference or by setting up alternative practices and redefining behavioural code. Equality of expression, right to relate directly to an outer world, control over the body and the freedom to choose one's course of life—all these need not be based either on isolation, segregation or celibacy. The relationship with the body—one's own body—becomes as important as the relationship to the mind. Wifehood and motherhood are not necessarily ruled out. One may as well ask the question: why should freedom be experienced only in isolation, why not within social and sexual life? Affiliation to a guru may or may not imply subordination. In the Indian tradition of learning, the notion of 'guru' both as a sounding board and a source of knowledge is accepted as a legitimate route. There is a saying, '*Bin guru gyan nahin*' (without a guru, there is no knowledge). The *Guru Granth Sahib* also mentions that as long as one does not feel the emotion of relationship, knowledge cannot be acquired.

The Bhakti Movement, stretched over several centuries, carried on a process of questioning of the institutional structures and social divisions, of caste and gender inequality, of the categories of purity and pollution and the boundaries of inclusion and exclusion. And for the *bhakta*, even rejecting and suffering are means of knowledge. Muktabai writes:

In the world, know that one for a sant
Who is the image of compassion, forgiveness;
In whose mind greed and ego are not,
Know such to have turned aside from the world—
Happy in this world and the next,

145

Pure knowledge ever on the lips.

Pour away all false ideas—

Open the door, O Jnaneshwar. (Muktabai 52)

Janabai goes one step further. She addresses Vithal or Vithoba as Vithabai, feminising the name, and talks to her as a friend. She imagines that Vithabai is with her, sharing her hard labour of grinding, pounding, washing clothes, making cow-dung cakes, going to the forest and cleaning (Vanita 55). Whatever the gender of God, he is called upon to perform other roles—of friend, sister and mother. Janabai sings:

One day I went to bathe there was not enough water to mix

God came running, gave me cool water,

saying 'Here you are',

mixed it with his own hands,

poured it over Jani, over my hair,

I had not been able to bathe for many days.

He washed my hair well, saying:

'Sit still, I'll do it',

Jani says, like a mother

He plaited my hair with his own hands. (Vanita 57)

Internalising the 'other', imagining various roles, singing, playing and dancing together, are ways not only of experiencing God but of setting the caged notion of the 'self' free. But everyone was not able to combine the two worlds of the inside and the outside in this manner. Some of them had to struggle with their circumstances all along. Bahinabai, who came almost two centuries later, was married to a man who came from a Shakta family, and was opposed to her religious pursuits. Moreover, it was a very unequal marriage. She was three when she was married to a man of thirty. She joined him some years later and was mortally afraid of him and, as the story goes, her husband got angry at her because a *swami*

146

had patted her head. He objected also to Bahina's (who was brahmin by birth) devotion to Tukaram, a shudra. But due to a vision, Bahina took Tukaram, a person she had never met, as her guru and thus emotionally moved out of her restrictive family circle (Vanita 58). It was much later that her husband was finally won over to her side (59). During these years she became a mother and also fulfilled other duties of wifehood. There were moments when she fretted against her fetters. She resented the brahmanical taboo against women's listening to the reading of Vedas and pronouncing the sacred word 'Om' (59).

Reflecting the freedom of folk songs, which are often abusive and bold in their expression and criticism, and at times even bawd, Eknath Maharaj, a sixteenth-century *bhakta*, crosses over to a woman's feelings of restriction and writes:

Save me now, Mother—
I'll offer you bread, Bhawani (1).

Father-in-law is out of town—
Let him die there (2).
I'll offer you bread, Mother Bhawani.

Mother-in-law torments me—
Kill her off (3).
I'll offer you bread, Mother Bhawani.

Sister-in-law nags and nags—
Make her a widow (4).
I'll offer you bread, Mother Bhawani.

Her brat cries and cries—
Give him the itch (5).
I'll offer you bread, Mother Bhawani.

I'll give my husband
Free me, Mother! (6)
I'll offer you bread, Mother Bhawani.

Eka Janardan says,
Let them all die!
Let me live alone! (7)[19]

Except for the fact that it is addressed to the goddess Bhawani, the only inkling of its religious character, the rest of it reads as 'a married woman's bitter, ironic and quite funny cry for release' (Zelliot, 'Let Me Live Alone', 60). It subverts the image both of the devoted wife and the one projected in romantic folk songs where the husband's whole family is rejected but not the husband himself.[20] Here she is willing to give away even her husband.

Bhakti in Gujarat was somewhat late to begin and recorded history is hard to come by. The influence of Sufism, which travelled to this region through Sindh, is also evident. Sonal Shukla comments on the work of three women *bhakta*s, whose work is still alive in the oral tradition—Gangasati, Toral and Loyal. Shukla also mentions a Muslim woman, Ratanbai. All of these women 'sing *nirgun bhakti*, possibly because of their distance from the temple tradition' (Shukla 65). These women emphasise discovery of self, compassion for the other, pursuit of knowledge and humility in the process of knowing. One has to prepare oneself for the idea of *bhakti*, for devotion to take root in the self. But of the Gujarati/Rajasthani *bhakta*s, Mirabai is the one who is most popular and on whose life story several films have been made. Mira's *bhajan*s are widely sung. Kiran Nagarkar more recently has also written a novel about her life titled *Cuckold.* Moreover, the contemporary feminists in Rajasthan have picked up Mira as a symbol of protest.

Mira belonged to an aristocratic family, thus caste and economic hardships were not her main worry. Primarily, it was her conviction that she was Krishna's bride and as such was already married. It is said her marriage into a royal family was not even consummated. She had no children. It is uncertain whether she walked out of her house while her husband was alive or walked out after his death, rejecting the rites of sati. In either case it was a bold step. There can be several explanations of her conduct in psycho-social terms. Perhaps it was her fear of or an abhorrence of the sexual act; perhaps her husband was impotent; or more likely, it was her conviction of being married to Krishna, something her mother had told her once with half an intention to distract her from her persistent childhood questionings. Whatever the reasons, there can be no doubt that she must have been persecuted by the orthodox forces for her continued resistance to married relationships as well as her pursuit of Gopal's (Krishna) worship. She also took Ravidas, a *bhakta* from a lower caste for her guru, which again was a point of contention. To leave the premises of the family home and move out was objectionable enough in itself, but to top it up with an association with an outsider, that too from a lower caste, was cause enough for further persecution. Thus, whether placed within upper caste or the lower, women had to contend with different kinds of problems, all equally constrictive. In Rajasthan, the self-image of the Rajputs as heroic men, embroiled as they were in class wars, and the legendary tales of women who were even more heroic in their support of their men, ready to commit sati or *jauhar* as the circumstances dictated, added both to their orthodoxy and practices of gender discrimination.

Against this backdrop, the immensity of Mira's resistance and protest becomes clear. The dominant note in Mira's poetry, however, is romantic—a single-minded, romantic devotion to Krishna, expression of an intense desire for a union, a playful flirtation and also a total submission. She refers to herself as a *dasi*, a slave, very consciously adopting a position of subordination. Neera Desai, commenting on this, has pointed out the way the imagery of Mira's *bhajan*s celebrates womanly duties (Tharu and Lalita Vol. 1, 91). Moreover, she never questions brahminic orthodoxy, caste segregation or the 'degeneracy of ritual' (91). Why then is Mira picked up? Is it because of the scarcity of information about other women *bhaktas*? Or because of her popularity? Parita Mukta points to Mira's place in the oral tradition and the peasantry's imagination—for them she is a symbol of resistance. Once again—the point will stand repetition—in some ways Rajput aristocratic orthodoxy is even more ruthless and formidable than brahmin orthodoxy, perhaps because it also exercises political power.

Mira's poetry combines the romantic with the ultimate, making her desire the vehicle of union:

> Mira's Lord is Giridhar Nagar,
> I am longing to reach the ultimate
> How can I throw it [body] away?[21]

In another verse, she uses the phrase of having been 'sold into the hands of Giridhar'.[22] In yet another verse she talks of having been 'dyed in his colour' (76), 'dyed in the dark one's hue' (79). If the choice between home and devotion has to be finally made, she'll choose the latter, indifferent to the Rana's wrath. Defiantly she asks, 'What will he do to me?', but if Hari is angry 'I will wither away' (79). She simply cannot live without him. The family frowns on her behaviour, 'They have a watchman sitting at the door, and a lock fastened on it. / Why should I give up my first love, The love of my former life?' (80). The right to love and the refusal to recognise marriage as a ceremony that calls upon the surrendering of all freedom go hand in hand. There is an obvious concern with the right to pursue her identified desire. The word 'I' features almost in all her positioning vis-à-vis the lord. Miracles or miraculous protection is associated with Mira. Her brother-in-law compels her to drink a cup of poison which is said to have turned into nectar. And when a serpent was sent to her, coiled up inside a basket, it turned into the image of god (Kishwar and Vanita 82).

Gulzar's film version of Mira's life also locates her in history, in the midst of the Mughal–Rajput alliances and counter-alliances. The Mughal emperor (the enemy) is seen to be visiting her outside a temple. It is immaterial whether it is actually true or not; what is significant is the historical juncture of ideas and the fact that she has not only crossed into public space, outside gender and class restrictions, but also into political space. Parita Mukta, during her researches on Mira, visited Chittorgarh where the Mira temple is located inside the fort. The people she interviewed spoke about the social taboos that had been imposed on speaking of her or singing her *bhajan*s. The upper classes forbade it and the poorer people fell in line. The subordinate sections—weavers, leather workers and the like—Mukta believes, are the ones who have kept her memory alive. Mira's rehabilitation came through colonial intervention and the changing political scenario in the nineteenth century (Mukta 97).

In her discussion of the Varkari Movement of Maharashtra, Vijaya Ramaswamy observes:

> The notion of women's subordination within a patriarchal structure is ideally reinforced in the concept of 'the bride of the lord', in which the devotee male or female is the eternal subordinate/surrendering/loyal bride to the superior protecting/demanding groom, the almighty. The notion of the bride of the lord is however conspicuous by its near absence with the Warkari tradition. (Ramaswamy, *Walking Naked* 215)[23]

But it is overtly present in Mira's poetry. Why? Do we dismiss it as a case of individual desire, submission or belief, or see it as a regional difference, a social class difference or a regressive orthodoxy within which even protest takes more conventional forms?

Ramaswamy's view that with the sixteenth century changes began to take place which denote the gradual transition of South Indian societies into colonial structures partially supports this retreat into growing conservatism (233). But this is not applicable to the North. Here the forces that pushed the orthodox to strengthen their positions were power and territory vis-à-vis the Mughals.

Kiran Nagarkar locates his novel *Cuckold* against the backdrop of succession wars, and the narrator, rather than being an omniscient one or the consciousness of Mira, is the 'Cuckold' himself, Mira's husband. The novel opens with a complaint in the royal court from a *dhobi* about his wife's infidelities. The man is old and wrinkled and reminds him of the *dhobi* of the Rāmāyana (Nagarkar 1). Thus the theme of public gossip, slander, sexuality and adultery are all introduced together. The husband, suspected of impotence, is sent to a brothel to prove his prowess, thus introducing the possibility of impotence. Additionally, the need to prove infidelity—which we discover is impossible to prove in the case of Mira—is also stressed. The atmosphere of decadence dominates. Very early in the novel, Maharaj Kumar's stepmother refers to the 14-year-old Mira as a 'nautch girl' (9) and *tawaif* (11), meaning a prostitute, a much stronger word than the earlier nautch girl, meaning a dancing girl. And all because the young girl has a flowing grace, is capable of concentrating on her object of worship, is indifferent to all else and is unconscious of the inhibitions imposed on female behaviour. The prince defends her by stating, 'My wife has a mind of her own' (9), thus allowing her an individual status.

As the narrative unfolds itself, the complexity both of Mira's character and of the husband–wife relationship is revealed. Mira is living more than one life. On one hand she is the model Indian wife, the perfect Rajput princess, the subordinated woman who removes her husband's shoes, bears his rebuffs in silence, is perfectly and elegantly dressed, keeps up all appearance with the perfect decorum, is jealous of her husband's second wife and manifests all feminine emotions. On the other she doesn't allow her husband to touch her, and the marriage is not consummated as she states she is promised to another. Her resistance induces a temporary impotence in him. She holds on to him yet does not give of herself. There

is also a third aspect. She has an inner emotional world—she writes poetry and sings and dances before her Giridhar Gopal, the blue-coloured
flautist. Music is a dominant feature of the Bhakti Movement, both in
its Sufi manifestations and the more subdued pilgrimages and worship
practices of the poor. Music is both self-absorbing and world-distancing;
it draws a circle around one.

The prince, who himself has no hesitation in taking other men's
wives, is cuckolded in a way by both his wives. In Mira's case, his rival
is outside his reach. On one occasion he tells Mira:

> You are going to tell me who it is. Now, I'm going to kill him and then I'm going
> to kill you…. Have you no shame carrying on under your husband's roof?…. Who
> is it, who is it who ravishes you in this very palace while you deny your husband
> his conjugal right? (89)

Male insecurity on sexual rejection and the blow it strikes to his ego and
sense of superiority lead him to suspect all men around him. Mira also
experiences sexual desire but the principle of fidelity to one restrains
her. The division between her role of a wife and that of devotee/lover is
complete and unbridgeable. She forms her own community of devotees,
becomes their leader and is transformed into the little saint. The narrator
comments:

> How the times had changed. Nautch girl, slut, the royal whore, the people of Chittor
> had called her every dirty name in the language. When they ran out of them, they
> invented new ones. Finally her name itself became synonymous with the faithless
> wife as mine became interchangeable with cuckold. Now she was called Chhoti
> Sant Mai. (316)

Mira's interplaying of the several roles she inhabited was itself a challenge to patriarchal and priestly authority, feminine sense of *dharma* and
pativrata, and moving in direct opposition to them, she put into practice

the right to her body, her mind and her emotional self. Her resistance to and disapproval of it also exposes the double standards applied to moral and social values on the grounds of gender. Kiran Nagarkar's Mira turns back on her husband and asks:

'What if I want to?'

'Want to what?'

She knew I was being deliberately obtuse but she was not fazed.

'Remarry?'

'There are enough rooms in the palace and I believe a wing has been redone'. I continued to talk at cross purposes. I had, however, merely played into her hands but it was too late to do anything about it.

'For whom? Me or you.' (461)

No wonder Mira had to face a great deal of social criticism. She was not willing to live, or it was simply not possible for her to live, in anonymity, or with both her marriage and devotion living side by side, not interfering with one another. No question of bearing children, or becoming a mother. She chose to inhabit two worlds without dividing herself. This was possible because she was from the upper classes; this was remarkable and conspicuous on that very count. Her courage, her ignominy and her later fame, divided across class and caste, were possible because of her location in caste and class.

Mira has acquired a multilevel symbolism: she is the symbol of the woman on whom marriage is imposed—the unwilling, reluctant wife; the symbol of the creative urge expressed in writing and kept secret, of devotion that wins a grudging admiration, of sacrifice to the notion of respectability among several others.

Shashi Deshpande in her 1993 novel *The Binding Vine* uses the story of an absent character, Mira, to reinforce the continuity of this symbol and the various meanings it evokes. Deshpande uses it for addressing the practice of the male's prerogative in choosing the marriage partner (irrespective of the woman's wish), for examining the untimely suppression of creative expression due to an early and forced marriage and finally for the issue of rape within marriage. The discourse has shifted from Rukhmabai's resistance to the restoration of conjugal rights to rape within marriage. Mira is Urmi's—the central character's— dead mother-in-law. As Urmi negotiates her own bereavement on the death of her daughter and tries to rework her own space within her marriage, she discovers the poems of her dead mother-in-law, uncovers the past and attempts to make sense of it. Her father-in-law had caught a glimpse of this young girl, proposed marriage and the proposal accepted by the parents, much against the girl's wishes. An imposed marriage, an early motherhood, unfulfilled wishes and a life cut short were the natural consequences. Mira dies in childbirth, leaving behind a few scattered poems expressing her anguish, which fall into Urmi's hands and compel her to rethink the whole notion of romantic love. Mira has also left a diary, and the excerpts all talk about women's self-effacement and self-governed marginalisation that the cultural patterns thrust on them. What then is the relationship between the self and the other? Does it always have to be governed by masculine desire and patriarchal frameworks? Women of the Bhakti Movement question just that, and as each one struggles against a specific set of circumstances, the separated spaces of the home and the world often clash, and at times collapse and come together.

Retellings: Moving into Political Spaces

The brahmanical code kept women out of Sanskrit learning, priesthood and the performance of other religious ceremonies, permitting them to participate only as married women. But one aspect of feminist protest is to claim this space, appropriate this task and shape it accordingly. Located in their own biological difference, do women perceive the epics differently? Earlier, we have already seen how women's folk songs reflect different concerns. In the sixteenth century, a woman from a potter's family wrote a new version of the *Rāmāyana*. Atukuri Molla is believed to have written it in Telugu in five days. Part of the Virashaiva Movement, she was inspired by her devotion to undertake the task. The composition *Molla Rāmāyanan* is surrounded by many a legend (Tharu and Lalita Vol.1, 94–98), some believing her to be a brahmin foundling, others framing the composition by stories of contests between villages. There is no way of verifying them. It is the epic which alone supplies some information about her—the tribute to her father, the direct address to Rāma (not to any patron) and the immediacy of her diction. Molla looks at the narrative through Sītā's childhood and 'celebrates her vitality, her strength, and her joyousness' (95). In short, she discards the more dominant purpose of the fight between good and evil and moves into the world of nature, the growing up years of Sītā, and her coming of age; she fills in the gaps in the *Rāmāyana* story and creates more space for the woman who was at the centre of the narrative. Tharu and Lalita state, 'Sources in the oral tradition make it clear that Molla was a rebel. She lost her mother quite early, we are told, and was reared by her father, whom she loved greatly. So she grew unwomanly and bold in her ways' (95). Apparently, the bringing up did not stress the internalisation of the female code of behaviour emphasising silence, modesty and control. One can well imagine the kind of womanhood likely to emerge if household patterns and social structures were more equal.

Molla's *Rāmāyana* was different in language and style in its development of and focus on the female eye and psyche. But Chandrabati, a near contemporary of Molla, who lived in Bengal, also wrote a *Rāmāyana* which ventured into describing contemporary economic conditions. An unfulfilled love relationship led her to get a temple made for herself, and she asked her father's permission to remain unmarried (Tharu and Lalita 102–103). In another long poem, 'Sundari Malua', she comments on the injustices against women. She moves

into more harmonious relationships between women, thus giving birth
to the principle of solidarity (103–104), one which is now being taken
up as one possible solution of feminine issues.[24] Tharu and Lalita, commenting on this, observe:

> The relationships between women too are refreshingly unstereotypical. Indian liter-
> ature of all kinds is full of the enmity between daughter-in-law and mother-in-law.
> But in this story, when Malua is released from the hauli, her mother-in-law stands
> up for her and argues in a remarkable passage, against the elders of the village, who
> want to exile her. Chandrabati also depicts the village women as joining together to
> argue Malua's case. (Vol. 1, 104.)[25]

This early intervention into the political sphere (in the sixteenth century) is the beginning of an aware female consciousness, outside domestic concerns. The shift from personal space—right to body, right to
choose, to stay unmarried, to resist exploitation of the body, to insist
upon a direct relationship with god, the right to express creativity to a
more public injustice that used women to cow down men and which the
villagers also used to chastise women—is obvious here. Perhaps, solidarity is much easier to attain where public causes are concerned.

Malua's story falls outside the Bhakti Movement as such and connects up with the narratives of the partition when the rehabilitation of
abducted women became a state matter. But it looks at the law of purity
as defined along caste and religious lines:

> The brother of Binod's mother, Halwal Sardar,
> A village elder, decreed: 'Taking this woman back
> Will cost us rank and caste. For three long months
> She lived between Muslim walls. The shame of it
> Would shatter a tiger! Who can save a doe
> Caught in the wild beast claws? We can do

Nothing once chastity and caste are gone.

Have we not turned away other weeping

Women who came back in shame from the Hauli?' (106)

This passage exposes the same mindset that prevails in *Rāmāyana* when Sītā was banished or when Iphigenia was sacrificed by her father Agamemnon without even informing her mother Clytemnestra of the intended sacrifice of their daughter in order to please the gods (the Greek dramatist Euripides [484 BCE–407 BCE] has written a play about her, 'Iphigenia in Tauris').[26] Such incidents expose the hollowness of masculinity. The concern with individual preservation dominates. Binod's mother, the mother-in-law, steps in to redefine the whole notion of chastity and declares her daughter-in-law to be a true *sati* (107).[27] It is true the norms are still *pativrata* and *sati*, but the shift in these norms has been transferred from an excessive focusing on the purity of the body to emotional values. Morality is being redefined and contextualised.

Where does one place Muddupalani, whose *Radhika Santwanam* (Appeasing Radhika) is midway between *bhakti* and sexuality? She is believed to be the first woman to have written an erotic epic, reinforcing the subjectivity and subjecthood of a woman, which marked a shift from the total surrender to one's god to a more conscious location in a social structure (see the earlier discussion on Chandrabati) and in the actual experience of sexual desire. Tharu and Lalita have commented in fair amount of detail on *Radhika Santwanam* and the controversy that surrounded it when it was reprinted in 1910 (1–12, 116–118). Muddupalani was an eighteenth-century poet, and Nagaratamma, who reprinted it, was a courtesan living in the twentieth century—the two women connected on the basis of aesthetics. The prohibition on the book and the order on destroying all copies were on the basis of 'obscenity'; thus, the question that was under debate was: what is it that shifts eroticism into obscenity? The narrative poem was about love and the principal *rasa* was *sringara rasa*, it foregrounded a woman's sensuality instead of a man's. Victorian prudery had by now (1910) taken hold of Indian society,[28] which

158

is far more liberal where the Radha–Krishna relationship is concerned. Colonial authority had by now begun to intervene not only in matters of political writing, such as Gandhi's or Vir Savarkar's,[29] but it was also deeply engaged in the task of restructuring gender. There is then this factor to be taken note of.

Visiting God's Abode: Pilgrimages and Ashrams

Ashapurna Devi's *Pratham Pratishruti*, the first of her trilogy about three generations of women in the turn of the nineteenth century, is about a woman who, in resentment of her husband's decision to marry off their young daughter, Suvarnlata, leaves home and proceeds to a pilgrim centre where she begins to teach in a school. This woman who goes into self-exile is Satyavati. The story of her daughter, Suvarnlata, forms the second part of the trilogy. Suvarnlata lives in a joint family and struggles for her space within it. The third novel is focused on Satyavati's granddaughter Bakul, who chooses to remain unmarried, becomes a well-known and respected writer but, in every other way, is dependent on her brother and sister-in-law. The trilogy raises several questions: Why do women leave home? Why do they choose to go on a pilgrimage or why do they live in ashrams, religious centres or pilgrim centres? Apparently, going on a pilgrimage is one activity that offers escape from the tyranny and the closed space of family life. Leaving home is only one part of the action; the next question is where to go from there. In Tagore's 'Stree Ka Patra' (discussed in Chapter 3), the woman finds the courage to express herself only when she leaves home and goes on a pilgrimage to Jagannath Puri.

Pilgrimages serve an important function in religious societies at more than one level. They allow the distancing from home, a certain contact with a community and independence and freedom within that; a contact with nature, a peaceful atmosphere away from the city humdrum and everyday pressures; and also a freedom from routine. Moreover, it is a legitimate, socially approved activity. Yet, it can be used as a means of escape, for expressing protest and seeking an alternative refuge.

In Anita Desai's *Fasting, Feasting*, Uma, the eldest of the four siblings, feels happiest when with her Mira Masi she visits a temple or goes on a pilgrimage. When she is reluctantly permitted to visit an ashram for one week, she extends the period to a month. Going to an ashram is, for her, quite in line with her other adventurous escapades: her overcharged enthusiasm for studies, the enjoyment of a tonga ride, the abandon with which she jumps off a boat and the pleasure of a dip in the river. The restrictions of everyday life lead to epileptic fits, to her becoming a failure in almost every sphere of life—studies, daughterhood and wifehood. Why? She is not as docile as a good woman should be; her need for freedom, privacy and love is intense. Her protests are ineffectual, hence the joy of escaping from her prison and the dip in the river which connects her with the creative powers of nature. Water stands for the maternal principle. In the Vedas, water is referred to as *matritamah*, the most maternal (Cirlot 364).

Ashrams are the rightful place for refugees of all kinds, be it Sītā (*Rāmāyana*), Śakuntalā ('Abhijnānāśakuntalam') or a more 'modern' woman like Girija in Rajam Krishnan's *Lamps in the Whirlpool*. C.T. Indra, in her introduction to the English translation of Krishnan's novel, looks at the centrality of the word *madi*, meaning purity of body (and mind), and the manner in which it debilitates a woman's life, alienating her from the pleasures of everyday life as well as from spontaneity and warmth. It is 'an oppressively exclusive system' (xii).[30] Thus, one day Girija, who lives in Delhi, leaves home to go to the market, but instead boards a bus to Haridwar in search of peace, spontaneity and freedom. She has various kinds of experiences—an old couple takes her into their care and she reciprocally becomes their guide and interpreter; a former student recognises her; another old woman, a stranger, shares her life experiences with her and offers her hospitality. Amidst all this, she also discovers the pretentiousness of those who exercise religious power, the hold of superstition and the way religion is used by some for absolving themselves of their sins. Domesticity has pushed her into obedience and a myopic, self-alienating existence. Her five days in Haridwar and Rishikesh, the dip in the river and the commingling of different waters seem to restore her connection to the living. For this she does not need the mediation of a swami. But, what now? She had left home because she was angry, because she had a strong need to get away. 'She had torn herself away from her family with the implicit faith that she would find peace on the banks of Ganga. Even as she was savouring her freedom, the question of what the future held for her tortured her' (Krishnan 45). Men can leave their families, become wandering sadhus or ascetics. But can women have the same freedom? Can they leave or go back at will? Women escape to ashrams for survival, or they are sent there by families who are reluctant to support them. Behind this lies the tragic tales of the widows who are ghettoised in Benaras or in Vrindavan, subjected both to humiliation and exploitation.[31] But there are others who voluntarily seek these collective community places for it helps them retain a sense of usefulness, belonging and piety with a little more of personal space and choice thrown in. It offers them the security and the companion-ship of collective living, and is perhaps the only other alternative to domesticity.

The old woman tells Girija,

> But I had made up my mind not to go back, come what may. I did not want to face the abject poverty in my parents' house, the cruelty in my husband's home and above all the inevitable barbed insinuations that I was responsible for my husband's drowning. (Krishnan 55)

But Girija does decide to go back, only to find that she has no place there. The doors are closed. She has, however, learnt to take a stand and is not going to be cowed down into feeling guilty (especially for crimes that she has not committed). What was the real meaning of freedom and what

was the interpretation given to it by orthodoxy? Were goodness and freedom to be seen as opposites? The conflict is also a triangular one with
cramping orthodoxy on one hand, permissive morality and materialistic
pleasure on the other and an individual morality based on humanistic
values and the element of choice in the middle.

We have a similar problematising of this feminist conflict in Kundanika Kapadia's award-winning Gujarati novel, *Seven Steps in the Sky*
(1982). When the novel first appeared in a serialised form in the Gujarati
daily *Janambhoomi Pravasi*, it was amidst several kinds of protests. But
it also received praise because it touched the core of many a woman's
existence as, through its multiple sub-narratives, it brought out into the
open the inequalities that held the institution of marriage in place—confined spaces, absence of choices, overpowering claims of duty, lack of
economic independence, no freedom and no right to individual friendships, a total erasure of all earlier claims and a persisting subordination. The answer, at one level simplistic, is Anandgram, the ashram. The
author wrote a lengthy introduction to the Gujarati publication of the
novel, which has not been fully translated in the English version. This
introduction goes into the everyday constraints that hedge a woman in,
many of which are described in the novel. There is the double pressure—
from the elders in the family as well as from the husband—the drudgery
of routine multitasking, inability to choose one's moment of relaxation,
and male ownership of the family, children and property, not merely in
legal terms but one which is proudly announced at moments of achievement, especially if the success is that of the male child. The woman is
excluded from any part in the family's achievement. Men only use the
singular 'I' or 'mine'. In middle-class households, there is also no economic freedom; a woman cannot at will invite a friend to come and stay
with her, or advance a little loan to a relative or friend in need. When
these 'little' issues come together in collective pressure, they blow up
into a personal crisis. Several novels depict this reality of the claustrophobic atmosphere of domesticity—Kundanika Kapadia's *Seven Steps
in the Sky*, Alka Saraogi's *Shesh Kadambari* (Take Over, Kadambari)

and Rajam Krishnan's *Lamps in the Whirlpool* being only some of them. When they engage with these multiple problems, they seem overloaded. At times, the aesthetic aspects are subordinated to the cause. But they do make a statement about the causes for unhappiness as well as the thrust of feminist protest. It is not directed towards a major shift in the family institution in legal terms, but works towards a more reciprocal relationship and a greater degree of equality. Kundanika Kapadia in her 'Introduction' makes several comparisons with the status of women in other countries, the provisions for child care, day crèches and the like. She makes it abundantly clear that she is targeting the way the seven steps around the fire of the marriage ceremony are misinterpreted in everyday life. Some of the ways which are anti-women are their exclusion from an equal, participatory role in decision-making, dowry demands and denial of economic liberty. *Dharma* cannot be interpreted from a single feminine perspective—it is a universally applicable moral law.[32]

The institution of the ashram as it exists from beginning to end, modernised by Gandhian ideology through mixed populations as at Phoenix Farm, Wardha ashram and Sabarmati, needs to be reexamined both for its persistent projection as a solution to personal conflicts—in this case, feminist conflicts—and for the oppressive authority such institutions may exercise by practising life-denying isolation and concentrated spiritualism. In Gandhi's reference and in Bankim Chandra Chattopadhaya's novel *Anand Math*, ashrams can also be seen as the bringing of people together in a political context, and their use as locations of collecting like-minded people for a common cause. Thus, they can also be used as protest centres—not necessarily abdication or withdrawal from the social world. Rajam Krishnan, however, does not end her novel with Girija deciding to stay in an ashram. Girija comes back, confronts her family, makes her choices and walks out of the house with the intent of taking up a job and becoming economically independent. Girija had been a school teacher for eight years before her marriage, she had related to her pupils very positively and she is confident of relocating herself.

Education, from this aspect, is important even for the *bhakta*, for writing or reciting was also a crossing of exclusionary boundaries. The annual Varkari pilgrimage, with its freedom and openness, has other equivalents in society. I remember once my mother undertook a pilgrimage to all the main Gurudwaras, including the ones in Pakistan. This was her way of finding her space away from the heavy claims of a large family. And this was a way sanctioned by society, religion and patriarchy. The frenzy of temple-singing, the madness of the *faqir*, the constant repetition of God's name as for instance in 'Mast Qalander',[33] the rhythm and the abandon of the singer's movement liberate one from other pressing and obsessive concerns. The deterioration, when it happens, takes place in any practice through misuse, misinterpretation and, at times, backlash.

The Shakti Principle: Trance, Possession and the Devi Syndrome

I begin with a passage from Baby Kamble's autobiography, *Jeevan Hamara*, which carries a detailed description of the manner in which women are possessed by gods and goddesses. Even as this description critiques religion, it recognises the fact that the act of being possessed allows a woman an escape from hunger, subjugation and inhibition. As the month of Asadh (July) begins, hordes of women are possessed and move around as if in a trance, stepping outside all docile roles, careless even about their clothes, and dancing away merrily, oblivious of all else:

> At the time when the mother-in-law would set about the task of cooking the food, the gods would take possession of the women's bodies....
>
> The women who were possessed would, oblivious of all else, run blindly like buffaloes towards the square where the *Potraja* would be beating the drum....
>
> Flinging their open hair, tossing their heads wildly the women would accompany their frenzied dancing with loud shrieks. (31–33)[34]

The enactment of such rituals serves a double purpose: it gives the women a sense of self-importance and simultaneously permits anonymity, providing freedom from the socio-familial roles as well as subjugation. It also acts as a safety valve, preventing their resentment from boiling over. In fact, this applies to the social function of such moments of festivity, the role they serve for the whole community, irrespective of gender. They allow space for a temporary forgetting. One can compare them to the role of carnivals and masquerades. Possession evokes awe and terror; it calls for ceremonies for placating the angry individual. Rituals, moreover, contain a non-verbal element and mark a 'reclassification of reality...and man's relationship to society, nature and culture' (Turner 52). Kamble believes it is a ritual the dalits have borrowed from upper-class Hindus, but whatever be the origins, being possessed or experiencing a trance is both an expression of protest and a route to freedom, given the widespread practice of Kali worship. One can work oneself into a trance, that is, it can be self-induced, but in the scene referred to above it is mainly the auditory channel, the sound of the drum combined with the change of season which allows the young, sexually alive women to respond to the moment and move out of normal states of consciousness into an out-of-body experience defying all conventional social norms of behaviour and hierarchies.[35]

My purpose here in taking up this spirit possession or this trance-like state is threefold. First, it is also a way of opting out of conventional frameworks, roles and constrictions and should be considered, in the case of women and the marginalised, as a means of protest, because it subverts authority, relocates it in the dislocated personality and empowers it. There is a role reversal in this. Second, it links up directly with the image of *Shakti* and the *Devi*-worship which exists all over India under different forms, and the mother goddesses, who with their ambivalent powers combining both the benevolent and the terrifying, are worshipped. We have Durga, Kali, Amba, Bhiwani, Shitla Mata and Vaishno Devi. There are others, but these are the ones who have to be appeased or who at least control evil forces. Mata Vaishno Devi is also called Sheranwali Maa, the mother with tigers, because she rides a tiger. And third, witch-hunting or considering a woman a witch is the negative side of possession and can be seen as a backlash by the dislocated power structures, especially when mainstream society, in order to preserve its power, victimises the marginalised sections.

In 1927 when Katherine Mayo wrote *Mother India*, she opened her narrative with a description of the Kali Temple in Calcutta where the many-armed goddess, with her garland of skulls, reigned supreme, bloody and gory, with her tongue hanging out of her mouth. Who is Kali? And what is *shakti*? There are many legends and myths surrounding the origin of Shakti, but the majority of them agree that when the Mahisasura was granted a boon as a reward for his years of penance, immortality couldn't be granted. Subsequently, he asked that no male should kill him, and he should only die at the hands of a naked female. Accordingly, when Durga was created out of the consciousness of the gods, Durga had to disrobe herself in order to destroy him:

> After killing him, a terrible rage entered Durga's mind, and she asked herself, 'what kind of gods are these that give to demons such boons, and apart from that what kind of gods are these that do not have the honesty to tell me the truth before sending me into battle?' She decided that such a world with such gods did not deserve to survive and she took on the form of Kali and went on a mad rampage, devouring every living creature that came her way.[36]

Views of believers also differ. There is another story which gives the whole credit to Śiva, and not to the collectivity of gods, for creating Durga out of his consciousness (Caldwell 20). Menon and Shweder point out that one interviewee stressed that Shakti cannot achieve anything by herself, she has to 'combine with consciousness for the process of creation to take place, and so consciousness as symbolised by Śiva has a unique position' (84). But another 74-year-old brahmin interviewee persists:

Sakti is indivisible, Śiva has no *Sakti* of his own, it is all Devi's and who is Devi? She is Kali, she is Durga, she is Parvati. She is self-creating, self-generating; while he is born of her, he takes his strength from her. And yet, he does have something that is uniquely his—he is pure consciousness—if he is fire, then she is the energy with which the fire burns, and so it is foolish to talk of him being stronger or her being stronger; they need each other, and we can't talk of one without talking of the other. (86)

Even the earlier interviewee does talk of interdependence. There is an inbuilt ambiguity (typical of patriarchal positions) in the whole myth. Shakti has an agency of her own but apparently no consciousness. If she is seen as an independent entity, both equality and creativity are possible; if Shakti is seen as a delegated power, then she is subordinate. From one point of view, both are incomplete in themselves, for consciousness needs a manifestation, just as action needs a consciousness. But from another point of view, Śiva can be seen as superior, as in the first instance, he is believed to have generated Shakti.

Kali herself is a double-faced goddess, a benign protectress but also capable of revenge and vindictiveness. Thus, she evokes awe and fear, is pictured as a blood-thirsty revengeful deity and as a war goddess. Her role in destroying the demon is crucial: she is the deciding factor. Again, the image of the naked body itself is a strong strand which runs through Indian writing, both religious and secular: from the *Mahābhārata* to Mahasweta Devi's 'Draupadi', and is thus the representation of female sexuality. Its opposite, the covered body, modest and docile is created by culture for the protection of man. Female sexuality is seen as a danger trap, thus the need to control it, suppress and tame it.

The Kali image through its transformation into Mother India during the nationalist struggle became a political symbol. In Bankim Chandra Chattopadhaya's *Anand Math* (1882), Kali is linked directly with the resistance to colonial oppression,[37] as she demands sacrifice from her children. Aurobindo, during his years of revolutionary activity, brought out a pamphlet, *Bhiwani Mandir*, and the thugs of the nineteenth century had Bhiwani as their goddess.

During this period both the nationalists and the imperial rulers used Kali for entirely different purposes. The nationalists used it for inspiring sacrifice, the revolutionaries for violence and the imperialists to critique India and Indian culture and dismiss it into primitiveness. She came to represent the 'dark and terrifying—yet also strangely seductive and alluring powers of the Orient' (Urban 170). She formed a part of 'the broader project of "imagining India" as an Other of the West' (170). The Indian imagination used her image for inspiring nationalist fervour, but in an attempt to tame her sexuality also locked her up in the image of the mother.

This ambivalent use of the image of Kali, her creative and destructive powers, her sexuality, which according to the male mind needed to be controlled and tamed, the burden of motherhood—all were regressive steps trapping women into images and stereotypes, framing them in subdued, subordinate roles and subjugating them to both native patriarchy and colonial power. The Western encounter, even if it was seen as a liberating force by the caste-oppressed sections of society and other victims of tradition (like Jotiba Phule, Pandita Ramabai and later Ambedkar, to mention a few), all those who converted to Christianity not on basis of belief but as an escape from a moribund tradition, was for feminist causes, a dark period. The gradual deterioration of open practices, the growing rigidity of tradition (especially the views of Manu) and the use of the woman question as a debating ground for reformists and imperialists alike have left behind their own legacy. One needs to realise how the dark tunnel, which always perhaps existed, was beginning to close in from all sides. So much so that the Bhakti and the Sufi Movements, which encouraged liberal values and communal harmony, were now almost dry streams.

In all this the image of the *devi* became a manipulative and a manipulatable prison. In 1960, Satyajit Ray made a film titled *Devi*. The same year saw another film released, Ritwik Ghatak's *Meghe Dhaka Tara*. Ghatak's film uses 'the popular Bengali legend associating young married women with Durga, the mythical provider, to reveal how history and culture create the oppressive social spaces determining women's lives.'[38] Set against the backdrop of the partition (1947), the film focuses on a refugee family where the eldest daughter Neeta is sacrificed to the needs of her family and condemned to die of loneliness and tuberculosis.[39] Satyajit Ray in *Devi* works on another kind of domestic scene where the old father-in-law's own sensual appreciation of the beautiful young daughter-in-law begins to frame her as an incarnation of the goddess Kali. Her husband's arguments are brushed aside and the young girl is trapped within an iconic image for the villagers to worship. She gains a reputation for performing miracles. In the process her wifehood and motherhood are neglected and destroyed. When she fails to protect her own nephew from the hands of death, Dayamoyee, the goddess incarnate, goes mad. This is a parallel reading to Ghatak's of the cultural situation and the growing negative hold of the Kali legend. There are several aspects of this depiction. The father-in-law's possessive sexuality, which destroys the marriage of his son; the blind faith of the people who believe miracles are actually being performed; the destructive self-image, created and fed by others, but which finally destroys the woman; the disadvantages and deprivation inherent in the concept of *devi*, which is life-denying; and a culture which is caught up in its own web, refusing to evolve, as if the flow has dried. There is also the materialism which is attached to this iconicity.

Indian feminism, thus, is constantly engaged in deconstructing images of *devi*, of the Supreme Mother, the Virgin Goddess and the like, even as it contests other socio-political and legal systems. In the game of politics, women paid the heaviest price as native systems yielded to Victorian norms and colonial imagination on the one hand, and, on the other, surrendered before the presence of nationalist guardianship, which evoked the Vedas in every breath. But at individual levels resistance surfaced in myriad ways as writing, journalism and travel became possible, and as the freedom struggle began to open out alternative spaces. The obverse side of *devi* is the *dayan*, the witch. Persecution of a woman as witch closes all doors upon her and it is usually the people in power who do it—priests, landlords, wealthy and rich people—often to camouflage and hide their own sins. Natural disasters like an epidemic, flood or famine are attributed to the presence of these women. Suspicion, mistrust and fear pervade the atmosphere. There is no question of a collectivity of resistance; instead, there can be a coming together of the persecutors. This is a kind of social backlash.[40] People who are poor look for survival on the outskirts of a town or village, or make a living through an unusual occupation—like women guarding a cremation ground (as in one of Mahasweta Devi's story)—and are soft targets for this kind of persecution.

In a story titled 'The Witch', Mahasweta Devi exposes the phenomenon of witch-making and the atmospheric pressures which are created by exploiting natural disasters. The crowding in of incidents, of the hammering in of notions of insecurity, the spread of distrust from the other to oneself (because of fear and uncertainty) and the mounting desperation unfold themselves in this beautifully written story. Months without rain, the monsoon is dry, wood crackles with dryness, the drought is expanding itself into a full-fledged famine. The villagers as they wait for some relief, food supplies, or work on daily wages are also possessed with thoughts of migration from the village. And then superstition takes over: 'Everything that happened along with the famine is due to the *daini*.... All because of the *daini*' (58).

Anyone can suddenly become a *daini* or a *dain*, people we meet everyday. Unnatural things begin to happen. No one sees them but everyone hears about them. In the midst of this, on the very second page, is a sentence about the missing daughter of the tribal priest of Tura. The brahmin priest dramatises this disappearance through a dream vision of a naked woman, who announces her identity as 'famine'. This is the *daini* who has to be hounded. The narrative comments upon the manner in which the blame always falls on the marginalised sections, never the upper castes (59).

In this hour of trouble, families crack up, men watch their women with suspicion, and all relationships, human concerns are given the go by. Men have become beasts; therefore, a common prayer has to be performed. Outsiders come, people die, water is scarce. The upper castes don't allow people to use their wells; the tribals are looked down upon because they don't follow the caste system (68–69). The village community decides to chase the witch and stone it to death. The pursuit goes on and the foreign press descends on them (a side effect of globalisation), essential facts remain hidden, and surface happenings are narrated.

Finally as they chase the *daini*, it is discovered that she is the missing daughter of the *pahaan* (the tribal priest), a woman who is dumb, and who had been exploited by the *thakur*'s son. Now pregnant, hungry and naked, she is being hounded. She escapes into a cave, and there delivers a child. This is when the father recognises her and the village discovers she is not a *daini* but a victim. The whole religious system, the futile performance of *puja*s, construction of temples and the intervention of the media, and foreign aid are all means of obscuring the main issues. Superstition is fed by the exploiters, its flames fanned. The community decides to boycott Hanuman Misra. This is how resistance is born, out of local contexts. The world of nature, so mysterious, had really not changed, it 'was exactly as she had always been in a dry year' (122). The 'witch' is a creation of the power-wielders, and a woman—the naked body of a woman—the right incarnation of this terrifying image. This is how 'devi-worship', 'witch-hunting' and the theme of the naked female body come together.

V

The Nineteenth Century and After

❧❧

Feminist struggles and issues underwent a change in the nineteenth century, which was simultaneously the period of colonialism, cultural encounters and the Bengal Renaissance. The various strands often seem to be running contrary to each other as urbanisation, modernisation and the pressures of a foreign culture and language mount. It is a period broken up into different contrary movements on account of ideology, language, class and region. The term 'colonial' does not signify a unified concept or a mono-directional flow of time. The year 1857 marks a shift of power and a change in the Indo-British relationship. It also signifies a shift in the dominant flow of ideas of the Indian elite as the earlier fascination with a foreign culture yielded ground to a concern with nationalism and native culture and identity.

How did colonialism come into being? The beginnings are traced to 1757, the Battle of Plassey. But in bare skeletal terms the whole episode is a ridiculous play of events: spasmodic incursions for the purposes of trade end up in the building of an empire. The aggressive determination of the newcomer and the almost foolish yielding and hospitality of the native marks the true difference in cultures and its laws of morality and hospitality.

True, India was torn in its unending wars of succession amongst the different clans, royal houses and power centres. True also that moral principles were not strictly followed in the wars of the *Mahābhārata* and

172

the *Rāmāyana*. Yet, they were no match for the history of piracy, adventure and need for territory of the islanders. Shortly before 1947, during the final phase of the freedom struggle, Sheila Bhatia, a Punjabi writer, wrote an opera which became very popular. One verse ran as follows:

Aaye ag lain nu;

Bhaite ban gharwale

(They came to fetch an ember, And took over the house).[1]

The two cultures were different at many levels: philosophical traditions, territorial limits, family systems, religion and attitudes towards travel were only some of them. The subtlety of the interaction which brought these very differences centre stage, to be reshaped, interpreted, absorbed or reformed is admirable.[2] The rivalries of the native princes were fully exploited. The interpretative task, which the British took upon themselves and which cast itself like a veil on indigenous forms of knowledge, is one manifestation of the process of colonialisation. Enough scholarship has emerged to allow us to accept that (*a*) these interpretations, whether of law, tradition or text, or of the forces of history, have played a considerable part in shaping our responses and our history; (*b*) all reform measures pertaining to Indian law, the woman question and inheritance were not necessarily progressive, some of them were disruptive of traditional practices; (*c*) similarly, all reform movements that rose in response to the colonial interpretations, especially religious reform movements which attempted to rationalise the practice of traditions, were not necessarily beneficial. At a later stage, at times, they developed into fundamentalist positions and ended up as separatist movements.

The first half of the nineteenth century, the period of the Company Raj, and the intellectual stirrings it brought about, especially in Bengal, is a period which is known as the Bengal Renaissance. It has been perceived as the beginning of modernisation. It was a movement largely limited to the English-educated, urban elite. Right from the 1830s to the end of the century, one has to discriminate between writing as felt response, or written as explanation to the foreign 'other', or under the pressure of patronisation, or consciously directed towards nation construction. Indifference to these conditions is likely to lead to misreading of history.

The second half of the nineteenth century marked a shift in the British attitude, with Company Raj giving way to the direct control of the British authorities after the 1857 war. The British attitude was now both more cautious and more ruthless. And the coming together of the various resistance movements strengthened nationalist aspirations. This was a period of debates about national identity, language, territory and grassroots movements. While the first period was dominantly attracted by foreign ideas, the second emphasised the cultural difference, concentrated on recovering and writing histories and interpreting the past both for us as well as them.[3] However, it would be a mistake to think that a criss-crossing or a contrariness was absent. It was not. The lower classes, sections of the oppressed and converted populations looked upon the British as saviours.[4] For them it was a choice between two oppressors and whatever little edge one had above the other was the main point of affiliation.

The gender issues were common to both periods—pre-1857 and post-1857—and played a significant role in nation construction as several writers including Partha Chatterjee ('The Nationalist Resolution') and Meenakshi Mukherjee ('Gender and Nation') have stressed. Chatterjee traces the development of the nationlists' approach and feels the 'relation between nationalism and the women's question must have been problematical' ('The Nationalist Resolution' 233). It shifted from the early modernisation tendencies to increased conservatism, resulting in a split in the public discourse. We have an example of Tilak's orthodox position in the case of Rukhmabai.[5] Tanika Sarkar works through a different interpretation of the situation; she points out to the continuing pressures of caste, family and social institutions, which practised reform only symbolically.[6]

Chatterjee suggests that we need to look more closely at the nationalist ideology and pursues Sarkar's argument that the acceptance of Western liberal ideas was selective. He asks, 'How did they select what they wanted? What, in other words, was the ideological sieve through which they put the newly imported ideas from Europe?' (P. Chatterjee, 'The Nationalist Resolution' 236–237). It chose to separate culture into two spheres—the material and the spiritual—thus incorporating the Western systems of scientific thought and technology, but preserving the identity of the national culture. This emerged as a separation between the outer and the inner, the home and the world (238). Expanding on this idea (which has been enacted in some measure, even through a shift of gender roles in Tagore's *Home and The World*),[7] Chatterjee argues that a 'new patriarchy' came into being, an indigenous one, which aimed not merely at social reform but at producing a more cultured version of womanhood, different from the one projected in the common woman, who may be vulgar, loud and coarse. Thus, it aimed at self-improvement. Towards this aim it stressed education (244–245).

Mukherjee focuses on historical writing, which, in her view, is a reaction to the coloniser's account of India's past, 'In order to counter the teleology of this version of history a different emplotting of the past was necessary', a rewriting which would create a counter-narrative ('Gender and Nation' 117). She comments on the glorious projection, which crystallised 'a sense of nationhood through the valorization of both the physical prowess and the spiritual strength of the community', an effort at retrieval of a sense of self-respect. Mukherjee focuses on the way women were 'used/perceived/deployed/represented in this predominantly masculine project' (118). As a counter between masculinity and femininity, a certain orthodoxy and idealism of 'Indian Womanhood' was created, a stereotype which continues to haunt us even now and which feminist resistance at both collective and the individual levels is engaged in dismantling. Women upholding sacrificial values, obedient, subjugated, almost asexual, living permanently for others—the Sītā–Savitri, the *pativrata* model—as in the *Laws of Manu*, became increasingly codified. The nationalist movement again was not a monolithic construct. It incorporated ideas and ideologies of various hues and colours—the reformist, the revolutionaries, the moderates, the grassroots leaders, religious groups and groups of the marginalised categories. These multiplicities lent themselves easily to being played against each other and provided room for the strengthening of divisionary forces.

The nineteenth century was in several ways a break with the Bhakti Movement, but the issues remained the same. Only now there was an additional aspect to the whole thing, the legal aspect related to the prevention of sati, age of consent, widow remarriage, restoration of conjugal rights and inheritance laws. Other issues which the feminists were more concerned with (despite overlappings) were the right to body, to choice, to personal space as well as to participation in the public space (the freedom struggle), the right to education (thus knowledge) and to economic independence; above all there was the right to life (as opposed to sati and the restrictions on widowhood), right to action and various other emotional concerns.

It is amazing that despite early marriages and limited formal education, we do come across women who made the effort to educate themselves and acquire learning. Both formal and informal systems (supported by religious bodies, local societies, personal initiative and government effort), existed side by side.[8] The attempt to codify law also highlighted the visibility of other minorities. It is a matter of concern that scholarship has veered towards a projection of Hindu culture, but there are other cultures also which have a long tradition, like the tribal, the Parsis and the Muslims, people who are part of Indian society. Currently, the Aryan invasion of India is being dismissed as a myth, but whether we accept it as fact or not, the tribal presence in the *Rāmāyana* and the *Mahābhārata* exists on the margins to remind us of the incursions. Further, they are shown to be receding into the forests, or living in remote areas, and at the end of the *Mahābhārata* war, Kunti, along with Gandhari and Dhritarashtra, chooses to live in the forests. Shashi Deshpande has a story about this phase, which is like a confession, 'Hear Me, Sanjay', but it is focused on Kunti's monologue. Mahasweta Devi has another story about this episode, 'Kunti and the Nishadin', where the same episode is seen as a confession to the Mother Earth and the Nishadins.[9]

Mahasweta Devi's narrative contrasts the world of the palace with that of the forest. Each is governed by two different laws and moral values. The world of the palace is one of power, therefore it rules; it does not reach out and is self-absorbed. There is a certain ruthlessness behind this authority and an adherence to what seems right (may or may not be so). Kunti, as she fulfils her duty of a younger sister-in-law looking after her elder brother-in-law and his wife, recalls the many roles she has played, with never anything to call her own. Now, all she wants to do is to unburden herself and confess, and she decides to 'tell the forest, the river, the birds, murmuring leaves, the wind and the Nishadins. She will talk in her language and they won't understand, nor will they ask questions' (86). Thus, the act of unburdening and not that of public confession or penance is important; neither accountability nor punishment matter, only the confession.

Reviewing her many roles, her motherhood—with each son sired by a different father—she now tries to comprehend the meaning of *dharma*. Can one feel for others without experiencing loss? Can there be confession without a sense of guilt or remorse? Why, she wonders, did she not publicly mourn for Karna? Karna was the only son who was not fathered by a proxy for Pandu; he was born of pure desire. There is an underlying feeling that the act of birthing the other three was not as enriching as the birth of Karna, even though he had to be abandoned. Kunti realises that she has not fully comprehended *dharma*. The laws of chastity and unchastity do not make any concession to desire. Her sins are many; they have multiplied one after the other as she has not listened to her heart. Even when she asked for Karna's help, she did it for her own selfish purpose. She never had the courage to acknowledge him openly. But there are other sins she is not even aware of. She has looked down upon the Nishadins (tribal women) as limited beings, dumb and unreceptive. An elderly Nishadin woman approaches her and speaks to Kunti, who is astonished that the language is the same. For once, she is made to realise that the Nishadins are humans like her and her equals. Kunti, in the eyes of this elderly woman, is guilty of denigrating human life and of judging everything by the shallow moral values of the palace. Kunti is also guilty of having conspired, along with her sons, of doping the elderly Nishadin woman and five men, leaving them to be burnt in the hut. This was in order to provide a concrete evidence of the Pandavas' death (this refers to a well-known episode of the *Mahābhārata* in the fifteenth chapter of Ashram Vasik Parva where the burnt bodies send a signal of their death and facilitate them in a fresh beginning). The woman rejects Kunti's plea for forgiveness (95). Sins obviously have to be paid for. This story examines the underside of the narrative, a subaltern's point of view, and mocks at the sense of right and wrong that dominates power discourses. Madhu Singh observes that the story 'challenges, interrogates and subverts the hegemonic structures of *Rajavritta*, exposing the social and political injustice towards the abused and the marginalised sections of society'.

Tribal customs, practices, values and gender morality are different and they need to be recognised as such. Mahasweta Devi has pointed out that tribal people have their own versions of the epics as well ('A Tribute to Jaidev'). Dalits, similarly, having been excluded from the brahminic language and culture, have a parallel value system (Illiah). The overpowering presence of Hindu culture and its projection as Indian culture is an over simplification. Minority cultures, resistance movements and other religious traditions need to be recognised as part of it, even as the *margi* and the *desi* are. Except for Islam, Christians, Jews and Parsis, the Indian constitution brushes all other minority religions into the category Hindu (Kale). This has periodically led to questioning, resentment

1. Sita's *swayamvara*—Rama wins her hand (Courtesy: Street Art).

2. Celebrating the destruction of evil: A view of the Dussehra festival (Courtesy: Molina).

3. Crushing all opposition: Hanuman on his way to Ayodhya with Rama and Sita
(Courtesy: Street Art).

4. After the victory: Rama and Lakshmana return to Ayodhya—a Ramlila procession
(Courtesy: Bhumesh Bharti).

5. Ramlila performance (Courtesy: Bhumesh Bharti).

6. Draupadi's *chirharan* in the *Mahābhārata* and the benevolence of Krishna
(Courtesy: Shabbir).

7. Kathakali mask (Courtesy: Shabbir).

8. A dome depicting the *Rāmāyaṇa* in Shekhawati region (Courtesy: Molina).

9. Continued histories of the *Rāmāyana*: Worshipping through art (Courtesy: Molina).

10. Understanding good and evil at a young age (Courtesy: Molina).

11. Śakuntalā and Duhsanta in the hermitage (Courtesy: Shabbir).

12. Durga Mata in all her glory (Courtesy: Molina).

13. Worshipping Mata Vaishno Devi amidst domestic bliss (Courtesy: Shirish Batra).

14. Hansa Wadkar. (Courtesy: NFAI).

15. Women protestors arguing with the police (Courtesy: Vividha).

16. C.S. Lakshmi speaking on oral narratives at Jaipur with Gitanjali Chatterjee in the chair (Courtesy: IRIS).

17. Setting up shop with the support of a Self Help Group (Courtesy: Renuka Pamecha).

18. Collage: (*a*) Fighting legal battles, (*b*) Protest march in support of Bhanwari Devi, (*c*) Circulating information—*Ujala Chadi*, (*d*) All set for a leap forward and (*e*) Solidarity—politics at work (Courtesy: Vividha and Renuka Pamecha).

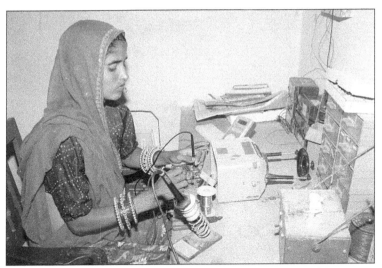

19. Empowerment: From illiteracy to technology (Courtesy: Renuka Pamecha).

20. Taking down notes—Mamta Jaitly at a public hearing (Courtesy: Vividha).

21. Protest march on the streets of Jaipur (Courtesy: Renuka Pamecha).

22. The arm of law and the protestor's self-defence (Courtesy: Renuka Pamecha).

and controversy. As cultural units they have either separated, dented the mainstream culture by bringing about marginal changes in it, or been absorbed by it through passage of time, pressures of power or social pressures and ambitions, at times by the simple notion of a singular concept of respectability. In these minorities, the position of women, restrictions imposed on them, marriage laws, concept of chastity and the right to remarriage may also differ. Tribal culture permits and even encourages remarriages; some tribes encourage the coming together of young people of both sexes; tribal communities also allow women to work. Some of these tribes exploit their women for economic purposes, as amongst the Kolhati caste, the eldest daughter is often a dancer/courtesan and supports her parents and brothers (Kale). Cultures that worship the book (as opposed to idol worship), as Islam and Sikhism, do not ordinarily believe in goddess worship or observing of frequent fasts, either as penance, a compulsion or with the aim of achieving some goal or objective as we have in the *vrat*s for weekdays or at times to appease some particular god or goddess.[10] Indian culture is a multi-stranded culture and the position of women, discrimination against them and their own strategies of resistance accordingly reflect these differences.

But despite these differences, non-accessibility to education, confinement to domesticity and the pressures of the notion of respectability are by and large the same. If they differ, the difference lies more in economic status than in religious belief. Else stereotypes emerge on the grounds of this difference as in the case of Christian and Anglo-Indian women. Both media and literary texts seek to present them as more modern—in dress and moral behaviour—and free and often fix them in particular social roles such as teachers, cabaret dancers, nurses and other professions which take them into the public arena. Not afflicted by a sense of purdah or *antahpura*, they occupied a more visible space but this visibility may not necessarily have social respectability.

The variegated strands of social life make it obvious that resistance, whether individual or collective, was much more secular and context specific than its placement in the Hindu tradition would make it appear. The Islamic presence where the gender question is concerned became increasingly visible with the British codification of different laws on the grounds of religion. An attempt will be made to locate resistance in multi-stranded Indian culture.

The Aspirations for Equality: Negotiating Tradition

The feminist movement has all along had male interventions in support, in the form of public voices and as gurus and reformers. But women too have spoken for themselves and we have already traversed this ground through the Upanisads, epics and the Bhakti Movement revealing a continuity in its persistent questioning and seeking the removal of exclusionary boundaries. At about the time when Pandita Ramabai, Savitribai Phule (another social activist) and the anonymous writer of *Simantni Updesh* were raising issues related to social injustice and gender discrimination, Tarabai Shinde wrote *Stree-Purush Tulana* (1882), focusing on the double standards of morality. Shinde writing in Marathi, talked about female desire and the sexual repression of widows, and hit out at the endless debates of the reformers and their unsympathetic moral censure. Shinde's work falls in between Pandita Ramabai's and the *Simantni Updesh.* She writes in a regional language, addresses both men and women of her own country and makes abundant use of myth and history. Neither is it a fund raising exercise nor does it suggest that women should take the initiative. Her primary aim is to make the men realise the injustice in their models of womanhood and to critique the restrictive patriarchal impositions, which seek to deprive women of the very basic freedoms (J. Jain, *Feminizing* 125–129).

While Partha Chatterjee pointed out the construction of a new patriarchy in response to the colonial encounter ('The Nationalist Resolution' 244–245), Malini Bhattacharya points out that women did not 'necessarily submit passively to its revised contingencies' ('Introduction' 3). She points out the resistance offered by women's emerging subjectivity in several works of the period. The term 'power' did not have the same meaning for men and women, it is sought 'not merely to serve the revised needs of the family and the home, but for self-development and self-expression; it is a conceptual tool which allows the woman to critique effectively the various inequities of her social condition' (3). There was no clear break from tradition, instead, some of the writers praised it fulsomely; a few moved away from it and a majority worked for more space and equality within it as well as for a greater role in decision-making. There was also a constant attempt to attack all kinds of stereotypes, the *pativrata* as much as the lax modern woman seen as the new product of Westernisation. Their major concerns are with access to education, protest against oppressive social practices (like purdah) and looking afresh at the institutions of marriage and family through women's perspectives.

With the growth in literary culture and education, it was not long before women started writing and publishing essays in the magazines and journals that came into existence. Malini Bhattacharya refers to this phase as a period when the literate woman appeared on the scene (*Talking of Power*). Self expression, creative writing, autobiographical and argumentative writing or participation in social debates were acts of transgression and resistance. There was a felt need by women to participate at a more public level. In their negotiation with traditional value structures, they can be seen to be creating a counter discourse to the 'conduct' books that abounded in every language, mostly written by men, often given as wedding gifts to women and used for the processes of socialisation, such as Maulana Ashraf Ali Thanvi's *Bihisti Zewar*.[11] Metcalf in her introduction to the English translation refers to its reputation as 'a guide for respectable women', one which sought 'to standardize a respectable morality throughout a large population during a period of social change'. *Bihisti Zewar* differed from other conduct books as it also 'encouraged female competence and self-confidence in a domestic sphere' (Metcalf vii). When women began to write on similar areas, they explored the concept of freedom, brought into debate a direct participation in political matters, wrote about patriotism and expanded the range available in male discourse by bringing to it their own concerns and gender perspectives. They compared their situation with women of other times, cultures and different castes, thus simultaneously building up solidarity (in terms of gender) and pointing out the possibilities of a more equal social system. They travelled to and fro in terms of time and space. As Tanika Sarkar writes:

> Their writing went in all directions: prose, poetry, drama, polemic and discursive essays, imaginative fiction. From within their secluded homes—for very few were widely travelled as Krishnabhabini Das or linked to renowned families and public roles as Swarnakumari Devi and Sarala Devi—they observed the world and confidently judged it. Perhaps, what more successful public achievers could express in their working and public lives, housewives would grasp and construct through writing alone: a new identity, a new relationship with the word and the world. (xi)

One of the earliest writers of the mid-nineteenth century is Bamasundari Devi. Herself a Brahma, she was greatly influenced by the additional space and freedom Brahmo Samaj offered women as also by its rationalistic spirit vis-à-vis the superstitious beliefs that pervaded the social structure at large. It is perhaps a little too unrealistic to expect radical thought from her, but there is an openness and a plea for rationality and a degree of humaneness. In one of her articles she strongly condemns *kulin* polygamy and the segregation of women on grounds of pollution. She holds a brief for female education, pleading that it was important for improved social condition, for happier and more equal marriages. She also advocates widow remarriage. The essay "What are the Superstitious that Must be Removed?" was written in 1861 and reflects, despite its conservative attitude in placing women amidst domesticity, an awareness of their emotional and physical problems related to exclusion and segregation. It needs to be noted that her criticism of caste hierarchies and prejudices was not necessarily subscribed to by many reformers themselves even as they engaged with religious reform or the woman question. Her argument that our caste and race arrogance is the greatest hindrance to our betterment (23), is as valid today as ever before.

Social mores also come in for criticism from Kailashbasini Devi. In her essay 'The Woeful Plight of Hindu Women', once again *kulin*ism, treatment of the girl child, child marriage, forced celibacy on *kulin* women, the hollow sense of honour, loveless and unequal marriages, inheritance laws—all are critiqued. Written in 1863, the article reflects an amazing amount of social awareness. And Kailashbasini Devi's writing, like that of her contemporary Bamasundari Devi, is in the form of a dialogue. Constantly they address the listener/reader. As for instance: 'Ah me! Widowed on account of education? Can the might of knowledge kill a husband and deprive a woman of the apple of her eye?' (46).

Her reference is to the superstitions that surround the fact of women's education, that an educated woman brings an early death to her husband. There is a slight satire and mockery, even as she proceeds to load her query with multiple other questions. Freedom, again, is a term which needs to be explored more rationally. Most of the exclusionary practices are justified by society on the ground that women who move out of the home whether in search of education, a career or independence are likely to neglect their home: hence subjugate them, keep them ignorant and in mortal fear of fate. Patriarchy—in the interest of its own power position—upholds the traditional power structures. Kailashbasini Devi's criticism precedes works like Marcus Fuller's *The Wrongs of Indian Womanhood*, which appeared almost four decades later or Pandita Ramabai's work which also caught up with Kailashbasini Devi more than two decades later.

Education was one area which most women writers insisted needed to be opened out. We have similar arguments being put forward in other regions and languages. In Malayalam, N.A. Amma wrote, at the close of the century, 'The Demerits of Female Education: A Refutation' and Abanti Rao took up the same subject in Oriya when she spoke at a conference on the reform of women's education:

> Women experience a feeling of incompleteness, a sense of non-fulfillment at home, in society and the nation, and proceed on the path of reform: this is the aim of this conference. But who gets a sense of incompleteness of her knowledge? The ignorant does not understand the limits of her knowledge. Therefore it is clear that knowledge alone propels us along the path of reform. We must first understand this truth. (42)

She goes on to build up a case for universal primary education. A century later, we can see that as a society we have not yet been able to achieve this goal, despite constitutional and legal provisions. The emphases on education, knowledge and learning in order to build up self-confidence and provide for a sense of personal freedom is evident, despite the fact that familial and societal reasons are also paraded all along.[12] Abanti Rao came from a Brahmo background and had the full support of her husband. These women then were twice privileged—education and male support—and as such were keen to acquire agency towards the improvement of the general condition of women.

It is not always that they addressed only other women, they freely moved from genre to genre and mode to mode—satire, comedy, skits, dialogues and open letters. Kusumkumari Devi wrote a rebellious letter, addressed to her father—a letter published in *Somprakash* in 1872. She addressed 10 questions regarding the absence of choice in choosing a husband, the guilt of the parents for the unhappiness of their daughters, marriages based on all kinds of deprivation, the mode of marriage and the possibility of divorce. Building up a case for marriage of choice she asks: 'Between man and God—who ought to be feared?' (54). The letter is an appeal to the male conscience and pushes them towards the realisation of their own guilt in constructing a system so loaded against women, and in the process using the scriptures selectively for that purpose, often deviating from them in principle.

As one reads these writings from different parts of the country, one realises that women are not blind advocates of tradition, uncomplaining or passive victims, not even only armchair critics, but are conscious of a wider world and seek to inhabit it in their own right. Towards this end they claim an equal status, access to education and insist on being located within the category of human (not subhuman). Girindramohini Dasi writes:

> We find that whenever a woman driven by her own nature gives up the dependent, retarded state of a doll, tries to open the eyes of knowledge, puts a step forward towards the attainment of humanity, male society confronts her with obstruction, hindrance, examples, judgements and other weapons in its arsenal. What does it mean? I ask, is women's existence not their own?.... If men need freedom and self-reliance—a great deal of knowledge for self-improvement—to enter a profession and a trade for security of life, why do women not need the same? (71)

The concerns with social and familial justice, education and freedom persist working as an independent category outside political ideologies and the nationalist movement. We have in 1933 a Malayalee writer writing about 'womanliness'. Moving freely between myths, scriptural stories and the present, Sarojini argues that women are 'a cut above men' (58). In 1934 Sarala Devi wrote *The Rights of Women*, wherein she places her argument in a much larger context as she discusses Roman law, Chinese practices, conditions in Italy and other countries before zeroing in on the oppressive environment of the *antahpura*. She observes:

> Today, the inner self of the woman aspires to freedom. She is determined to overcome all the obstacles that stand in the way of liberation. The continued closing in of her inner self can never be accepted. This has become intolerable, especially now. And because it is unbearable now, there is a fire of rebellion. (157)

185

There are others who adopt a similar position as K. Mary Thomas in 'Women's Independence' (1927) and Kochattil Kalyanikutty Amma in 'Some Obstacles in the Way of Equality between the Sexes' (1938). Both argue in favour of a more equal position. While K. Mary Thomas recognises the differences between men and women (106) and thus picks up a point, which men had always used to their advantage, for her own purpose, and as such is one of the earliest proponents of a positive evaluation of 'difference'. Men view woman as 'a caged bird' but women ask for equality and freedom and resent this confinement. Further, Kalyani-kutty Amma draws attention to the association of women with sorcery and the goddess image, both limited and negative perceptions, for when they come together they project woman as 'a concoction of the Goddess and the Devil'. A science graduate and a teacher, she introduces a psychological element in her perception: 'The mystery of the rhythms of the female body—menstruation, pregnancy, and childbirth—challenged the human powers of comprehension…. The fear of Woman's dark powers that sprung up so vigorously within ancient Man have condensed into certain misgiving in the Unconscious of modern Man' (175). Kalyani-kutty Amma goes on to place the woman question in the socio-economic reality. There has to be a degree of industrial culture and institutional structures dismantled and reconstructed (176–177). And of what use is equality? Because it creates a more rational universe, it helps to move away from prejudices towards more widespread opportunity to develop individually and socially (178).

The myth surrounding the power of women in matrilineality is also exposed. Anna Chandy, a law graduate, who became a District Judge in 1948 and a High Court Judge in 1959, actively participated in the debates surrounding women's issues. She adopted the legal format of a court judgement in one of her speeches, 'On Women's Liberation', as early as 1929. She was also the founder-editor of a magazine called *Shrimati*. In the above-mentioned speech, she argued for the right of women to employment and public space and built her case on the unequal position of women and the need to rectify it. Men feel threatened by the earning capacity of women as much as by their competence. Chandy writes:

How is one to claim that women in Kerala are not in bondage? Women in the numerous castes and communities in Kerala occupy distinctly different situations. Antherjanams who are confined to the inner quarters with bronze bangles, the cadjan-leaf umbrella and the servant girl; Muslim sisters who suffer eternal hell in purdah, ridiculed by their menfolk as the soulless herd lacking the Adam's apple; Brahmin girls trapped in wedlock at an age in which one plays at mud-pie making, to become widows at the door-step of youth, and condemned to live on with shaved heads, heaping curses upon life; Christian women, forever accused by the harsh-ness of dowry—all these are slaves who live in Kerala. (115–116)[13]

She then proceeds to look at the 'Matrilineal Domestic Empresses', the Nair women. Even when the property is inherited through the fe-male line, they hardly have any control or authority. They are 'passive holders'. They are not free to attend public meetings though they can go to temples. This kind of hollow privileging does not lead anywhere: 'Women should not be worshipped as Goddesses; they must be treated as mere mortal creatures', for men who worship them, also condemn them to suffering ('On Women's Liberation' 116–117).

Several years before this, a Muslim woman belonging to Bengal had taken up both the fact of goddess worship in an essay, 'The Worship of Women' (1906) and purdah in 'Sultana's Dream' (1905). Purdah was also the major link in her essays put together in *Avarodhbasini* (1931). While adhering to the image of a respectable middle-class woman, Rokeya Sakhawat Hossain is radical in two aspects: her mode of writ-ing—humorous, fun-loving and mockingly satiric, a strategy through which she subverts authority; and in her open criticism of both Hindu and Muslim practices. One might as well add a third, her use of dialogue and fantasy. In 'The Worship of Women', a set of women enter into a drawing-room debate where the myth and reality are placed side by side.

Sītā and Savitri became famous 'because of their own good qualities' but no one really worshipped them during their lifetimes. Similarly, other women have risen to exalted positions on grounds of their learning or virtue often accompanied by a lot of suffering. The reality of sati, of child marriage, of ignored and oppressed wives and condemned widows shows no indication of a society inhabited by women worshippers. The discussion then unhesitatingly takes on Muslim practices such as purdah and other practices which are abhorrent, but all along there is the false pretence of goddess-worship linked with them. In 'Sultana's Dream', she projects a feminist utopia where the world is all topsy-turvy. With the men behind purdah and women in the open, roles are reversed and national calamities call upon the women to prove their worth, which they are able to do through their intelligence and education. They harness and control heat, sunlight and rain water for the purposes of development and protection.[14]

The ruling house of Bhopal had a series of female rulers. Each ruler, in her own way, negotiated the movement from closed/private space to public space in terms of relationships, purdah, politics and patriotism. Nawab Sultan Jahan Begam of Bhopal, the fourth in the line of the Begams was a contemporary of Saraladevi Chaudhurani, Cornelia Sorabji and Rokeya Sakhawat Hossain, among others. She participated in the Bharat Stree Mandal and worked towards building a network among the women of the subcontinent. And her royal status helped her to reach out to other royal families including Maler Kotla and Loharu. Admittedly, these were elitist circles, but wealth is an easy partner of conservatism and all the more necessary that those with resources be shaken up and brought in.

Sultan Jahan Begam was clearly of the view that women must take the 'responsibility for their own reform through independent women's organisation' (Lambert-Hurley 162–163). One needs to go back in time in order to gauge the enormity of these tentative moves outside the models of conformity as well as to appreciate the courage with which these

188

women went ahead with their demands for independence even as they conformed to dress codes and remained anchored in religious faith. Lambert-Hurley comments on the half-and-half measures of Sultan Jahan Begam's reformist thought. The Begam supported purdah, advocated a separate sphere for women, did not contest polygamy and did not support suffrage on one hand, but on the other was a strong supporter of education for women, and their active participation in nation-building and social reform (164–175).

But the women who were articulate saw to it that their voices were heard. They were bold not only in their dreams but also in their actions, imagination and activism. They were not afraid to adopt definite positions on questions of social and legal reform, or to form associations for the purpose of expressing solidarity. The nationalist movement was an additional spur but even when outside it, they were conscious of themselves as members of a larger body called nation. It is often said that Indian women got all the constitutional rights on a platter at the time of independence. But if we read some of the essays, speeches and journalistic writings of this period, many of these rights were fought for through a variety of channels as they resisted both patriarchal hold and colonial domination along with the conservatism of religious or semi-religious practices. Their struggles were many and widely spread.

In Private Domain: Looking at the Past through the Lens of the Present

In this section, I want to begin with a discussion of five texts; of these, the first is *Phaniyamma* which is a fictional presentation of a real life story of a woman whose life spanned nearly or more than a century, written by her great grand niece. The second is *Fragments of a Life*, a biography of Subbalakshmi, a Tamil brahmin who, married to an officer working in the Civil Services, sought to carve out some personal space for herself.

189

This is also written by a granddaughter, a third generation representative. The period covers the first half of the twentieth century and runs parallel to the freedom struggle. Ashapurna Devi's *Suvarnlata*, covering almost the same period, is a novel (the middle one of a trilogy) and is the third text I propose to discuss. In this we find Suvarnlata constantly resisting her environment and circumstances and reshaping them as well as herself. Lalithambika Antherjanam, a Malayalee writer's autobiographical pieces of a Namboodri girl's childhood, brought together in *Cast Me Out If You Will* is my fourth text, and Ismat Chughtai's autobiographical account *Kagzi Hain Pairahan* is my fifth text.

Except for the last two none of them is an autobiography and even these do not follow conventional frames. All are written by women, all concern themselves with struggles for some breathing space; as these women watch the world outside them, they often find it equally suffocating and then choose to transgress some of the restrictions imposed on them. In the process they break free of conventional frames. Earlier in this book, several autobiographies, especially of film artists and singers, have been considered as also Rassundari Devi's *Amar Jiban*. But these works differ from them as they do not focus on a specific interest or an art but on the self as it stands surrounded by hostile traditions and practices. The 'self' consciously or unconsciously is in the process of breaking out of the old mould.

Phaniyamma is a child widow, whose marriage has not even been consummated. The bangles she bought at a fair were broken the moment the news of her boy-husband's death arrived. And then she was doomed to a life of widowhood—a single wrap to cover her body, a single meal to keep her alive and a shorn head to single her out as a widow. A prematurely terminated childhood has no time to blossom into womanhood. She has never learnt the meaning of freedom or experienced sexual relationships. How does one *grow* in circumstances such as these? Over the years she trains her body to want less and less, to do with the basic minimum, and looks for substitutes for all her needs so that she is not financially dependent on anyone. Socially invisible, she strives to become even physically invisible. Outside all normal familial structures, Phani exists only as an appendage. Despite this exclusion, she is still bound by the moral code, which reaches out to margins such as Phani, with a vengeance. The narrative travels back to the nineteenth century, capturing some of the social issues.

Born in 1840, she lives to be 112 years old. And the wisdom of horoscopes not withstanding, she is widowed as a young child (Indira 45). Despite the fact that her sexuality is permanently to be denied expression, her body is still centre stage. The wait for her to be raised to the status of a *madi*[15] ends only with the onset of her menstruation at the age of 13. Before that she is neither here, nor there—not a child, not a wife, nor a widow, neither pure nor impure. *Madi* women avoided the touch of others and had to take extreme precautions regarding purity, uphold all orthodox traditions and observe all rituals; in fact, she was always to be on the edge of life. Women like her were an economic necessity for large households to run comfortably—unpaid labour round the clock. All food likely to arouse passion was forbidden and the senses starved. It is at the age of 40 that she realises the meaning of copulation and at 82 the process of birthing when, on account of her slim hands, she is called upon to assist at the birth of a baby and pull the baby out when other methods have failed. This, too, at a lower caste woman's delivery. She feels totally alienated by both these experiences. The baby's birth makes her think: 'This pain this filth—do women forget it all when they go to their husbands? What a strange forgetting! I don't want a human existence and specially not a woman's' (Indira 87–88).

Phaniyamma has, over the years, developed her own epistemological questioning. Deeply conscious of the contradictions existent in the religious code and in the social acceptance of superstitions, she is aware that the façade of respectability is a matter of convenience. She feels bold enough and free enough to change them and step out. If all else around her was changing, the railways and the roads coming in, and other changes in the social and economic environment, family structures and hierarchies, why not rituals?

There are other women in the novel—Subbi, who is rejected because she is believed to be barren, as if the sole purpose of womanhood was to give birth; 16-year-old Dakshayini, widowed soon after her marriage and one who resists all pressure to shave off her hair and turn her into a *madi*. Phani takes up her defence but to no avail. Finally Dakshayini works out the solution herself by breaking all rules. She has a relationship with her husband's younger brother, conceives and gives birth to a son, takes charge of the household and refuses to budge or be thrown out or to adopt a widow's role. True, she uses her sexuality to work out what she wants, but this is not helplessness or dependence, on the other hand it is the adoption of a role—that of a married woman—and it is the exercise of power: over the man, over her body and over the house. For, what is freedom? Not living alone, or doing penance, or abstaining from sex and all kinds of emotional relationships—it means exercising choices, and her choice is a refusal to be dismissed from life.

What about Phaniyamma? She too steps out of the confines of upper caste prejudice. She learns to resist both gently and through subterfuge; she crosses the boundaries of 'purity', assists in two deliveries, one that of an untouchable. Age also comes to her rescue. No longer does she have to be subservient; people ask her for advice. She ordinarily refrains from interfering but when asked, gives her opinion unhesitatingly. Her sense of freedom also comes through the use of her mind, through a resistance to traditional wisdom and knowledge. Everyone's true salvation lies in working out the solutions through one's own experience and judgement. She tells Banashankari that she has distanced herself from all rituals:

What kind of happiness did the great mother Sītā experience, having wedded the Lord Rāma himself? A life of trouble she had. And did her husband give her joy? He made her jump into the fire and sent off a pregnant woman to the forest. And Draupadi, did she not suffer? (Indira 118–119)

This reverses all moral values because they have been generated through justification of Sītā's and Draupadi's sufferings. Patriarchy and tradition both are critiqued. Life long abstinence and practice of rituals have distanced her from them because they are hollow, directionless and lead nowhere. There is no rationality, logicality or inevitability about tradition or patriarchal power. She moves away from them because there are discrepancies, because gender discrimination as defined by the *ashramas* and on the superiority of the husband or as defined by the sacred thread has no validity. Phaniyamma evolves for herself a humanistic system of belief, based on her own impulse for action or non-action and by locating the living human being at the centre of life.

Suvarnlata is a much longer and more complex work. When the young nine-year-old Suvarn is married, her parents' home breaks up. Her mother, who is against the idea of a child marriage, is unable to accept this or forgive her husband for deciding to do this without consulting her. She leaves her home, moves to her father's place, opens a school and teaches there in order to be economically independent. This is her resistance to and a non-acceptance of her husband's decision; she walks out of both—wifehood and motherhood.

The newly married Suvarn is not allowed to forget this act of her mother which attaches itself to her like a shadow. In fact, though the novel begins with Suvarnlata's death, the very opening refers to her mother: 'Suvarnlata knew none of this. She had entered her married life with the burden of her home-abandoning mother's ill-fame. That is why she is leaving this world with the regret of an unfulfilled life' (A. Devi, *Suvarnlata* 2).[16]

The Hindi word used is *grah-tyagni*, one who abandons the home. With the mother not there, the father doesn't send for her after her marriage. Thus, she is truly deprived of her parental home—abandoned and left entirely in the hands of her in-laws. The basic question is does one live for oneself alone or is one responsible to and for others? How is one's courage affected by the choices forced on one? Is an act of

193

resistance a selfish act or a matter of principle, or just an assertion of one's right?

By locating the beginning at the end and tracing the history of women from mother to daughter and then to the daughter's daughter, a kind of matrilineage is established. Suvarnlata's life was lived in the shadow of her mother's act, constantly reminded of it and affected by it, and now Bakul, her 17-year-old daughter, sits by her deathbed, compelled to make a new beginning from this legacy. The need for personal space had been a life-long desire, and is fulfilled close to the end, when she had already lived the best years of her life. Suppose for a moment that she had got this space—this south-facing verandah—when she was young, energetic, growing, the course of her life may have been entirely different. Open spaces are contrasted with caged existence—the journey from cages to open areas is a long arduous one.

How does a child of nine, who is transplanted into an alien environment, grow? How does the child develop, learn and nurture her positive strengths? Placed against the son's devotion to his mother, she has to push every inch of the way. Why are the wishes and desires of women ignored or subjected to a perpetual subordination in the household? Her one source of contact with the outer world is through books, which she has to read surreptitiously, hiding them from the rest of the family. If it had come to the knowledge of her sister-in-law or mother-in-law they would have raised hell (5). Her world is shut in, closed, for patriarchy believes that women should not be given any opportunity of interaction with the outer world, lest their minds get polluted.

Suvarn can never get over the fact that her school-going was interrupted and that her father had betrayed her mother by negotiating Suvarn's marriage without consulting her. All her dreams were swept aside by one act—and here she was confined to a small space in an overcrowded joint family. Lack of space, of freedom, absence of outside contact, the abrupt change in the course of life, the indifference to the needs of women—these constitute the dominant discourse in the first few pages as the early years of her marriage, from age nine to fourteen, are described.

She is also the subject of envy. Prabodh, her husband, doesn't give any thought to her desires but loves her very much. He can't go beyond the physical, but there is a prominent romantic streak in him as he fixes appointments with her during the day and skips office in order to spend some time with her on the terrace. This is another aspect of 'closed' family structures, the denial of all normal expression. But it also highlights the conflicting attitudes of husband and wife. Suvarn has to look for her sustenance elsewhere—borrowed books, magazines and her own dream world. She is constantly described as 'mad', 'stubborn', 'obstinate'—words that are used to describe her dreams, aspirations and determination.

Another strand in the novel is the motif of pilgrimage. Muktkeshi, her mother-in-law, is all set for a pilgrimage to Jagannath Puri. She is the all-controlling figure who rules the household. When these preparations are afoot, Suvarn also expresses a desire to go with her. She wants to see the sea, she wants to go out, in search of some fresh air. But the expression of this wish also recoils on her and the whole family, including the children, turn against her. Many years later, when she is actually about to undertake a pilgrimage, she is summoned back on account of her husband's illness. There are only blind alleys, no open lanes.

On one occasion when she learns that her father is ill, she expresses a desire to go and visit him. Then all hell is let loose the skies fall. Once again the reference is to her mother having abandoned her home. And her whole family is criticised. Later, they decide to send her but not to fulfil her emotional need, instead only to be free of her presence in the house. Either way, Suvarn is compelled to resist. When she refuses to go, she is forcefully sent. She looks for a compensatory factor by wanting to take her son with her but he is not allowed to accompany her. There is no forgiveness for her. In her father's home also, she is not welcome, mainly because she is unaccompanied and has been sent to her father's home like an abandoned woman. Her father, Nav Kumar, bitterly reminded of his wife, first cajoles, then scolds and sends her back.

At every step her own will is thwarted. The male world, the conventionally brought up women, the ones who have internalised all social prejudices, follow all the distinctions between purity and impurity, whose minds are closed to reason—all join to condemn her. Suvarnlata is a representative figure of every young child exposed to alien surroundings, of every woman growing up with a husband who has little time for her as a person beyond the physical relationship, every mother whose children's loyalties are divided between their mother and the forces hostile to her, and every person who has a mind with which she can think and who is capable of nurturing dreams. She jostled from one position to another, one household to another—as all conspired to break her will, but all along she refused to ask forgiveness for a supposed wrong. She is punished for having an opinion of her own and her refusal to fall in line with the falsity of appearances. Amidst this, her husband is blamed for giving her a free hand and the view is expressed: 'He on his own accord will send Sītā into exile' (87), indicating how deep rooted is the belief that Sītā was in the wrong and deserved to be sent away. Women are held responsible not only for what they do, but also for what others think of them. It is not possible to trace the history of Suvarnlata in a chronological manner, nor is it possible to treat it as a well-bound book; instead, her life was loose-leafed with all the pages strewn everywhere (88). I borrow this image from Ashapurna Devi, for tracing the struggles of women, struggles which need not take place on the wide canvas of public leadership but struggles which take place in communication, relationships, family ties, that is, at every step in the course of a normal household life. (Incidentally, this is also where writing by women has the possibility of differing from the writing by men about women. The latter can write about the oppressive nature of reality but not about the experience of being oppressed.)

Gandhi's Non-cooperation Movement doesn't affect the household at all. And when the cheaper mill-made sarees are given to the servants as Dussehra gifts, even the maidservant is better informed and more patriotic than the men of the family who do all the purchasing (126–129). When Suvarn wants the children to learn 'Vande Mataram', the children are forbidden from learning it, because of the fear of British persecution (242). Closed houses, closed minds—collectively bring down a nation. There is also a widespread feeling of caste and economic hierarchy.

In this life full of constant struggle, when she longs to unlock the door and find freedom (136), when she longs for a moment of quiet peace and enjoyment (227), she is humiliated over and over again and is treated like a bonded slave (238). Suvarn still finds people she can relate to—Kedarnath, her sister-in-law's husband, her husband's uncle, the maidservant and some of the children. She finds people who loan her old magazines. Through reading she carves out an escape route. The reader can sense the manner in which these closed structures affect marital relationships and the roles that husbands play in making life difficult.

When Suvarn starts writing her memoirs, there is a narrative within a narrative. Though the main narrative begins with Suvarn dead, this narrative on the first page records her first real encounter with her mother-in-law who forbids her from weeping and says, 'Your mother is not dead, then why are you crying.' A consoling hand comes in the form of the daughter-in-law of a relative, the wife of a cousin, who lives just on the other side—there is a wall in between—who, introducing herself, also informs Suvarn of the family quarrel which forbids communication. She has been sent only to attend this wedding (348–349). This lays the foundation of a friendship sustained through occasional meetings through a narrow skylight in the wall, when the two would talk for a minute or two across the opening. Suvarn had to clamber up on a support of bricks. This girl, just a few years older than her, is another source of books for Suvarn. Her husband is different from other men (349). The other women in Suvarn's own household—except for one of her husband's sisters—are all well schooled in the patriarchal way of thinking. This friendship with the cousin across the wall is, however, short-lived. Suvarn's family wins the legal case, receives the compensation for the family property and shifts house, thus closing this little skylight in her life.

How does masculinity play up to the public image? It also acts divisively. Prabodh, instead of taking his wife's side, is motivated by the desire to be an ideal son. He is conformist in his role and displays what Sudhir Kakar has referred to as the underdeveloped male ego (Kakar 107). But when this mother's boy or a person without a sense of righteousness or pride makes love to a wife whom he has publicly denigrated, what happens to the wife? The whole body is on fire. One wants to throw away everything and run away (A. Devi, *Suvarnlata* 351). Marriage is something more than sex. Even Rassundari Devi writes how her relationship was governed more by fear than by any understanding (*Amar Jiban*).

Patriarchy and its closed structures distort both masculinity and femininity. Women too falsify their real selves and are never able to discover their own true nature. Ashapurna Devi, through the process of writing *Suvarnlata* and through her voice, writes:

Women are the enemies of women. Housewives if they had been a little bit sympathetic, a little more maternal, then perhaps the whole society would have been different. But no, she only assists the tyrannical patriarchal structures. And men don't consider women of any greater importance than brick and mortar. And use them as such...

Fools, Fools. Women are the greatest fools. They don't realise how they are being moulded.

They think—oh, how valuable I am. He loves me. He worships me, he brings me ornaments.

My body is a place for gold to find a storehouse—she doesn't think that this decoration is an advertisement of his pleasure, she doesn't realise that she pleases him with her clothes and jewellery and get charmed by his expression of love. Chi!

Not for nothing do I say, that women are the greatest fools. (Translation mine, 351–352)

Suvarn, despite all odds, finds time to write and then asks Jaggu to publish it. These are all acts of transgression; the discerning eye can recognise their worth. Jaggu, the press owner, her husband's cousin, is surprised and full of admiration and presents an evaluating process which runs counter to the model of the submissive and/or the over-decked woman. This model is based on qualities of mind and action—not of appearance. He tells his mother that Suvarn is not the one to brag about her virtues, 'I am astounded by her intelligence. She is a veritable Lakshmi who blessed Bua's house. God has given her in abundance. It is the mind's quality that is true wealth. Blessed is the man who is her husband' (368).

As a new bride, once when she had learnt that her father had come to fetch her but had been sent back without her, she had fought and rebelled and had wanted to run away. 'But where? To her mother? Where was she? To her father? Go back to school? Be laughed at by her classfellows. She didn't know the way, but once she was on it, she would find it' (376). But she hadn't left her married home and it was now after so many years, so many pregnancies, childbirths, marriages of her sons, that she had found a way.

The process of writing is not merely going over the stock of her experiences or memories, she also reviews her relationship with her husband and her children. She looks back at her own lost childhood, how her mother's efforts at training her as a good social being had been converted by her mother-in-law into becoming a good, silent daughter-in-law who was not to feel thirsty or hungry, not even to laugh or to communicate. And her own children—did she know them?

The book (Suvarn's), when it is published, is on rough paper, and the printing uneven. And when her son reads aloud from the book and the whole family laughs at it, Suvarn is upset. Infuriated, she makes a huge bonfire of all the five hundred copies on the terrace. One has to pause and think, what does one feel at the end of a life, one as this? A life spent in a futile search for a mind one can relate to, leading a choked existence constrained and restricted from all natural expressions—how does one get over each crisis and continue the act of living? Where does one find peace? Is it patriarchy, ritual, conventional ideas, the harshness of control, child marriage, lack of education, absence of a relationship to a larger construct like society or nation—what is it that destroys talent and stifles all creativity?

Suvarnlata is held together through its motifs—Satyavati's rebellion (Suvarn's mother, the subject of the first part of the trilogy *Pratham Pratishruti*) has a recurring presence, pilgrimages and failed pilgrimages another and Suvarnlata's conscious reflection on her life forms a third. These control the flow of the narrative. From within, the narrative is held together by the recurring image of space, both closed and open spaces—kitchens, *ghunghat*s, skylights, corner rooms, verandahs—and finally, the haunting image of the bonfire of books. Ashapurna Devi works through domestic environs, the existing social practices and women's everyday situations in order to trace the line of resistance and the various ways in which women resist—through anger, asserting independence, subterfuge, search for alternative sources of support and strength, taking hold of their life and even walking out of a marriage. Satyavati's stance is the refusal to tolerate betrayal and to be treated as someone whose opinion is of no importance in the decision affecting her child. In Suvarnlata, we see a woman who resists every unreasonable claim. A tremendous self-effort is involved.

Mythily Sivaraman reconstructs her grandmother Subbalakshmi's life through some of her letters, the people who had known her and by locating her in her time. Regions may differ, languages and levels of education may differ, but the social environment is reflected in the lives of the women of this age. Githa Hariharan writes in her 'Foreword' to *Fragments of a Life*:

...I felt a jolt of recognition. The specific contours of Subbalakshmi's life were unique to her; so was her accomplishment of carving out a small political space for herself. But there were, in her life, those other achingly familiar features that have shaped so many other women's lives: the overwhelming opponent, convention, that Subbalakshmi had to wrestle with everyday of her life; the inevitability of her dreams being thwarted in the end (vii).

The struggles of ordinary women to find expression in the very ordinariness of life are evidence of the intense fire burning inside them, of the enormous involvement they bring to the act of living. They also reflect on the ways feminist tradition has shaped itself as well as the way we need to trace its history—not only through visible collective struggles, mass movements and documents but through individual struggles, acts of transgression, strategies of connection and reaching out to the future. If nothing else, these women have carried out lone battles which redefine an individual's relationship with society as well as the concept of feminism. They explored the silences of their selves and of their history.

Mythily Sivaraman's own 'Preface' begins with a confession—her sense of regret that she never had a 'typical' Indian grandmother. She never made many of those gestures that children have heard of, or all the things other grandmothers did. It was Subbalakshmi's husband who filled the role of a good grandfather. But as one grows up one learns to read the subtext and Mythily also began to do the same. Subbalakshmi's life spanned the period from 1897 to 1978. Married at age 11, she became a mother at 14, which was the lot of many a child wife. She was intelligent—what happened to her education? How did she equip herself with learning to enable her to develop her thinking, to read Tagore or relate to Gandhi? As also to writing a diary for the years 1924–1926? Did this activity—like Suvarn's—have to be hidden or secretive or be camouflaged in some other way? Sivaraman describes how she had to read her terse one or two-liners and cajole them to yield their meaning. One could choose to write a diary boldly, provided one took care 'to note down only harmless minutiae like daily accounts, shopping lists, religious rites, menu for the day, sickness in the family and such. All these were safe and within the female territory approved by Hindu orthodoxy' (xv). Subbalakshmi talked freely about her visits to the art exhibitions, but in other respects she noted down the hospital visits, the chores of the household, a piece of embroidery and, now and then, a bird she had identified. If silence can be deafening, it was so in what Mythily feels in Subbalakshmi's silence about her major disappointments and could be heard loudly enough. Like Satyavati (Ashapurna Devi's fictional heroine in *Pratham Pratishruti*), who had to live with the lifelong regret of her failed ambitions about her daughter's education, Subbalakshmi also had to live with the disappointment of not being able to educate her daughter Pankajam at Santiniketan. There are brief references to her frustrations or a line or two from a poem to mark these moments of pain and of coming to grips with it.

The Tamil brahmin culture 'silences the woman effectively and denies her personal warmth' and Subbalakshmi was as much a victim of this as any other (xvi). Widowhood and consequent dependence prevented Subbalakshmi's mother from fulfilling her husband's (Subbalakshmi's father) dream of educating their only daughter. Subbalakshmi acquired her early learning in her grandfather's house, a learning which was to stand her in good stead in later years and encouraged her to take membership of public libraries. Even with the loss of one parent and with brahminic culture restricting her, her upper class placement gave her some social advantages. There were times when the husband and wife lived alone, without the demands of a joint family and she accompanied him to some of the places he travelled to. Their sons died very young—one at four, the other at one—and this loss resulted in the epileptic fits she was afflicted with for the rest of her life. As her husband did not have much faith in Western medicine, she was perhaps not 'adequately' attended to. This affliction—like fits of insanity—condemned her to a more confined existence.

She developed a political consciousness early in life by reading the newspaper to her grandfather, a consciousness which developed into a more involved relationship with Gandhi's Non-cooperation Movement in 1919–1921. Subbalakshmi—it is believed—marched with a black flag in her hand in the protest against the Prince of Wales's visit (52). But as her husband and brother both were in government service, a more persistent involvement was not possible. A public display was not to be risked (53). We have examples in fiction of this kind of activity on part of women who knew where their loyalties lay. Kamala Markandaya's novel, *A Silence of Desire*, has the wife of a civil servant join the freedom struggle, wear *khadi* and work in the villages. Similarly, Mukul Kesavan's *Looking Through Glass* has the narrator's *dadi* wear *khadi*, join the Non-cooperation Movement and even draw the pension of a freedom fighter for the supposed participation in the Quit India Movement, 1942, a pension which her conscience doesn't allow her to keep and she feels has to be returned. How did these women find the courage to step outside their homes, for neither were they anonymous nor were they leaders or wives of political leaders. But they could wear *khadi* and this they did. The public issues that touched women's lives were child marriage, right to property and equal laws of morality.

Mythily Sivaraman, even as she stresses Subbalakshmi's courage, her interest in art, her deep sense of loneliness and being alone in her grief for her two sons, quotes from her grandfather's poems, his comments on political issues and his pride in being a volunteer at a Congress gathering, leaving us with the picture of a man who was sensitive, mourned his sons with an equal sense of loss but failed to build a bridge of communication as his image fell into the pattern of an authoritarian Tamil brahmin. Men suffered perhaps as much as women on account of the impositions of convention. PRG, Sivaraman's grandfather and Subbalakshmi's husband, wrote a comment on the women's page of *The Hindu Illustrated Weekly* (1933), in which he expressed the view that pictures of decked up women clashed with the new ideals they were propagating (Sivaraman 164–165). Despite this realisation, he was not willing to go very far into modern spaces. For him women were guardian angels on whose frail shoulders the whole cultural and religious edifice rested itself (165). Apparently they could not or should not follow in the footsteps of the British feminists (165). Native movements consciously disassociated themselves from Western movements and sought to work with their own circumstances in order to find their own solutions.

Was Subbalakshmi insane, as her husband contended, or were these seizures epilepsy, as her daughter maintained? Most probably the latter, with loneliness, frustration and depression all playing their part, especially when freedom and outings were limited. How do women learn to live under the constant surveillance of family and society? Ever imagine a constant living under the gaze? There is this conflict between visibility—in terms of being valued as a person—and being watched as someone in perpetual need of guidance, protection and advice, bringing to mind Foucault's *Discipline and Punish* with its ever-watchful and all-controlling eye.

Lalithambika Antherjanam, a reputed author, is widely known for her short story, 'The Goddess of Revenge', a story that delineates the life of a Namboodri wife, her compulsion to tolerate her husband's multiple affairs, along with a permanent imprisonment inside high walls, where she is not even able to see the sunlight. Many fathers felt the harshness of these caste practices when their daughters were growing up, even if they had not experienced similar feelings when their wives were young. Here I propose not to discuss her stories but her memoirs—rather autobiographical essays, many of which 'had first appeared in magazines; others were radio talks. She also included some pages from her diary....' (Krishnakutty xxvii). She never got down to writing a proper autobiography, instead she collected together these pieces, some of which have now been translated and are available in *Cast Me Out If You Will*. Lalithambika is a contemporary of Ashapurna Devi, and was also born in the same year, 1909. She was exceptionally fortunate in both—her parents and her husband—who were supportive of her activities. Most of her stories deal with her social milieu and the particular problems of the Antherjanam women, women who with the onset of puberty become indoor inhabitants confined to the house. She recalls an anecdote associated with her birth. When her father learnt that a daughter had been born, he exclaimed angrily, 'No, I will not live here any longer. I'll go away, may be to Madras, become a Christian, and marry an English woman' (*Cast Me Out* 134). The Namboodri practices so incensed him. In the essays there is a section titled 'The Caged Bird', which is about the onset of menstruation:

> The events that her parents had dreaded took place at last. The day she reached puberty, the house looked and felt as if someone had died. Her mother wept, so did the rest of the family, and the servant women, and seeing them, she too could not help crying. Even her father, usually confident and assured, lamented: 'I feel as if I have to cage a free bird.'
>
> She was like one dead now, as far as the outside world was concerned. She might not go to the temple, or play under the champakam tree. She might not talk to her favourite swami. (Antherjanam, 'The Caged Bird' 138)

The manner in which both caste and the life of a human being were being governed by the natural cycle of a woman's body points out to the unnaturalness of the whole system as well as the primitive orthodoxy of patriarchy. That this practice could survive well into the twentieth century in upper class, educated households indicates the rigidity with which the caste laws were applied and the helplessness of the individual—in this case whether the parents or their daughter.

The closed life compelled her to watch the other women closely and forced her into reading a great deal. Tagore is one of the writers she read. Written in the third person, her autobiographical essays attempt to describe this life from the outside, as an observer:

> She reflected deeply and compassionately on the contradictions, the joys, and the
> sorrows, the ideals, desires and experiences of all the people around her: her im-
> mediate and extended family, her society and the labourers in the village…
>
> She wrote a novel in the narrative style of *At Home and Outside*…
>
> She had no companions of her age at all. (138–139)

It is natural to ask why Lalithambika chose to write in the third person. Was it the fear of reliving the same experiences again, an inability
to confront the past through the first person 'I'? The third person permits
her the objectivity and the distancing from her subject and allows her to
see it from the outside. As she speaks about her marriage and the sense
of freedom she felt on account of her husband's support, it is clear that
there is no history of personal oppression but that the average life of a
Namboodri woman is under the scanner. There is a recognition of the
fact that a social revolution is also afoot:

> It was a period when a group of young revolutionaries were actively engaged in
> trying to change society…. People began to see that art could be used as a powerful
> weapon. The waves of this impassioned social and national struggle swept through
> the darkest corners of the inner rooms and roused them into a new awareness of
> freedom. (140)

It needs to be recognised that women's issues were closely linked
with social practices; also the desire for change and the reflective process
this desire set in motion went a long way in raising levels of awareness and social critiquing. Political movements affected almost all parts
of India—books, ideas and revolutionaries travelled—and linked India.
Western education helped only marginally—it helped as a window to the
outer world—but the local movements were rooted in and emanated from
local causes. Men cannot always be seen as hostile. Ideological beliefs
may have been conservative or liberal, but in several cases men took the
initiative in raising issues of social reform related to the oppression

of women. Gita Krishnakutty points out that in the late nineteenth and early twentieth century 'struggles against the oppression of women were focused mainly on the plight of the anterjanams' (xviii). Several plays were also written and staged for public viewing, depicting the life of Namboodri women. Even though the female roles were enacted by male actors, the orthodox remained critical of these performances. In one of her essays, Lalithambika refers to some of these performances. One important one is *From the Kitchen to the Scene of Action*, a play by V.T. Bhattadiripad. She recalls how the 'winds of a momentous change swept through the whole namboodri society'. Her own life was also deeply affected. The youth was conscious that not much progress was possible if the women were left in the seclusion of the *antahpura*.

In 1932, a meeting was organised in honour of those women who had done away with the Ghosha. The legal resolution had been passed, but hardly anyone had put it into practice.

> Nor did we believe that we would ever be able to go out without our umbrellas and shawls. We all had limitations to contend with: the tyranny of family relationships, opposition from orthodox members of the community, a constant fear of being cast out of society.... (Antherjanam, 'A Writer is Born' 147)

Inspired by the action of two young women who had discarded their umbrella, she also attended the meeting. This incident is described in the third person in another essay, 'We Cast Away Our Umbrellas': 'She pretended she was going to a temple, started out with her umbrella and shawl, and threw the umbrella away as soon as she left the house' (140). This was the first time she had to face the disapproval of her mother. For a while it appeared that the matter 'may lead to a legal dispute, or even partition of the family property' but her father sided with her (141). In 'A Writer is Born', the first person takes over: 'Amma wept, beat her head, and lamented, "I wish I never had a daughter. If only she had died as soon as she was born...."' Lalithambika had to pay the price for this defiance. Her brothers treated her as if she was an outcast. Her in-laws were strongly disapproving. Her father had to come to her help, buy a piece of land and make the young couple a separate home (149).

Looking back at this period, she writes:

> Meanwhile, there were babies every year. She brought them up. She wrote, read, and made speeches. When I look back, I see the young mother crouched on the ground, writing as she rocks the cradle. I see the wilful, ignorant young woman standing on a public platform, holding her baby close to her while she makes a speech—the impudent woman who did not agree with her, who used her art as a weapon against her adversaries, who stoically accepted the blows and wounds that her enemies in the literary world aimed at her. ('We Cast Away' 141)

This essay was written in 1969, at the age of 60. It describes the life-style of many a woman activist, intellectual and writer, in fact, of all women—Rassundari Devi, Lalithambika and the fictional Suvarnlata. Most families had hordes of children to be looked after and fed. Amidst this, a public function in honour of the two women who gave up the Ghosha and came out of seclusion was also a public recognition and visibility. They were like 'messengers of god' and the public leader—Mannath Padmanabhan—organising it said it was a public blessing. ('A Writer is Born' 147)

Almost all her work is resistance to the existing social ills and the oppression against women, whether Namboodri, Nair or any other. There is no way a writer can stay away from society's conditions and experiences:

> I think it is because they represent the consciousness of society that writers are si-multaneously able to feel the emotions of the individual as well as the multitude.... Art is a force that awakens all the powers of expression that are within the self and addresses them toward the entire universe. ('Lessons from Experience' 162–163)

The only play she is known to have written was about widow remarriage. Written in 1934, it coincided with the remarriage of a widow ('An
Account of a Performance'). Lalithambika is of the view that talking
openly about unpleasant things (implying suffering) is in itself a purifi-
catory ritual (171). But though this was staged, it was never published.
The reasons for this temporariness bestowed on the play can at best be
speculative.

In an article addressed to her mother, 'Sesame Seeds, Flowers, Water', she recollects her childhood. This woman, who was otherwise so
conventional and tradition-bound, exposed her young daughter early to
revolutionary ideas. Her mother had also saved the issues of *Swadeshab-
himani* (a newspaper which was fearless in its tone and whose editor
was exiled from Travancore in 1911 for writing against the government),
because it was a paper that caused a revolution in her mother's youth.
Her mother even saved copies of books that had been banned, political
novels such as *Parappuram* and *Udayabhany*, for Lalithambika to read
when she grew up ('Sesame Seeds' 174). She asks her mother (who is
now dead), 'Was it because your daughter had access to such books that
she later walked so easily on dangerous terrain and became a rebel?'
(175).

But Amme (Lalithambika's mother) lived in fear—fear of others, of
her relatives, the older generation and of social criticism—all her life and
kept herself from doing things she so much wanted to do; fear stopped
her from giving her daughter the freedom to go to school. Similarly, fear
treads like a ghost behind every woman (and man). Not for nothing did
the poet wish for a country 'where the mind is without fear' and Gandhi
work on non-violent *satyagraha* to drive away this sense of fear. Writing,
like all forms of resistance, requires boldness and fearlessness. Almost all
her work faces trouble frontally, and this essay, addressed to her mother,
is a reconstruction of the past, continuing the matrilineal heritage so pow-
erfully depicted in Ashapurna Devi's trilogy. All of Lalithambika's stories

have a subtext that connects up with her resistance to society. I cannot resist a brief reference to 'The Goddess of Revenge', which is a story about a visitation from Tatri (a real life woman) to a Namboodri wife harbouring writerly ambitions. Tatri too was a Namboodri, whose case had come in for trial in 1905. Abandoned by her husband and faced with the choice between humiliation in her husband's house and dependence in her parental house, which was already over-inhabited by widows, she carved a third course for herself and took recourse to prostituting herself, waiting for the day when her husband would come to her. At last the day came and Tatri revealed herself. At the trial by the community, she gave abundant proof of the infidelity and loose morality of 60 very 'respectable' and 'respected men'. It was at this point that the trial was abruptly called to a halt, with the whole community faced with a sense of collapse. Tatri was of course cast out, but the community also had to indulge in some self-reflection.[17] In Lalithambika's story, Tatri visits the writer when she is just looking around for a subject and narrates her story, asking her to write about her, if she dare ('The Goddess of Revenge'). The act of writing in a busy household, with a day full of household chores, is itself a test of will. The story strangely reminds one of other similar situations both at home and abroad. Charlotte Perkins Gilman's 'The Yellow Wallpaper' with its claustrophobic atmosphere, Luigi Pirandello's *Six Characters in Search of an Author* and Virginia Woolf's *A Room of One's Own,* all crowd in. Tatri is motivated by a strong feeling of hatred and a desire for revenge. At the end she exclaims, 'Oh, my sister, what I did was as much for your sake as for mine. For the sake of all namboodri women who endure agonies' (Antherjanam, 'The Goddess of Revenge' 25). The narrator discovers, at the end of the story, that Tatri's visit was a dream, like Rokeya Sakhawat Hossain's 'Sultana's Dream'. The dream frame gives a certain freedom, a degree of distancing and more significantly, courage. It leaves scope for a certain ambiguity and at the same time enters forbidden territory. Actually, Tatri's and the narrator's story make two frames, the first is embedded in the second and is also a counter discourse, the first (Tatri's story) representing reality, the second (the narrator's vision) universalises this to apply it to other similar situations simultaneously contrasting the social condition (collective) with the individual's action.

B. Chandrika, a critic and a well-known writer in her own right, begins her essay 'In Search of Infinity: The Parallel Strands in Women's Fiction in Malayalam' with a quotation from one of Lalithambika's short stories, titled 'Kathayengil Katha' (A story of that is what you want). I quote from that:

> It is not easy for a woman like me to get the title of an artist. Even if I get it some-
> how, it is not an easy thing, nor a comfortable one, to live with. There would be
> several suspicious, restraints, fears, that would hover round an artist. Along that
> thorny path which a man could walk easily, we the women have to move cautiously,
> fearfully.... (Chandrika 343)

In Chandrika's view, 'indirection' is a way of writing and this is the tradition Lalithambika developed for women's fiction, the tradition of the 'Invisibility of the Author' (Chandrika 344) as contrasted to another parallel tradition of experiential writing merging life and writing. Resistance expresses itself in multiple ways—direct and indirect, dream and reality and, as Tatri demonstrates, even with the body. But one needs to locate the resistance manifested in this period, which one can tentatively define as 1870–1940, as running parallel to the nationalist discourse and at times crossing it, being influenced by it and even resisting it.

The discourse of the body which one sees in Tatri's revenge continues in other ways in Ismat Chughtai's work. Her autobiography titled *Kagzi Hain Pairahan* (The Clothing is of Paper), carries a title which itself debates the reality of the visible and juxtaposes nakedness and transparency with what is seen, appears to be or is used as a cover. In 1941, Chughtai wrote a short story 'Lihaf' (Quilt) which was charged with obscenity and she was tried on this charge. The story was about a young woman married to an old man who was incapable of satisfying her in anyway. The poor woman, deprived and lonely, resorted to a lesbian relationship and the pleasures of massage. The story hit out at unequal marriages, brought out the nature of sexuality and critiqued the constricted life behind the purdah. Written at the age of 26, this story was based on a real life incident and was quite in line with Chughtai's own rebellious stand concerning gender inequality and segregated existence. She was bold in action as well as in thought and when, at the age of 15, her parents wanted to get her married, she wriggled her way out of it, pushed her way to being educated and began to write. *Kagzi Hain Pairahan* opens with a juxtaposition of the oppressed and the oppressor, an image which represents the colonial situation as much as it does gender. It is an image she had harboured since childhood, a real life memory which forced her to realise early that it is a world based on power. The strong dominate the weak and power can be of physical strength, economic wealth or simple aggression. A crowded family brought home the misery of motherhood. This is also reflected in her novel *Tehri Lakeer* translated into English as *The Crooked Line.* The language she uses is strong and open:

> We were so many of us that our mother felt like vomiting on seeing us. One after another, we came along trampling on her womb. The endless pain and morning sickness she had been subjected to, rendered us into symbols of punishment. At a young age, she had spread almost into a huge mound. At the age of thirty-five she had become a grandmother and was subjected to a super punishment. (Chughtai, *Kagzi Hain Pairahan*, 7)[18]

The almost crude representation of birthing and motherhood, bereft of all romanticism and noble emotions, gets to the other side of the story— the woman who suffers endless pregnancies and is trapped inside them. It is a male indulgence, but also a powerful method of subjugating women to domesticity and childrearing. *The Crooked Line* is a fictionalised autobiography in the sense that the novel takes up her own sprawling family with all kinds of relatives walking in and out, her own experiences of teaching in a school and the complicated relationships (verging on the lesbian) amongst the students.

The objectification of the body as a sexual object has more than one side, and somehow as the focus is shifted from beauty and desire to the innards, a move is made towards subjectivity (provided the subject mind is one's own). But young Ismat could sense the sense of alienation between mother and children with life leaving hardly any time for indulgence or cuddling. The world around her was one of the powerful and the powerless, the rich and the poor, the Hindus and the Muslims (who worshipped differently and ate different kinds of food), and between the upper class and lower class. These divisions were abhorrent and suffocating. Behind the façade of conviviality there were these subtly managed differences.

This world pushed her to rebel, question, resist and cross boundaries in almost every sphere. She would argue and act stubbornly. Her mother often reprimanded her for her boyish manner and unwomanly behaviour. She was afraid of the future—where could such a bold woman find a place in a man's world? Ismat knew why her mother was afraid:

> This is a man's world, man has created it and spoilt it. Woman is but a part of this world whom he has made a medium of expressing his love and hatred. He, in accordance with his moods, worships her and also rejects her. Thus woman, in order to find a place in this world, has to work out various strategies—patience, cleverness and intelligence. (*The Crooked Line* 14)

She doesn't add 'cajoling, connivance and manipulation or even craftiness', strategies which women often employed to get their way. The responsibility for distorting feminine virtues can safely be laid at men's door.

But Ismat refused to pretend—she went on to behave as she wanted to and soon realised that friendships were not dependent on the cosmetics one used or the way one was decked up or not. Education seemed to her to be one way out of the whole situation of pretence and inequality. One finds in her autobiography mention of several friendships across the class gap—a servant's or the washerman's daughter—people to whom she related in different ways, sympathised with, shared a world of storytelling and from whom gathered experience and knowledge; all this was possible because she was bold and daring and believed in going over, crossing boundaries, refusing to be intimidated by behavioural or religious conventions.

The writing of 'Lihaf', as already stated, led to a court case on the charges of obscenity, charging her, her publisher and printer with obscenity. Ismat and her husband Shahid Lateef were in Bombay in those days, the publisher and printer in Delhi, and the trial was to be held in Lahore. At about the same time, Sadaat Hasan Manto was also charged with a similar charge and he was also summoned from Bombay to Lahore. There was a great deal of pressure on both to apologise and pay the fine—but none of the two obliged. In fact, their lawyer, by playing on words, reduced the trial to a farce. Ismat's husband was concerned with the ill fame the case was creating and thus when there was a second appearance, after two years, he asked her to apologise. In the face of all this, she still went ahead, refused to bend and was willing even to go to prison. What is striking about her is her whole attitude, not subdued, tentative, subtle or yielding, not even patient, but playful, bold, argumentative, ready with a counter-reply, marked by a sense of curiosity and a feeling of anticipation—willing to go the whole hog.

The chapter which describes this whole episode—right from the woman, her family and her servant Rabbu, the writing of the story, the trial and then a meeting with the woman, now divorced, remarried and the mother of a child—is titled 'In the Name of Those Married Women' and is followed by a quotation from one of Faiz Ahmed Faiz's poems and carries the meaning 'whose bodies unloved are tired of lying in wait on those pretentious beds' (24).[19] The story had received a mixed response depending on who the reader was and whether the reader was conservative or liberal. By no means obscene or pornographic, it proceeds to delineate the deprivation within marriage, the hollowness behind social respect and brings in the theme of same-sex love. It also exposes the suffocation attached to the word 'ideal'. This chapter concludes by referring to the ideal image of the Indian woman.

> And I began to think—where is that great woman of India! The goddess of purity Sītā, whose lotus feet put out the flames of fire.
>
> And Mirabai who stepped forward to put her arms around God's neck.
>
> That Sati-Savitri who won back Satyavan from the God of death and Razia Sultana who chose a slave to the many aristocratic suitors.
>
> Is she now hiding under the quilt or caught in a violent street-riot? (43)

Ismat Chughtai was deeply influenced by Rasheed Jahan, her senior by a few years, an active member of IPTA and one of the contributors to the ground-breaking Urdu anthology *Angare* (1931), which contained some of the most radical writing of the Urdu Progressive writers (Tharu and Lalita 117–119). Rasheed Jahan was the eldest daughter of Shaikh Abdullah, a Kashmiri brahmin who had converted to Islam, a lawyer and a staunch supporter of women's education. He was one of the founders of the Muslim Women's College at a time when support for women's education was difficult to find. He was also the editor of a journal *Khatun* which dealt with women's issues. In the autobiography of one of Rasheed's younger sisters (they were five sisters), *A Woman of Substance*, there is a whole chapter on Rasheed Jahan, a pioneer in her own right (Mirza).

A Woman of Substance: The Memoirs of Begum Khurshid Mirza, is much more than an autobiography or a biography remembered, written and compiled by several hands, for it tells us a great deal about upper caste Muslims and their efforts to change conservative mindsets. All along, the attitudes of men have mattered—as fathers, husbands and brothers.

Even as initiators of educational institutions. But they alone could have not achieved anything without the dreams of women like Subbalakshmi and the strength of women like Rasheed Jahan, Ismat Chughtai and Lalithambika Antherjanam, women who resisted every unfair imposition, extended help to others and went on to enlarge a woman's world.

VI

Articulating the Self

C.S. Lakshmi (Ambai), a committed writer and feminist, has set up
a centre, Sound and Picture Archives for Research on Women (SPAR-
ROW), with the purpose of giving visibility to 'the voice and the visual'
as much as to the word, and bringing orality into historical narration.
How does one write women's history, or more particularly the history of
their resistance? The usual principles of historiography do not necessarily apply. The norms of selection, or deciding what is significant, require
a total overhaul. History writing, as Gandhi said, in itself is one-sided,
a history of conquests. Or one can extend it to call it a history of power
shifts and of violence. Subaltern historians have focused on histories
from below, creating in the process a parallel history or casting new light
on the smooth surface of narration of events in order to draw attention
to the hidden underlayers.[1] One needs to ask the question: have then the
definitions of valour, heroism and power also undergone a change?

There has to be some point of interaction between parallel histories,
whether they are political, social or emotional, and mainstream dominant histories. When we explore autobiographical voices, the impact of
family, custom, religion, politics all converge to mould the response, to
instigate protest, to inspire the self to articulate its innermost feelings.
Border conflicts, different ways of administration—during the colonial
period, when the princely states had an independent identity—different
religious streams and conversion trends, and different languages and
local cultures also influenced the histories of gender. Rajat Kanta Ray

in *Exploring Emotional History* contextualises emotions in the social context where only expression and interaction establish a visible outer connection. Written literature in the form of fiction or poetry is only one kind of source. Diaries and letters are other ways of recording social reality, personal circumstances and emotions for the educated. Additionally they also need leisure and freedom. Women's diaries are not always so explicit. The veil of secrecy and the habit of silence prevent them from talking about their innermost thoughts. Other fields of expression are in action and public participation and depend on public/external sources for validation and verification.

Mythily Sivaraman, when she went through the diary of her grandmother, had to read behind the cryptic entries ('Preface' xiv–xvi), and Rassundari Devi wrote hardly anything about her husband. Early women diarists, even in England, wrote about the outside world, centring their world on the outside or their husbands' and lovers' interests or the dull, daily chores.[2] A public face and a private face may also be different. The assisted and aided autobiographies of Begum Khurshid Mirza, Malka Pukhraj and even Zohra Segal render accounts of events that are visible. There are hardly any recordings of emotional conflicts or debates going on in personal life. A strange kind of reticence, and at times the notion of respectability, constrains women in the expression of their innermost selves, the expression of hatred, love or guilt. The two autobiographies which strike one with their candour and openness are of Hansa Wadkar and Ismat Chughtai, who are least conscious or concerned of what the world thinks of them. They are self-analytical, critical and at times ruthless. Chughtai is more structured than Wadkar. She is educated and a writer and the selection of events she wishes to discuss has been carefully considered; Wadkar is fragmentary and her reflections are a collection of the bitter-sweet moments, selected at random, episodes that stand out in her mind.

There is the problem of writing the self. Women carry out a multiple-act of writing the 'self', through body language, response, action and last of all the act of writing.[3] One can understand why Lalithambika An-therjanam chooses either to write in the third person or to fictionalise her response. Several dalit women have also written their lives in the form of fiction. But the kind of archival research possible in historical formula-tion is not possible on the same scale. True, official records, especially of the last few centuries help us to understand the past as do written accounts of court poets, nawabs or begums, or travellers. They all sup-ply a brick or two towards the construction of the history of gender as well as of resistance. Veena Das in *Critical Events* uses parliamentary speeches in order to support her study and Urvashi Butalia in *The Other Side of Silence* depends on the method of recall, when her contacts are called upon to explore the emotional structure of their feelings, depend-ing heavily on memory. Is there a difference between this kind of recall, fictionalising an event, and writing of oneself in the third person? I have a feeling, yes. All three activities call in for different faculties and skills. The writer, while fictionalising the past, is writing about events she has lived with; her relationship with her material is a felt one and it has obvi-ously affected her deeply; the distancing mode allows the writer to see herself from outside and locate the inner being in perspective, but the method of recall does not cater for amnesia or selective and willed am-nesia, especially when the events concerned have been traumatic. There is a certain unreliability about memory, and one is hesitant to open out in interview situations for the fear of exposure, or for fear of upsetting the balance established with great effort in family and social relationships. There is likely to be a gender difference even in memory recall.[4] Oral histories, folk songs and sharing sessions are other ways of articulation. They work in more intimate and natural situations. However incomplete the process may be, each process also has inbuilt advantages.

Women have traditionally been perceived as ahistoric, as outside time, and rendered silent and invisible. They have been excluded from public domain through domesticity, seclusion and subordination. Con-sequently, when they began to be visible, the concepts of heroism were layered with a sense of stoicism, sacrifice and noble suffering—such as in the cases of Joan of Arc, Panna Dai and Sītā. These portraits are laden with histories of self-denial and a superhuman ability to ignore the self, in fact, a total erasure. Histories of desire, of self-perception, of individual motivation are rare. If we wish to trace histories, there is a need to look at their ways of knowing and the epistemological frameworks which they evolve or which are accessible to them and above all their experiential realities. Women learn through experience, through sharing, through the cultural perceptions of themselves as entities and bodies as much as they learn from ritual, and if lucky enough, from exposure and education. But knowledge and resistance are likely to begin from the body. I have in mind grassroots revolutions, which are not always necessarily collective, but also individual. The casting-off of the umbrella by the Antherjanams is one such gesture, indicating how important the matter of dress is. It falls in line with casting-off the veil or purdah and freeing it from the rootedness in either religion or respectability (J. Jain, 'Purdah'). Walking out of a wife's role is another. If on one hand we have the case of Rukhmabai, who resorted to legal measures, on the other we have Phoolan Devi, a woman beaten by her husband, starved, subjected to humiliation and rape, and who responded by becoming a dacoit and then journeyed back via surrender and a prison sentence to become an elected member of Parliament and finally death through assassination.

Mala Sen has reconstructed Phoolan Devi's life with the help of interviews with her, her police record and newspaper coverage in the book *India's Bandit Queen* (1991). The articulation Phoolan Devi found through action needed help for articulation in a verbal discourse. Mala Sen's work is also one kind of the double-edged hijacking that takes place in subaltern discourse. It makes it visible, provides it with accessibility, at times glamorises it and very often succumbs to market forces. The mediator is caught in a tight wedge between sympathy and the desire to share on the one hand and the difficulty of sifting out her presence on the other. Reality, if rendered tolerable by art, becomes a falsification;

if close to the ugliness of life, it is unbearable. Shekhar Kapur made a film on her life which attracted both censorship and controversy (*Bandit Queen*) and Mala Sen's reconstruction of Devi's life cannot be viewed merely as a biography. It does not trace the life of a hero. It is however an analysis of a woman's life and her battling against the patriarchal forces aligned against her primarily because she is a woman, because her body can be used for labour and because sex is a marketable commodity which can be sold and bought. Sen is also not interested in her political career. I read the work as story of a victim, a woman who can be seen as a representative of countless other women who continuously struggle against the atrocities committed on their bodies, and whose real life happenings contrast sharply with the idealistic cultural presentations of marriage, family and kinship ties. The sole possession of such women is their body which experiences its own desires and wants.

India's Bandit Queen comments on the gross inequalities in society. One could begin with unequal marriages. Married to a man much older than her, she is scared of him. The marriage runs an uneven course and she is reduced to the status of an abandoned wife. She was also an unwanted daughter, being one of four sisters. The children are caught up in the land quarrels and power struggles of the village. Another man, Suresh, tries to molest her and when she resists she acquires the reputation of a disreputable woman. Family protection, laws of morality and concepts of chastity propagated by cultural rituals and images all remain shelved. Instead, kinship ties, marital relationships, and caste-divisions become ways of harassment. It is just not possible to fight the upper castes. The middle-class feminist movement had simply passed by lives such as Phoolan Devi's. These women were, as Mala Sen has observed, victims of a fundamentally feudal society (54).

Subjected to beatings, starvation and police torture, passed on from one dacoit gang to another, Phoolan rebels and retaliates with violence. Covering a period of 10 years (1983–1993), it is a story of a string of moments—of frustration, insight, consciousness, compromises and helplessness. And of the consciousness to fight, resist and survive. Born into a community of fishermen, abandoned by her husband, she was meant to be submissive—instead, she chose to rebel, to transgress, to openly flout all rules and conventions and roles thrust on her and fight a lonely, violent battle. This too was resistance. Resistance by denying the procreative function of the female body, resistance by breaking bounds and becoming an outlaw. It is the struggle of one lone woman, fending for herself against all odds. One need not hold her up as a role model worthy of emulation, but that does not affect the realisation that her life was one long act of resistance and demonstrated a high degree of courage.

Right from the bottom of the social structure, we have other voices of resistance. Women who have struggled against their circumstances and caste prejudices to educate themselves, voice their feelings and relate their histories. Urmila Pawar is one such woman. In an autobiographical piece, 'My Four Enemies', she records how though they did not have enough to eat, she persisted in going to school even with her hair full of lice, ragged clothes and without a daily bath. Her four enemies are 'Enemy number one—my father! Enemy number two—my mother! Number three—my brother, and the fourth was my teacher—Harlekar Guruji. These four antagonists shaped my life, and whatever I am today I am because of these four' (298). Why does she consider them her enemies? Because they were always seeking new ways to tighten their hold on her. Her father was a strict disciplinarian and very good at giving a good beating, and he made them sit down to study. Her mother was a miser—or at least that is how the child's eye looked at their poverty. But she too insisted that the child attend school. Her brother also joined this effort. And her teacher likewise showed no consideration and used a free hand in beating her. These people strengthened her will (as much as her obstinacy), beat her into obedience but also aroused her resistance.

In the SPARROW workshop of C.S. Lakshmi, Urmila Pawar, a writer in her own right, participated in the group sharing sessions. When a person who has access to learning and language expresses herself in her own words (as Urmila Pawar does), it is a very different activity than when their feelings are translated by others (as in the case of Phoolan Devi). I want to reproduce a passage from this session, to recreate the image of the young Urmila:

> My mother could remember naught else but weeping and weaving baskets. Her only concern was with our education nothing else.... There were a multitude of lice in my hair bred by the dust in which I played. We would mix soda powder in hot water and wash our hair. As we poured the hot water, my mother would comb out the lice in hard strokes of a sharp toothed comb. When she did this, stars would appear in front of my eyes. It was if lightening had struck. (Pawar, 'Hum Nein Bhi' 53 [Translation mine])[5]

The role of parents, and the fact that education trickles down from one generation to another before it can spread to include the margins of gender or weakness, is stressed. Pawar's father was a teacher and when he died, his uneducated wife took up his mission. When resistance develops amongst the marginalised, it is more often than not in pursuit of justice, an effort towards social change; it is against a social structure, not against men or nations.

She goes on to state how social discrimination continued to persist. Employers still treated them as untouchables and refused to eat the food cooked by them (54). Her father was of the opinion that such discriminations were not to be tolerated. Even her mother could muster up her courage to protest against the discriminatory attitude of Pawar's teacher. The concept of dignity is present in every individual; only some of us compromise, guided by some other compulsion or likely gain. Gandhi's insistence on personal dignity and Periyar's on self-respect have obviously left their mark in some way or the other on thousands of people.[6] Again, breaking away from rural surroundings was another force towards personal liberation. One was marginally freed from caste oppression in urban settings.

Pawar also recounts the lack of medical facilities and the ignorance that surrounded childbirth. A woman having difficult labour was given hot fomentation, and if there was a tear in the body, a lot of salt was applied to it and salt-water and oil massage given to her whole body. In fact, Pawar says, giving birth was an ordeal for a woman in those days.[7] There was a high rate of mortality not only in childbirth but also due to illnesses—a clear indication of the little value attached to women's health.

One of the conflict areas was water distribution. Upper castes simply did not allow the lower castes to use the same well. And when women labourers worked in urban areas, no one would give them any water to drink. An illustration of solidarity (even across gender) for purposes of resistance comes to light in Pawar's father's attitude. He had got a well dug in their house and instructed his wife to keep it open for these village women who travelled to the city to sell wood. Women of the upper caste were a little more forthcoming than the men, highlighting yet another gender difference.

Pawar also refers to the attitude of shopkeepers. Pickles were normally made and sold by upper castes. Thus, whenever she went to buy some, the whole time-consuming ritual was performed, of distancing her, making her wait and then giving her the pickle by throwing it from above in order to avoid touching her. Once her brother advised her to move in and take out the pickle from the jar. The automatic result would be that the whole jar would be discarded. No doubt aggression, in such cases, had its advantages, even when it carried the risk of creating a riot.

Pawar's creative writing is a serious reflection on the caste and gender issues present in the society around her. There was hardly any literary tradition to fall back upon in her own family. She looked around and, as she states, she concentrated on issues closest to her: her first story problematised the issue of a girl-centred family, the second the pregnancy of a widow (Pawar, 'Hum Nein Bhi' 62–63). In dalit writing as a whole, the literary tradition is not very strong. In Arjun Dangle's anthology,

Poisoned Bread, women's presence is only marginal. The language most of the writers use is close to the spoken word.

In the course of the discussion, Pawar openly criticised the discriminatory treatment dalit men meted out to their women, the manner in which they treated them and expected them to fall into the role of the self-sacrificing, self-effacing wives. They too, like the upper caste men, practised a double set of moral values (Pawar, 'Hum Nein Bhi' 64–65). Patriarchy behaved in the same way; it really was of no significance whether the men were dalit or upper caste. Actually, in the second short story she wrote, 'Nyaya' (Justice), Pawar exposed the myth of dalit women having more freedom in matters of sexuality, control over body and mobility. The dalit widow is as much under social disapproval for her pregnancy as the upper caste widow whose case had roused Tarabai Shinde into writing *Stree-Purush Tulana* more than a century ago.

Lower caste women or dalit and tribal women were often forced into sexual exploitation by upper caste men. No social hue or cry is raised when this happens. Uma Chakravarti cites examples from early literature when 'dasis' (slaves) were freely used by their masters (*Gendering Caste* 85). We have examples of this kind of exploitation in a large number of novels of the nineteenth and twentieth centuries when the landowners exploited the bodies of women labourers including those of the married ones. Belonging to an upper caste worked as a social shield. In many sections of society, widows did not necessarily die a social death, but then forced cohabitation with a brother-in-law, which was one option, was also no easy choice. Chakravarti points out that 'enforced' cohabitation was the rule among 'untouchables' (83). Upper caste women were forced to commit sati in the interests of property and in order to eliminate their claim; similarly, the practice of levirate was also enforced in the interests of property or economic production or a continued claim to the male progeny of the widow and her dead husband.[8]

Kishore Shantabai Kale in his double autobiography in a single narrative, of his and his mother's—*Chora Kolhati Ka*—paints a graphic

225

picture of the exploitation of women, their bodies and their freedom for the support of the family, justifying it all on the basis of caste practice. Chakravarti is of the view that dalit women experience patriarchal oppression both individually and collectively (*Gendering Caste* 88). Women, no matter where they belong in caste hierarchy, either internalise the discriminatory practices (1),[9] are oppressed by it, or participate as mothers and suffer as daughters in 'honour' killings (157–159).[10] The moment they exercise some personal choice, women are seen to have violated the sexual norms of their castes.

Very visible as objects of desire, women are not visible in history. Aware that dalit women's role was ignored in the Ambedkar movement and dalit history, Pawar undertook to explore their participation. Almost everywhere she would be greeted with a blank statement that women had played no role. But persistence paid; gradually a great deal of information was unearthed about these silent workers and the result was the book *Amhihi Itihaas Ghadavlaa* (*We Also Made History*) (Pawar and Moon), which is a full-length book different from the SPARROW interview that she gave in the workshop, though both carry similar titles. Women activists worked for access to water and also joined in other movements, often against the wishes of their men. They not only attended to the household chores, looked after the children but also withstood the violent beatings of their husbands (Pawar, 'Hum Nein Bhi' 65–69; note the placement of the title within inverted commas to distinguish it from the full-length book).

Why do women need to recover history or have a history? Why and when does a class or a category desire to possess, write or recover its history? Often this happens when the need is felt for self-affirmation, for an intervention in the master narrative, for filling up the gaps in the knowledge available and for overthrowing hegemonic structures. There could be any one or all of these reasons. Without a history, it is difficult to trace a lineage. Matrilineal histories run parallel to this tracing of history. It is also a journey towards citizenship in one's own right, not as subordinated beings. The Greek word 'historia', which means learning or knowing through inquiry, at once calls attention to the methods of acquiring knowledge and conducting inquiry. The ways of 'knowing' for women are often through the men or through male perspectives. Pawar also refers to a case where an interviewee told her that often her husband would tell her to stay at home, and he on return would brief her about what was discussed in the meeting (67). Again, Pawar's interviewer, Lata, also cites an example of another way of knowing—of going out in the field and meeting women and asking them. A lot of effort has to go into this, and a lot of time invested. Lata also goes on to assert that the greeting *Jhujharu Narivadi* (militant feminist) emerged from such meetings (68).[11]

Caste has created its own outcasts. Partha Chatterjee refers to two different strategies that the Indian nationalists had adopted; one, to accept it as essential to the characterisation of Indian society, which will 'wither away' under the impact of modernisation and, second, to accept it as a basis for civilisational identity and as an attempt at harmonising the distinct sections of society[12]—the untouchables who were considered beyond the pale of *varna*. But time has shown that none of these two assumptions are correct or have materialised. Caste has not withered; instead, it has become more rigid, divisionary and separatist. Two contrary discourses are at work—one of modernisation and globalisation, the other of increased visibility of caste categories and large-scale agitations for more and more reservation. Only miniscule pockets have emerged where discrimination is not actually visible—but in such cases, it is either a situation where the dalit is in a position of power, or it is now a discrimination by their upwardly mobile section against their own kin.[13]

Alternate Spaces

When one converts to another religion, the reasons can be many. Faith, compulsion, survival, violence, resentment and desire to get away from an existing oppressive environment could be some. But what happens when one carries the load of past discrimination into the new faith or

227

environment? Bama, a dalit writer, is not a first generation convert. Born into the Christian religion, her relationship towards it was no different from that of any other individual who is born into a faith. But her auto-biography, *Karukku*, unveils before us the caste discrimination that has infiltrated into religious houses with all the inherent prejudices of upper caste Hindu society.

The word *karukku* literally means a palmyra leaf, which with its ser-rated edge is sharp. Bama uses it for multiple symbols—her life which has been one of struggle, poverty and discrimination as well as the actual experiences of childhood. In the author's 'Preface', she writes:

> There are many congruities between the saw-edged palmyra karukku and my own life. Not only did I pick up the scattered karukku in the days when I was sent out to gather firewood, scratching and tearing my skin as I played with them; but later they also became the embryo and symbol that grew into this book. (xiii)

Lakshmi Holmström, commenting on the title, points out that *karu*, in Tamil, also means a seed (Bama vii). Bama is critical of both the cor-ruption and selfishness which is fast invading houses of religion. The reference is to her experience as a novice in the convent which she had entered with the desire to be a nun. But the manner in which the nuns treated dalits and the contempt they displayed towards them left her with no doubt of the total absence of human understanding and compassion. They grudged them even their food and treated them as the lowest of the low. One needs to read the autobiography to sense the sensitiveness of the writer to the world around her. The very first sentence reads, 'Our village is beautiful.' She goes on to describe the mountains and hills, the practices, the division of lands, the owners and the caste hierarchy. She asserts, 'I love this place for its beauty' (1). People of upper castes are privileged, they build boundaries around their compounds, have wells and pump-sets. It is only the poor who are kept out, who have to collect firewood and have no steady means of livelihood.

Touch is a major taboo in Indian society; the whole myth of purity rests on it and when a person is born in a caste normally engaged in lowly and menial tasks that require contact with human and animal waste, raw hide and other related occupations, they are labelled *achut*s, the untouchables, and have little social mobility. The taboo on touch itself defines a dividing line between human beings marking them as low or high. Similarly, the concept of the *madi* woman rests on this purity. The frequent baths that women, cooks, widows and even priests are subjected to—if someone touches them—are also products of this taboo. In traditional homes, certain areas—like prayer rooms and cooking places—cannot be entered without having a bath, and entry is not permitted to everyone. We have several such depictions in late nineteenth-century and early twentieth-century fiction where grandmothers brush off their grandchildren in anger in order to protect the purity of their body!

Lata, the interviewer in Urmila Pawar's SPARROW dialogue, describes how even her own mother-in-law treated her badly, keeping the utensils she used separately, because Lata belonged to a caste that cultivated betel leaf! (Pawar, 'Hum Nein Bhi' 73–75). Ironically enough, even people of the lower castes discriminated against castes placed even lower than them in the social hierarchy. They too were desirous of marrying their sons into brahmin families. When men and women entered the field as educationists, it was a moot question as to what kind of moral values they were likely to teach their students (74). The ways of dissemination of discriminatory practices were many and subtle. And this affected all sharing, inside the family, among friends, other tenants, neighbours, all. Body and food are two major concerns and a general (and very ugly) practice has been to drop food from a distance for the poor so as not to come into close contact with them (73–75).[14]

Bama also refers to this practice and how what had initially appeared to her to be a comic incident when she saw a man walking along holding a packet of food from a string became for her a discriminatory practice when her brother explained to her the reason for this. Food received in charity and thrown from above attacked human dignity. When Bama told her mother not to lay herself open to such an insult, her mother replied, 'These people are the maharajas who feed us our rice. Without them, how will we survive? Haven't they been upper-caste from generation to generation, and haven't we been lower-caste? Can we change that?' (Bama 14).

Under such conditions, it was remarkable that parents—like Urmila Pawar's—and the young people themselves aspired to be educated and persisted in their efforts. The successes—as compared to the dropouts—are few, but this goes to prove the degree of challenge they were able to meet. Excellence was another conquest. Creativity, a third. These things simply did not happen on their own: a high degree of determination and strength of will were required to pursue these dreams against such heavy odds.

Bama recalls that when, for purposes of scholarships, she and another girl stood up to identify their caste origins, the whole class went off into a titter of contempt: 'I was filled with a sudden rage. At once I told the teacher that I didn't want their special tuition or anything else, and sat down' (19). On another occasion, she was refused permission to go and attend the First Communion of her siblings, which, in any case was to be on a weekend. She describes her reaction in these words:

> I grew hot with anger. I saw with my own eyes that they were giving permission for the wealthy children to go home. I lost my temper and challenged them head-on, 'How is it that you are allowing these others to go; why is it that you only refuse me?' The reply that I was given: 'What celebration can be in your caste, for a First Communion'. (19)

Bama, however, persisted in both her obstinacy and counter-questioning, thus displaying an unusual degree of courage as well as determination. The refusal to tolerate injustice, to stand up to authority and to hold on to individual dignity are remarkable qualities in a young school child, especially when the child is not equipped with a wealthy or an upper caste background.

Despite such incidents, her faith in God persuaded her to stay in the convent. Here too, among all those who were preparing to be inducted into the order, there were people who were curious to find out about her caste. She was shocked to learn that there was a separate (religious) order for Harijans, 'I lamented inwardly that there was no place free of caste.' After she had taken the vows of a nun, she discovered to her horror that in the school attached to the convent, people of her community were looking after all the jobs like sweeping the premises, swabbing and washing the classrooms and cleaning out the lavatories. The common attitude was to talk insultingly and dismissively of low-caste people and treat them shabbily. For sometime she bottled up her resentment, never retorted that she too was low caste. Bama writes that the battle continued within herself (22–23). She was respected on account of her efficiency, but because of the fear that low-caste people lived in, the servility and subjugation that had become part of their body language, everyday she became angrier and angrier. She realised that these prejudices and discriminatory practices not only attacked and eroded their sense of personal dignity but also acted as a mental block against aspirations for self-improvement.

> [Caste discrimination] stalks us in every nook and corner and drives us into a frenzy…. If you are born into a low caste, every moment of your life is a struggle. People screw up their faces and look at us with disgust the moment they know our caste. (23)

Bama's anger is rooted more in a collective anguish than in individual resentment.

Religion, religious conversion or personal faith, none of them makes a difference in matters of caste. It doesn't liberate one or free one from the cultural baggage it carries. Urmila Pawar quotes similar examples

231

when her teacher always earmarked her to collect the cow dung from the school compound (Pawar, 'My Four Enemies' 306–307). And Lata has voiced how their tenant's visitor went back with the food she had brought and returned the following day to whisk away the tenant ('Hum Nein Bhi'). Education or no education, constitutional provisions or not— none of this really mattered. *Manusmriti* was alive and kicking, running through in the blood of generations of the upper castes. It amounts to a social conspiracy to keep the lower castes subjugated. Power rests itself on oppression.

It is not only the living and the religious orders that are divided along caste lines but with the setting up of different cemeteries, even the dead are divided (Bama 25–27). Thus, inequality follows people even to the grave. I am referring to this kind of oppression mainly for two reasons: one, unless one realises the immensity of the problem and its multiple fallouts, it is not possible to realise the extent of human misery; two, this realisation is necessary for one to gauge the nature of resistance even in relation to gender. In fact, women may be more and not less oppressed on account of their increased vulnerability and the exchange they are subjected to in marriage, which may often be arranged and unequal. At the same time, I would like to point out that caste has infiltrated even those religions whose origins lie in the ideal of setting up an egalitarian society. Islam and Sikhism for instance. It is not only Christianity which practices caste discrimination. Separate colonies have come up where the well-to-do lower caste converts build their houses, and like the cemetery which Bama describes, even separate Gurudwaras (houses of God) have come up as Hindus and Sikhs keep the lower caste convertees out of their temples. This—with the low castes acquiring wealth—has become more of a power struggle than ever before. These also fan separatist tendencies and slogans of 'our people' and 'your people' are raised.[15]

Bama proceeds to ask, 'Are Dalits not human beings?' She also insists that the only way to find freedom or redemption is to work for it:

We who are asleep must open our eyes and look about us. We must not accept the injustice of our enslavement by telling ourselves it is our fate, as if we have no true feelings; we must dare to stand up for change, we must crush all these institutions that use caste to bully us into submission, and demonstrate that among human be-ings there are none who are high or low.... It is we who have to place them where they belong and bring about a changed and just society where all are equal. (25)

Bama gives several accounts of inter-caste skirmishes, the police atrocities that followed, the fear that stalked the land and the survival strategies that the women adopted (25–41). Caste discrimination coupled with poverty pushed her to stress the need for education and she planned to take the vows of a nun. Disillusioned with the system, she was left with no other choice than to walk out of it. When she first took her vows, it was with the ideal of service but experiencing this as another strong-hold of the rich, she decided to give up, not religion but the constrictive atmosphere of continued discrimination. This was no easy decision; em-ployment was not so easy to obtain. Caste, once again, came in the way. Then what does one do? Seek protection in a cage? '…words and rules in the convent, they cut me down and sculpted me, damaged me…. I don't know when my wings will heal and gain enough strength so that I too will be able to fly again' (104).

Talking of wings, another volume of workshop interviews from SPARROW is titled *Pankhon Ki Udaan* (The Flight of Wings). The in-terviews here focus on women who moved into unusual professions like photography (unusual in that time context), or move into those which were traditionally not considered respectable, like acting, and brought to it a respectability on account of their personal dignity. Esther Victoria Abraham, a Jew, moved in 1935 to Mumbai, became an actress and was also a photographer, perhaps the first woman photographer. Kanika Mur-thy works on sculpture, Damayanti Chawda went into dancing, Sushma into stage-acting. These women dared and not only fulfilled their creative desire, entered a different world, but also opened out new pathways for others (Arora).

Challenging Aesthetic Conventions

What happens when women, who ordinarily do not isolate their individuality from the community's, write an autobiography? Bama in *Karukku* often talks about her anger, her innermost responses to her surrounding and in the 'Afterword', she briefly talks of her loneliness, but nowhere do we see a highly developed sense of ego. Gender, over and above caste and poverty, plays a role in subduing it. Dalit women's autobiographical narratives raise some very important questions related to the genre, the construction of selfhood and nationhood. One needs to ask: how do they trace the process of self-evolution? Bama does it through narrating the discrimination around her and the hurt it caused her; others follow other courses.

Bama's autobiography was written at a fairly young age, but there are others like Baby Kamble's *Jeevan Hamara* (Our Life) and Kaushalya Baisantri's *Dohra Abhishaap* (The Double Curse), which were written when both these writers were past 60. Moreover, they place their autobiographies in the category of *upanyas* (fiction). They do give accounts of Ambedkar's movement, which was more of an enveloping movement than a local power struggle, but politics does not loom as large as it might have in male autobiographies. It is true that ideological differences between Gandhi and Ambedkar are there in the background, the differences that played an important role in national politics of the time. But their political understanding works mostly at a subconscious level. It is left to the reader to draw her inferences.

Both the writers give detailed descriptions of the way the dalits lived, their customs and practices, the food they ate and their domestic relationships. What is striking about these autobiographical narratives, no matter in which language or from which region, is that they are based on real life experiences, perceptions and history and are fairly objective and matter-of-fact in their narration. The main difference between men's and women's writing is the centrality of the self. Women do not spend any time on self-definitions, or projecting tales of achievement and progress. Even their achievements in education are underplayed; there is also no self-appraisal which announces their victories.

Urmila Pawar in 'Hum Nein Bhi Itihaas Racha Hai' comments on some of the Marathi women's autobiographies and has remarked on Baby Kamble's use of humour in critiquing blind superstition (Pawar, 'Hum Nein Bhi' 70). Though Baby Kamble does not discuss her life in the autobiography, Urmila Pawar narrates an incident about which she had told them. Once her husband was unemployed and she suggested that they should proceed to Bombay in search of employment. He readily agreed, but when on the way some young student co-travellers in the Pune–Bombay bus were laughing amongst themselves, he blamed his wife for their laughter. The moment they got off, he too got off and hit his wife with a stone which injured her badly. There was a lot of bleeding and as a result of the injury her face got swollen.

On reaching her sister's home, they realised that they were unwelcome. Her brother-in-law threw them out and told them to go back to Pune. Then again, her husband took off his *chappal* and gave her a thorough beating. When she asked why he was doing it, he replied by questioning why her brother-in-law gave her a 10-rupee note (which was probably given as a partial help towards their travel expenses, 70–71). Men, because they lacked self-confidence, felt insecure, and women found themselves hedged in from all sides, no matter how restrained their behaviour might have been. There can be no possibility of any companionship or compassion in such a relationship. Pawar also exposes the belief that dalit women enjoy greater freedom than upper caste women as a myth; it has no basis in reality. A candid autobiography, a rarity in itself, is by Mallika Amar Sheikh, who in her work, *Mala Udhvasth*

Vahachai (Marathi; the title could be translated as 'I Want to be Ruined'), has written about dalit men's attitude in an inter-caste marriage. In Pawar's opinion, women's autobiographies expose the flaws in dalit masculinity and patriarchy. At the same time, their extremely realistic descriptions of rituals, exorcism and other domestic practices offer a rich material to the anthropologist. These experiences also provide an insight into the various kinds of oppression which controlled them, shaped their lives and finally compelled them to resist. The act of writing expresses this resistance. It is a making of the self, a lifting off the veil that camouflages reality. And it stands in direct opposition to elitist writing in almost everything—motivation and purpose, ideology and aesthetics. It is shaped by an absence of power.

Jeevan Hamara moves at three different levels: the personal narrative, modest and underplayed, then the caste narrative which dominates the work and finally the third level of the gendered experience. Within this three-phased narration, Kamble uses several sub-narrators, both men and women, and works their lives through parables and folk stories, thus decentring the narrative voice. The work ends on a note of disillusionment. The long struggle seems to be unending. But even as it strikes this note of despair, in aesthetic terms it achieves two entirely different things. First, the narrator as a subject is decentred (and paradoxically, enlarged); the personal narrative moves into that of caste and through this route into the nation. Apparently, even if the margins are not yet the centre, they have begun to question the boundaries and are impatient to get out of their confines. Second, as the telling of a life story, defines a 'self'; and if accompanied by self-analysis, it becomes in itself a liberation. In this process, the writer/speaker is constantly engaged in an act of recollection, of events, personal perspectives and social contexts. It is evident that this writer–observer is likely to have been a different 'self' at the time of experience. But the action and now its remembrance, as they come together in the act of sharing, frame the past, give it shape and define its impact on the individual life. Thus, two processes, one centrifugal and the other centripetal, are simultaneously at work.

Dalit aesthetics, despite a fair amount of theorisation by the dalits themselves,[16] is falling into a rut even though their writing is ripe for more theorisation. One major mistake they commit is that they seek comparisons with Black Aesthetics and Marxism instead of working with their own writing.[17] Sufficient attention has not been paid to the rawness of their experience, the rituals they describe, the role the rituals play in the formation of their reality or the structures they adopt. The nature of their protest has dominated their theorisation.

Culture, Ritual and Empowerment

A group of scholars working together has researched on a selected number of communities in Gujarat—the Vankar, Bhangi and Koli-Patel women—and put together their findings and conclusions in *The Silken Swing* (Franco, Macwan and Ramanathan). Preoccupied 'with the phenomena of self-perception and self-fashioning', it seeks to work out how these constitute the subjectivity of a person. The editors are of the view that subjectivity 'may thus be seen as a point of intersection, an area in which an individual's libidinal energy is worked upon by the structures and categories of the outside world' (11). From this perspective, if a woman arrives at a realisation that she has a right to go out and work, and to stretch this point of view a little further begins to think about herself as a person, then even if she cannot go out to work or fulfil all her wishes, her subjectivity would still have undergone a change. Despite the gap between thought and action, a change does occur:

> Subjectivity is primarily a cast of mind, an interior state of thought and feeling. Any thought that enters a person's mental world and is reflected upon and accepted

will alter the person's subjectivity since it alters the perspective that person brings to bear upon the world. (2)

It is logical to presume that the building up of a subjectivity involves them as thinking beings, and in that measure it reduces their passivity. No longer can one expect these women to accept everything passively blaming it on their fate (*karma*) or womanhood. They respond to external conditions (including oppression) and subvert them or rebel against them—sometimes covert, at other times overt. As noted earlier (Chapter 4), possession by spirits is also a way of subverting authority; rituals and festivities become other ways. One could also add to these the songs women sing during weddings and harvest time. They are open, candid, critical and, at times, abusive. There is an expression of open sexuality and desire in them. Further, they sing them uninhibitedly.

All kinds of relationships come under scrutiny, the mother-in-law is accused of wickedness, the father-in-law of being a bully while the husband a no-gooder. The bride hammers the point that he is not like her— that is, not as good as she. Folk songs, as the noted folklorist Komal Kothari once pointed out, are that rare piece of art when the consciousness of a listener is absent. Women sing for themselves; they are their own listeners and hence not all self-conscious in the expression of their feelings and thoughts.

*Vrat katha*s, stories which accompany the observation of religious fasts, can be seen as a medium of both empowerment and disempowerment. This contradictory base is because they serve multiple functions. 'Fasting' as a practice, it is true, is absorbed into most religions—Hinduism, Christianity, Islam, Jainism—and men also observe fasts. We have examples of Jesus fasting for forty days and nights (Gospel of St Matthew, New Testament); Muslims of both genders fast during the month of Ramadan and Jains also follow this practice as a matter of penance, when they observe the annual ritual *priyushan*, a ritual of asking forgiveness for wrongs done. The final day is known as *Kshamavani*. Asceticism as a practice implies control of the senses and thus depends heavily on abstinence of all kinds, including food. Gandhi, by making use of it for political ends, brought the personal into the political. Despite the abundance of examples, the ratio of women observing fasts out of desire or compulsion is higher than the men. Fasting is an act which in Hindu practice, allows for a substitution. A mother or a wife can perform this on behalf of the son or the husband. Widows were (and in some pockets even now) compulsorily subjected to fasts. There are several fasts especially earmarked for women, as for instance, Karva Chauth, Teej, Gangaur, Vat Savitra, Hartalika and several others. Julia Leslie in her work *Roles and Rituals for Hindu Women* observes that out of a survey conducted on 108 women, 94 per cent observed fasts for marital felicity, 71 per cent for the health and long life of the husband, 65 per cent for having a child, 21 per cent for power, 37 per cent for drawing nearer to God and only 30 per cent for liberation (Leslie 79).

Fasts which are gender specific imprison women within gender roles such as wife or mother; they are also more often than not directed towards the well-being of the husband, son or family, or are aimed at disciplining the body of a widow. The stories accompanying them very often stress reward for strict adherence and punishment for any deviation, and thus seek to strike fear in the minds of women and persuade them to conform. They tend to establish a bargaining relationship with god. But the positive aspects lie in the attention the women may get, as well as the festivity or the community get-together which enables them an escape from drudgery. These privilege a woman, no matter how briefly. Moreover, some of the *katha*s (stories) can be interpreted variously. In a narrative like Urmila Pawar's or Bama's, one realises that fasting for any of the above causes is meaningless when food itself is in short supply. True, a fast is almost always followed by festivity or feasting; at times fasting becomes a necessity on the part of the mother for more food to be available for the children, but as Deth and Vandereycken have pointed out, women's self-starvation is linked to a broader issue of their position

239

within society and should be interpreted as a response to and struggle against male domination. 'Control' would be a basic issue to socially disempowered women who adopted relentless fasting as a vehicle for self-expression and simultaneously for manipulation.[18]

But at the same time, it needs to be acknowledged that the fasts are also disempowering, especially when they are accepted without any questioning or intervention of personal will and observed simply because they are there, and it is a common practice and needs to be observed. When they are undertaken with a specific aim in mind, they also reflect a material (and worldly) attitude even as non-worldly methods are adopted. The relation between the devotee and the object of faith may also be seen through multiple frames: as one between two friends (*sakhi*) or as a contractual one where the fast is the payment for the gain.

*Vrat*s, *vrat katha*s and the narratological techniques of the latter have interested me for more than a decade and, in their mixture of fairy tale and fable, they act as social pacifiers. Susan Wadley describes them as 'transformers of destiny'. Working with the theory of *karma*, she observes, '…it is believed that the performance of a *vrat* will alter one's destiny…past actions are transformed: the deity worshipped in the *vrat* is believed to destroy the sins that are being endured and causing present unhappiness' (Wadley 36). Thus, even as they indicate personal responsibility, they introduce the element of guilt and punishment, coercing the will to obedience.

Several fasts prescribe some kind of restriction or specification regarding food and at times passion-arousing food items are forbidden. *Satvik* food, that is, the kind that leads to purity of thought is allowed and *tamsik*, the kind that produces passion is taboo, particularly for widows and the growing girl child. It is surprising how a practice observed by an individual connects with religion, society and social relationships at several levels. *Nityavrat* fasts are the ones which are obligatory and are meant as self-purification and preparation for a new role or a significant ritual. *Kamyavrat* fasts are motivated by desire and are undertaken for

240

the fulfilment of a wish. Thus, it is obvious that 'fasting' as a practice recognises the motivation of desire, the control of the body as well as the mind and the role of the self.

The *vrat katha*s are in the main didactic and are constituted by a pattern of obedience/adherence leading to a reward, a boon or wish-fulfilment and any deviation resulting in punishment or loss. They follow a pattern of cause and effect and reinforce the theory of *karma*. Yet, it is possible to trace the presence of positive elements in the narratives. For one, they strengthen willpower; the protagonist of the *katha* is never really alone and despite a feeling of helplessness, the options are not closed. There is the consciousness of a super power, which comes to the aid of the sufferer; action on part of the character is seen to be the only possible solution. Very often, the performance of the action is in the face of opposition by the family or the social setup. The wife may perform the action without the knowledge of her husband; a woman may have to take an action against the wishes of in-laws. Thus, the *vrat katha*s recognise the need to oppose unfair impositions and encourage rebellion.

There are *katha*s for almost every fast: the specific fasts for the seven days of the week and the ones earmarked for festive occasions, especially religious ceremonies. *Satyanarayan katha* can be seen as a master narrative as it has several narratives embedded in it, narratives which generate other narratives. Additionally, both the fast and the puja are free-floating, they can be observed and performed on any day of the week and a public recital of the *katha* arranged.

Another popular fast is the Santoshi Maa fast observed on Fridays. Santoshi Maa is believed to be the daughter of Ganesh and Ridhi-Sidhi and has the virtue of making both the narrator and the listener content. The word *santosh* means contentment. Ashis Nandy has observed that this goddess is of recent origin, popularised as a counter-move to the growing materialism (Nandy, 'A Report' 147–148) and, I may add, also to act as an emotional alleviation of poverty. It has risen into popularity with the help of the media, the availability of devotional songs and even a film having been made on the subject (Das, 'The Mythological Film'). All of a sudden miracles have accumulated around the goddess. An analysis of this *katha* would allow us to trace the dominant pattern of *vrat katha*s.

Right at the beginning, after her lineage has been traced, the narrator cites her many virtues and the positive effect of devotion to her—she generates a sense of peace and contentment and facilitates tranquillity of the mind and a carefree life. The specific gender connotation is stressed by adding to these the additional benefit that may accrue to young girls. Observance of the fast, it is recommended, will lead to finding a worthy husband, enhance his longevity and also facilitate conception in the case of the childless. The preparatory rituals stress discipline, cleanliness and a general sense of purity. These are all incorporated in the narrative, reinforced through the act of recital. Total concentration is desired in the act of listening. Even the manner of concluding the recital is carefully laid down. These directions serve as the outer frame of the narrative and form part of all *katha*s even if they differ in some minor detail.

The main narrative is that of an old woman who has seven sons. Six of the sons are employed but the youngest is not. It is a happy, united family. Only the youngest, who is lazy and wakes up late, gets only the leftovers. When the son finds this out, he is both angry and unhappy and leaves home in search of a job. In his absence his wife is treated badly by his mother. This young, oppressed daughter-in-law becomes a devotee of Santoshi Maa. As a result, after she begins to fast, on the second Friday, she receives a letter from her husband; on the third, some money arrives. But the husband, increasingly absorbed in his new job, does not come back home. Now, Santoshi Maa is perturbed. She needs to fulfil her promise to her devotee. She decides to appear in the young man's dream and remind him of his wife. Then follows a sequence of events—the husband's return, the rituals of the puja not being adhered to and the repercussions, but later everything falls into place and Santoshi Maa visits their house.

The constant rise and fall of events is in rhythm with the performance of the acts of devotion. But it links action with discipline, emphasising the need to act. There is no undue homage to family ties or hierarchy; instead, interdependence of the husband–wife relationship is stressed. To that extent there is a message of empowerment. But if one were to weigh the advantages against the disadvantages, perhaps the latter would be heavier. In matters of personal discipline, the strength they impart is much less than the ordeal they present when compulsion motivates them.

Women, Nation and Citizenship

Women participated in several ways in the freedom struggle—as *satya-grahi*s, as workers, as members of political parties, as helpers and in multiple other ways. We have a history of women's associations crop-ping up in different parts along regional, political or national levels, right from the early years of the twentieth century, some in support of legal reform and some for political rights. It would be natural to ask if the free-dom struggle added to women's freedom or their sense of national worth and whether their struggle for political equality was a parallel move-ment, which had to be fought for separately. All these queries can lead to several debates. But with the advantage of hindsight, one can safely say that though the freedom movement provided more space to women than conventional social structures, and Gandhi with his work with the masses at the grassroots level inspired them to come out of their houses granting them a social approval and acceptability, it did not really alter gender roles. It is a fact of history that no major revolution ever attends to the gender issues with any continuity or even empathy—not even the most radical revolutions. The freedom movement did, however, lead them to think of the nation as an entity and to attach importance to issues like representation in the assembly, and economic and political rights.

243

In 1927, an editorial in *Vanitakusumam* (Kottayam) gave the wake-up call, 'Will Not Women Awake?' warning women that if they did not fight for their rights, the conservative would never concede them any:

> The work of intrepid struggle and sound bargaining to secure legitimate rights is the responsibility of women themselves. Any complacency on their part, induced by the hope that the government...will concede their rights and authority in full recognition of justice, and the mood of times, would be most foolish. (Devika 109)[19]

Women all over the country joined in the freedom struggle—as revolutionaries, as wives and daughters as well as in their own right. Many served prison terms; others worked in support. They donated their jewellery, spun the charkha, sacrificed their all and when India became a republic, they got equal voting rights and social equality was provided for in the fundamental rights, but both full citizenship and socio-economic equality still remained elusive. First the Partition, which reinforced the idea of a patriarchal state, then the first two Five-Year Plans, which did not follow the pattern of the pre-independence blueprints, managed to sideline gender issues. Despite this uneven post-independence scenario, one needs to go back to the early years of the twentieth century in order to understand and gauge women's role in the freedom struggle, which has left behind a mixed legacy. The 'mother' symbol which was thrust upon them and which they willingly adopted, both liberated and confined them. Radha Kumar in her marathon work *The History of Doing* writes:

> The first half of the twentieth century saw a symbolic use of the mother as a rallying device, from feminist assertions of women's power as mothers of the nation, to terrorist invocations of the protective and ravening mother goddess, to the Gandhian lauding of the spirit of endurance and suffering embodied in the mother. Here too we can trace a shift.... Gandhi's emphasis on the ennobling qualities of motherhood sought explicitly to curb or subdue the most fearsome aspects of femininity, which lie in erotic or tactile domains. (Kumar 2)

244

She also points out that women did not necessarily fall in line with the Gandhian idea of sublimation. Later, in the post-independence phase, the symbol of motherhood was to be replaced by the twin images: a daughter and a working woman (2). But the mother image has a longer history. One could perhaps go further back than Bankim Chandra Chattopadhaya's song 'Vande Mataram' for tracing the lineage of Bharat Mata. But it is a convenient take-off point both as a continuation of the mother-goddess figure and its political association. Written in the early 1870s, it went on to be included in his novel *Anand Math*, where the hymn is used as a war cry. It was sung in the 1896 session of the Congress and used as a slogan in the 1905 Swadeshi Movement in Bengal. It has had a lasting impact through iconic representations of the mother country as a goddess figure on the subconscious of the nation. It also shaped the image of womanhood. Women themselves conveniently resorted to it as a strategy of moving the self to centre stage.[20] The shift to the daughter image, Kumar feels, was especially significant because 'it moved into a new kind of self-exploration, starting from childhood itself'. She points out how through a series of exhibitions, plays and pamphlets, the focus was now on the 'pain and helplessness of being born a girl; the shock of puberty and the associated development of sexual fear; the terrible rejection of being "sent away" at marriage' and other related psycho-social areas (Kumar 2). To my mind, the events of the Partition also impacted this shift, but of that later. For the present, I wish to continue with Kumar's argument, which is very insightful as she draws attention to the 'new subjectivity' which entered the feminist discourse at this point. Women were now bold enough to express emotions hitherto suppressed.

Women's lives became the subject of patriarchal control once again during the riots that accompanied the transfer of population during 1946–1947, the period when the partition of the country was actively under consideration. No longer was it a direct relationship between a human being and the nation-state but it became, for women, a gendered relationship, via religion and patriarchy, to the nation-state. The woman's body, as Veena Das points out:

> Became a sign through which men communicated with each other. The lives of women were framed by the notion that they were to bear permanent witness to the violence of partition. Thus, the political programme of creating the two nations of India and Pakistan was inscribed upon the bodies of women. (*Critical Events* 56)

Many women were abducted, others committed or were made to commit mass suicide (*jauhar*), still others were mutilated or burnt alive, abandoned, sold or turned into public women. The two governments got together and began to negotiate the exchange of women. Subsequently, a large number of women were recovered from both sides of the border. But human beings cannot be transferred easily. Many women had been converted, had married and had borne children during the intervening years. Thus, recovery was problematic for both the women and their two families, rather three families—their parental, their marital (if they were already married) and their new families in the land where they were living at the time of recovery. Not only did concepts like family honour and purity become major issues, but emotional ties, a sense of belonging, the realisation of the full human being, paternity rights—all came into play. In several partition novels, these issues are debated. *Challia* (1960) was one of the earliest films on this theme. Amrita Pritam's novel *Pinjar* was also later made into a film. Several love tales—true life—have emerged out of it, such as the Punjabi film *Shaheed-e-Mohabbat Boota Singh*, which is based on a real life story.

Even when women were recovered, they were often rejected by their families and had to fend for themselves, or when accepted, the problem of their children remained. Many women were reluctant to come back as they had developed deep associations with their new families or guilt and shame forced them into self-erasure. Those who stayed there, converted and tried to belong, but were also at some stage rejected by both sides.

Khamosh Pani (2005) tells one such tale of the rejection a mother has to contend with when her son finds out that she was born a Sikh. The well she had refused to jump in at the time of the partition becomes her final destination after the rejection by her son. The combination of patriarchy and religion forms a deadly anti-human discourse.

Veena Das, through her researches, found that if the disrepute was not widely known, the natal family accepted the girl and then disposed of her in whatever way they could—which may well be through marriage to an unsuitable partner, either old or otherwise inferior and disadvantaged (*Critical Events* 64). Family and national honour forced women into a daughter's role. Revenge, legality and purity formed a tight net, leaving women hardly any option or choice (64–83). There were debates about treating women as adults or treating them as property—and as such re-sponsibility of the nation-state. In 1949, a bill on Abducted Person Re-covery and Restoration was placed before the Constituent Assembly. The debates that followed showed a division of opinion. Commenting on N. Gopalaswami Ayyangar's speech with which he introduced the bill, Das writes: 'This interest in women was not premised upon their definition as citizens, but as sexual and reproductive beings' (68), the focus being on their reproductivity. No relationship, no matter where they were, either compelled or of choice, could be free of the complex interweaving of love and hatred, alienation and belonging, legality and lack of freedom. Human relationships were shorn of all tenderness and compassion (79). The orthodox concept of *shudhikaran* resurfaced. The transition to the daughter image was fraught with pain and suffering and led into captiv-ity and dependence.

A great deal of literature about Partition is by men. For a sample selec-tion, I turn to *Stories about the Partition of India* (Bhalla). The volume contains 63 stories, only 9 of which are by women. In another volume, *Mapmaking* (Sengupta), only 2 out of the 10 stories are by women. Most of the stories written by men ignore the woman's perspective. They fo-cus on paternal anguish and on the body of the women. Amongst these men are sensitive writers like Sadaat Hasan Manto and Rajinder Singh Bedi. Women's stories, however, present very different issues and perspectives. They move away from power politics. They explore the nature of belonging: how does one belong? Jamila Hashmi's short story, 'Exile', works with multiple discourses and several refrains.[21] The dominant frame is the abduction of Sītā and the nature of forced exile. The story opens with the beginning of the Dussehra festivities and works through the consciousness of the nameless woman protagonist, a Muslim girl abducted during the partition riots. Memories of her arrival in the village, of Gurpal's offering her as a handmaiden to his grandmother, intermingle with the continuity of the Dussehra festivities, the burning of the effigies, the glow of fire, the swings in the fair, the setting sun and the noise of the crowd. She recalls how she had been brought to Sangraon amidst screams and lamenting, the reversal of all kinds of marriage rites and silence instead of celebrations awaiting her. Further back are memories of her own childhood, her brother's affection, her mother's love, her father's protection. Then there are other separations like her brother's trip abroad. Dreams, both conscious and unconscious, form a refrain in the story (Hashmi 51, 60, 63, 64, 66). There is a constant movement between the past and present. Short, clipped sentences punctuate the narrative: 'Exile is terrible' (51), 'Keep walking. Always' (54), 'Life is difficult' (57), 'I am terrified' (62), 'Seasons change' (65). And then there is the world of birds and trees, of the bond between the tree and the earth, the roots that burrow deep in the ground (51), of her own identification with a tree and of her home with a wilderness (54). The women singing under the *neem* tree (65) and the constant references to the change of seasons, all emphasise the persistence of roots. She cannot go back even when the authorities come tracing her, for suddenly she realises that besides everything else, she is also a mother and that too of a daughter (64). Her self-alienation is now complete: the body has been violated, dreams turned into disillusionment and kinships snapped. A

248

complete transformation takes place—'My heart has become empty. I have become Lakshmi' (57), trapped in the goddess image.

Lalithambika Antherjanam's two stories (in the same volume) work through metaphors of birth and motherhood. 'A Leaf in the Storm' is located in Punjab while 'The Mother of Dhirendru Mazumdar' in Bengal. Jyoti, the protagonist of 'A Leaf in the Storm', is one of the fifty women recovered from western Punjab. She is furious with herself and the world at large, and rejects food as she would rather choose death than life. Pregnant with the unwanted child of rape, her anger has turned inwards. The doctor coaxes her to eat, stressing the value of life and the human ability to endure. Accounts of her earlier self-assertion contrast sadly with her present state as she withdraws into her sullen world. Babies are born and babies also die or are killed. Guilt, crime, law—all have been totally erased from their lives. And then a distinguished visitor arrives, talks to them about the need for their social acceptance and advises them to think of their unborn children as the first citizens of a free India. And Jyoti thinks: 'How ironical…. Are they citizens of India alone? That is, of India as we conceive of her today?' (Antherjanam, 'A Leaf' 167). Memories of the past crowd her mind, memories of her home, her childhood full of freedom, the flight, the capture and the rape and they all come to rest now in the refugee camp where she is the prisoner of her body and of the unborn child. When the child is born, she abandons it, only to come back and hold the baby to her breast. The child is truly the citizen of free India, and the mother's claim to the nation is legitimised through the child.

There is a reference to an old woman in the story, mother of nine and grandmother of fifty. The authorial comment is, 'She has indeed been a mother to the whole village, to both Hindus and Muslims' (162). This woman appears in a different context in Lalithambika Antherjanam's other story, 'The Mother of Dhirendru Mazumdar'. She also has a parallel existence in Ismat Chughtai's 'Roots' with the difference that the refugee woman (in 'A Leaf in the Storm') has lost all her family while in 'Roots' the fleeing family is brought back. 'The Mother of Dhirendru Mazumdar' is a first-person narration in the voice of Shanti Mazumdar, mother of nine children, of whom five were sacrificed for India, four for Pakistan. In this manner she belongs to both the nations. Unwilling to leave, she has been forcibly brought to India—as a refugee, as an out-sider. Once again, words from Vande Mataram surface in the story: 'The divine mother as *Suphala, Sujala, Sansyashyamala*—we brought up our children as we meditated on the thousands of dazzling swords that adorn her many hands. We sacrificed them for her liberation.... Are they a part of your history?' (Antherjanam, 'The Mother' 512).

Dhiren is a revolutionary and once he provides cover to the leader of a terrorist organisation in his own home, who is disguised as a *sanyasin*. Shanti Mazumdar finds out the truth only when the *sanyasin* is taking leave of them: 'Forgive me mother, I am Surya Sen. Also known as Master-da. We worship our motherland in the form of Maha Kali. Swords in a hundred hands. The blood smeared head of the enemy! Intestines for garlands' (514). At this point, Shanti Mazumdar is transformed into an-other woman called Banglamata. Her son calls her a goddess and tells her to smile at his death and sing Vande Mataram. The region and the language acquire greater importance than religion. But Partition takes place: the country is divided and she is brought to India, as a refugee: 'If you tell me that this is not my country, I won't let myself die on this soil' (519). The question of nationhood remains unanswered: where does one belong and how does one belong? There is no direct route available to a woman. It is ironical that the helplessness and rootlessness of women is ruled over by the image of a goddess.

Jasodhara Bagchi in a very perceptive article on the Partition, 'Free-dom in an Idiom of Loss', quotes from Tagore's poem and refers to the vision of the goddess:

A scimitar shines in your hand
And your left hand quells our fears

Your eyes are tender and smiling

But your third eye scorches and sears

O mother, we cannot turn our eyes from you.... (Translated by Chandreyee Niyogi)

Bagchi goes on to observe, 'This extreme Hinduised form of the three-eyed mother goddess made cultural nationalism a strong divisive force.' Further, the identification of chastity with honour went on to make women 'potential victims' of communal conflicts, defining nationhood through wifehood and motherhood.

In Qurratulain Hyder's story, 'When the Prisoners Were Released, the Times Had Changed', expansion rather than division is centre stage in terms of both time and space. History is recounted from the pre-partition days through the childhood of the narrator and Andamans are taken into its fold. The struggles and sacrifices of the freedom fighters recall the proverbial Kala Pani (the Black Waters; political prisoners were sent to the Andaman and this was referred to as Kala Pani). Andamans have now become a home for refugees, a new home where they are trying to come to terms with their dislocation. The narrative moves from the memory of the childhood at Andamans, accounts of the island's history, its Burma connections and its political prisoners to a visit to Dehradun, recollections of Nehru, to the World Agricultural Fair in Delhi and back to Calcutta and the Lalit Kala Akademi. A mix of generations of rehabilitated refugees allows the narrative to embrace the whole of India. She wants to tell the freedom fighter she meets at the exhibition of her longing to write the history of India. In this story, there is a move from personal consciousness to a national one.

Debjani Sengupta in her 'Afterword' to *Mapmaking: Partition Stories from the Two Bengals*, comments on the difference in the situations of Bengal and Punjab. In Punjab there was a mass exodus while in Bengal there was a steady trickling in of refugees from across the border. Differences are reflected not only in the nature of the experience, but also in the response to it. Shared territories, shared languages and culture

251

had formed a parallel on both the borders, yet there were differences. Perhaps these differences were there because of the disparity in economic resources in Punjab and the different construction of masculinity, or the different histories of dislocations on the two borders. Sengupta observes that narratives and films from Bengal focus more on the refugee consciousness[22] and debate the notions of legitimacy and citizenship, the meaning of identity and belonging. There is a great deal that is submerged in memories or even in memories pushed aside, deliberately avoiding a direct confrontation with the nature of violence. Ashis Nandy, in his 'Introduction' to the same volume, looks for an answer to the avoidance of writing about the partition violence by some of our leading intellectuals and asks the question why this silence? Was it a deliberate effort to start life anew and 'contain bitterness, a way of repairing community life, interpersonal trust and known moral world?' Guilt is another area of exploration in several partition narratives. Trauma, insanity and coma, all are offshoots of this guilt. Partition narratives have explored the guilt arising out of a brutal act, but have not examined in depth the guilt experienced by a rapist. Jamila Hashmi marginally explores Gurpal's sense of guilt, but in the main, the male perpetrators of crime do not experience guilt. (Intizar Hussain's stories are an exception.)

Narratives by women writers do carve a subjecthood through memory, perception, recall and dream structures. They also constitute it through the body and the act of giving birth. But more than this, the narratives emphasise the flow of life by comparisons with the world of nature. The young adolescent girl in Attia Hosain's story, 'After the Storm', recalls only the journey of escape from the camp and the journey to the home of adoption. For the rest she is engaged in collecting flowers and stringing them together. The desire to revive life is apparent beyond the trauma and the amnesia. The Hindus protect the Mother Goddess, the Muslims, the ancestral graves, but women, falling outside both these categories, begin to examine their own rootedness. This process is strongly visible in Jamila Hashmi's 'Exile' and Lalithambika Antherjanam's 'The

Mother of Dhirendru Mazumdar'. And the consciousness of Raka, so sensitively explored through Alam's own consciousness in 'Alam's Own House', written by a man, is another narrative of rootedness. It is not only men who are hurt, but women too feel the pain of dislocation (85). It is this pain that binds them to the soil and the nation—an independent consciousness not routed through their male guardians. The meaning of Partition narratives emerges not merely from their themes or the subject–object relationships, but from their aesthetics, which move beyond 're-alism' and realistic description. They reveal psyches and subconscious selves through hallucinations, surrealism, images, and aesthetics of space. They unfold their meaning through the simultaneities they create with memory recall, flow of history, and individual response.

Krishna Sobti's short story 'Where is My Mother?' can be interpreted at several levels. Alok Bhalla categorises it as a story which is commu-nally charged because it denies 'the claim to holiness of all religions' (Bhalla xxvi). I would read it as a parallel account of male and female relationships to the nation. Bahadur Yunus Khan is fighting for the cre-ation of a new country, and this demands sacrifice, that too of the self. Even as he drives through this nightmare of violence and bloodshed, his heart goes out in compassion to the little girl lying unconscious on the roadside, her body torn by rape. He picks her up in order to save her. As she lay in his arms, a vision rises before his eyes, the eyes not of a mur-derer, but 'of a man full of veneration' as the memory of his little sister Nooran comes to him. He overcomes his hatred for the *kafir* and pleads with the doctors to save her, claims her as his sister but the traumatised girl is unable to transcend her fear of the 'other' which has inhabited her whole being (433–439). What does this story tell us in terms of nation and womanhood? What does it say for the relationship between the self and the other? While men sacrifice the self for the nation, women are expected to hold on to the body. Their bodily self is perceived as contain-ing their whole self. The relationship with the other is also perceived in limited terms of religion and otherness of the gender. Bhalla has missed the poignancy of the story where the man conquers his self, his upbringing, his limited sense of nationhood to experience a human emotion. But the girl, young and abandoned, is unable to transcend the fear of the religious other, which in this case is also the national and gender other, in her present state of trauma. Daughters of Mother India have yet to work out terms of belonging that encompass the whole self, the body as well as the mind. They need to reinterpret the body and expand the notion of space to include history and identity. The self-in-the-world has to outgrow inherited constraints of traditional moulds in order to reinvent itself.

The shift from the mother figure was part of this phenomena. There was a felt need to get rid of the all-controlling, goddess-like, strong self-sufficient mother or a sacrificing woman, willing to accommodate all unreasonable demands. None of the major women writers deal with strong, all present mothers. Mothers are either absent or ill or alienated or even marginalised figures.

The Inheritance of Activism

In an article titled 'Structured Silences of Women', Ritu Menon quotes the Palestinian woman writer Fadwa Taquan:

> Although confined and deprived of a homeland, my father wanted me to write political poetry…while the corrupt laws and customs insisted that I remain secluded behind a wall, not able to attend assemblies of men, not hearing the current debates, not participating in public life. Where was I to find an intellectual atmosphere in which to write political poetry?…I could not participate in any aspect of life unless I pretended to be another person. (Menon WS-3)

I have quoted Fadwa Tuquan at length to stress the denial of public space and the resultant need for an imaginative projection into another,

254

a different self. Again, it highlights the importance of both location and space. This is a projection of what her father desires for her in time present, but alongside runs the past described as 'custom' which hampers her freedom. Parallel to this runs the code inherited from the past, what she refers to as 'custom'. Indian women in the later half of the nineteenth century found themselves in a similar dilemma. Confined by custom to domesticity, limited by the colonial discourse to cultural laws, they temporarily worked out a negotiation between their societal roles and their inner selves as we have seen in the foregoing discussion of early writings, autobiographies and print journalism. Women were seriously concerned with issues affecting the socio-political life of the country. They came together, formed associations, uniting with the aim of giving support in terms of dissemination of ideas, gathering supporters, spreading awareness and debating issues of national importance.

Radha Kumar devotes two chapters of her work to women's active participation in politics: 'Towards Becoming "The Mothers of the Nation"' and 'Organization and Struggle'. Their work was three-pronged: social reform, especially where women's status was concerned, communal harmony and political freedom with equality for women. Some of the names that recur over and over again are women like Kumudini and Sarala Debi Ghoshal. Kumudini was a supporter of revolutionary terrorism. Brought up in a Brahmo family, she opposed the Bengal partition of 1905 and was the editor of *Suprabhat* (1907–1914). In one of the pieces Kumudini wrote in *Bangalakshmi*, 'What Women Should Do When the Motherland is in Distress', anthologised in *Talking of Power* (*Bangalakshmi* was a magazine she edited for two years 1925–27), she advocates a solidarity across language and region, recommends boycott of foreign goods, and advises women to be prepared to sacrifice (*Talking of Power* 94–99).

It is interesting to note that women did not only take up issues like demanding better education, economic independence, political franchise, but gradually they began to participate in political discussions, in the meetings of the Indian National Congress and also spoke against the British laws regulating prostitution. They took up issues like rape, race and racism. Sarala Debi Ghosal was very articulate in her advocacy of physical culture and especially invoked young men to take up the challenge of protecting their womenfolk (Kumar 37).

Women also formed independent organisations. Swarn Kumari Debi started an organisation, *Sakhi Samiti*, in 1886, held annual craft melas and in general worked for self-reliance and empowerment. Sarala Debi was her daughter. Kumar comments that she was 'one of the architects of a militant mother-centred nationalism which was to take to revolutionary terrorism in the twentieth century' (38). Sarala Debi had multidirectional interests. It is in the work of such women that the early seeds of modern feminism were sown. Writing and editing apart, education, its syllabus and quality of textbooks, handicrafts and their marketing, and political vision—all were of importance to them. An organisation like SEWA and other contemporary activist interests like dowry, sati, rape, domestic violence, right to property—all of them trace their lineage to the activities of these women. The image of a working woman—a middle or upper class working woman—was also created by them. Sarala Debi took up school-teaching much against her parents' wishes, wanting to flee the cage of home (Kumar 39). She was a thorough rebel. Not only did she organise a gymnasium in her father's house, she chose the figure of a Hindu landlord and parricide, Paratapaditya, and raised him to the status of a warrior hero, thus shocking the orthodoxy. But this resurrection of militant valour, in her opinion, was preferable to docility. This was also the period when the mother-goddess figures of Kali, Chandi and Durga were inspirational models. The glorification of the Mother Goddess is both empowering and disempowering. If it traps women into a role, it also, as Naomi Goldberg has observed, summons memories of a prehistoric past. This 'focus on the past is used to confer a sense of reality and legitimacy on contemporary women's experience' (Goldberg 147). Goldberg's point has a relevance because, as she observes, the myths not only draw attention to the complexity of the female experience but they 'dignify that experience by revealing its ancient roots' (147). In national history it carries on an interactive discourse.

Another woman, a Parsi, Bhikaji Rustomji Cama, was also involved in the revolutionary movement. Deeply influenced by Mazzini and Garibaldi, she held the view that militant opposition was justified. Her group started a journal, *Bande Mataram*, and published it from Geneva. The first issue came out in 1909, the year in which Gandhi's *Hind Swaraj* was published. Thus the non-violence movement and the revolutionary movement worked as parallel movements, partly rising in opposition to each other. Women were involved in both. Tagore's *Home and the World* and *Char Adhaya* give graphic representations, as does Sarat Chandra Chatterjee's *Pather Dabi*, of the early years of the twentieth century and the call of the revolutionaries.

There was Western contact but of an altogether different kind. Women like Annie Besant, Margaret Cousins and Madeline Slade (rechristened Mira by Gandhi) were also participants and took active interest. But they did not bring the British approach or even British women's feminist struggles to India. Each one of them found some other point of response and attraction in the Indian situation. Annie Besant, along with Sarojini Naidu, Margaret Cousins and eight other women, met Mr Montague in 1917 to demand votes for Indian women. In 1919, Besant founded the National Home Rule League and later, in 1925, drafted a Bill for demanding Home Rule for India (Kumar 48).

The freedom struggle produced a whole lot of women leaders like Sarojini Naidu, Kamaladevi Chattopadhyaya, Aruna Asaf Ali, Rajkumari Amrit Kaur, Kumari Lajjavati (who happened to be the Principal of Kanya Maha Vidyalaya when I joined the institution in 1959 as a young teacher), Sucheta Kripalini, Begum Shah Nawaz, Durgabai Deshmukh, Begum Kidwai and several others. Their personal lives also reflect a degree of rebelliousness, courage and determination. These women displayed an enormous strength of mind and determination of purpose.

Kamaladevi Chattopadhyaya resented Gandhi's instructions when he forbade women members from actually participating in the Salt March and Sarojini Naidu persisted in joining it on the last day in Dandi and was promptly arrested. The Congress Committee withdrew the veto on women's participation and women volunteers joined their male counterparts in picketing the legislatures, selling salt openly on busy streets and thus not only spreading a sense of patriotism, arousing the sense of dignity of the common people, both of men and women, but also succeeding in spreading the message far and wide and creating a grassroots revolution. Salt was manufactured by all kinds of people—tribals, children, urban and rural women. These women stood at street corners with packets of salt and said, 'We have broken the Salt Law and we are free! Who will buy the salt of freedom?'[23]

Many of these women had to face opposition from conservative fathers and possessive and strict husbands as now they were seen as stepping outside the circle of family obedience, but they went along. Male attitudes represented various hues: support, approval, pride as well as disapproval, rejection and insistence on choosing either family or country (Kumar, *The History of Doing* 81). Yet they (the women) boldly went ahead. One may notice that several of the marriages were inter-caste, inter-religious, inter-lingual or inter-regional. Thus to step into an unknown world, often against the wishes of the family, required a tremendous amount of courage and was a personal act of self-assertion.[24] From among the tribal women, Rani Gudiallo was one person who got involved in active participation at the age of 13 and led several campaigns (Kumar, *The History of Doing* 84), and the revolutionaries had several women who laid down their lives for the country or served life sentences. Durga Bhabhi, Bina Das, Shanti Ghosh and Suniti Chaudhary are only few of these names.

A mild flirtation with Western feminism that might have taken place was quickly nipped in the bud by nationalist feelings and the anti-British stand. Several women leaders of the early twentieth century firmly disassociated themselves from it (Kumar 88). Moreover, there was an awareness that different conditions and needs of women required a spreading over of strategies. Falling in line with this awareness are the shifts in the image of the Indian woman. Kumar observes that while Besant glorified the 'self-sacrificing Hindu women, Naidu the self-sacrificing Indian mother, and Cousins the proud representatives of the "great Hindu race and the strong Muslim people"', Kamaladevi Chattopadhyaya went on to glorify the self-sacrificing peasant woman (Kumar 79).

The concept of *shakti* entered the formulation of feminist strategy. It was a way in which women could simultaneously indigenise the movement and silence male opposition. Even now, one of the activist songs speaks of woman as a firebrand. '*Hum bharat ki nari hein phool nahin, chingari hain*' (We, the women of India, are not flowers but live embers). Joanna Liddle and Rama Joshi begin their book *Daughters of Independence* with reference to the Shakti cult:

> The women's movement has a long history in India.... The Shakti cults go back centuries, and the concept of Shakti—the female power principle—was recognised thousands of years ago. In this form the women's movement represents, not merely an oppositional force fuelled by anger, a rather negative reaction to oppression, but the development of a distinctive female culture, a positive creative force inspiring men and women alike. (5)

Earlier in this work I have commented on the concept of Shakti as a derived power. But here, the issue is not of the interpretation of the concept but the use which the women's movement put it to. Liddle and Joshi address the social issue of female subordination and locate the practice in class and caste, and distance themselves from the belief that the women's movement has Western origins. Why was such an idea circulated in the first place? One, because when the men disapproved of women's freedom, it was easy to lay the responsibility at other people's doors; two, the British prided themselves as liberating Indian women from the chains of orthodoxy; three, the missionaries reinforced it (6–7). But, in all respects, a movement which is grounded in socio-cultural situations cannot be derived from other cultures: 'Women's resistance to oppression in India neither began nor ended with the British Women's intervention, but had its roots in the Indian social structure and cultural heritage' (49).[25] Their struggles were against child marriage, for access to education and other social customs.

There is some debate about when the movement actually began. While Liddle and Joshi locate its origins in active political activism and label it the first wave, and the late 1970s as the second wave (20, 75), other thinkers work through three waves or phases. The reform initiative of the nineteenth century, whether by men or women, are identified as the first phase; the second phase begins with women actively assuming an agency and participating in politics and the third coincides with the international wave of feminism of the 1970s (Khullar). In each of these phases there has been a contact with the outside world: cultural encounter in the first phase leading to an analysis of social situation, the rise of different associations and group formations like Brahmo Samaj and Arya Samaj; the second was influenced and was in large measure part of the freedom struggle; the third is an aftermath of the lull of the post-independence phase. The post-independence phase threw up its own contradictions. The reinsertion of patriarchal norms in the post-Partition situation, the surfacing of woman-headed households and the emergence of the working woman, the growing materialism in society resulting in dowry deaths and other social atrocities—all gradually came together to form resistance forces.

Liddle and Joshi see the period of the first 30 years after independence as one when the movement disappeared. Women's subordination remained embodied in personal relations of the patriarchal family (75). The state also conveniently ignored their economic role. But salvage operations continued and organised groups worked for issues such as providing refuge to destitute women, battered housewives and other such categories (76).[26]

But it needs to be recognised that such programmes focused more on women's welfare and were coordinated by the Central Social Welfare Board, established in 1953. It was with the setting up of the Committee on the Status of Women in India (CSWI), at the UN's mandate for all member countries, that the women's movement became more analytic, now specifically focusing on women as individuals, and Women Studies Centres were established in major universities. The report of the Committee *Towards Equality* identified discriminatory practices, and wider social issues came under the purview of gender-based approaches. Violence against women, non-recognition of their economic inputs, population control policies—all came in for a critical analysis and were issues in public debate.

The Constitutional provisions often worked in contradictory directions. As several writers have pointed out, the equality conceded to women in Article 15 of the Constitution is contradicted by the application of different personal laws, inheritance laws, etc. The rising demand for a Uniform Civil Code was pushed into the background when the issue was hijacked by Rightist groups. It is obvious that the aspirations for equality were often thwarted by other considerations and fear of misuse of the women's agenda for other political causes.

The role of the state in rising up to the occasion and giving support to the women's cause is noteworthy. After its initial neglect and sidelining of women's issues, the sixth five-year plan document, for the first time, included a chapter on 'Women and Development' (1980–1985), the government set up a Department of Women and Child Development in 1985 and the UGC extended support to Women Studies Centres in major universities. They facilitated both consciousness-raising and research in women's issues from an interdisciplinary perspective. Further, recovery of lost texts and histories also became possible. One needs to admit that state support could at times also become a negative factor, limiting or controlling the activities of the centres. Several universities appointed men as Directors, thereby denying women leadership positions. Nevertheless, the general outcome has been good with some centres doing excellent work, publishing material and participating in national and international conferences. One needs to recognise the immense contribution that Women's Studies have made as a discipline and the excellent quality of research they have generated. Academic interest has been in constant touch with activism, each drawing inspiration from the other. The partnership has yielded a rich harvest. A constant process of questioning of structures, methodologies, approaches and age-old myths is at work. The best thing about it is that the really motivated have not allowed complacency to set in. The issues are not discussed or debated to meet individual ego needs.

Yet, as Mala Khullar points out, much remains to be done both where conceptual inputs are required and where grassroots analysis is concerned (26–27). The discipline still remains marginalised in universities and amongst student bodies. One may add to this that it has failed to develop into 'Gender Studies'; men do not play as constructive a role in it as they did in the nineteenth century or in the early decades of the twentieth. This change, and the changing nature of masculinity across class and caste, needs to be addressed. The causes for this are much deeper than a mere gender divide. One stands at a crossroad where, at some point, issues of globalisation and issues related to tradition need to be brought together in healthy gender equations. An important aspect of this is the direction the women's movement is likely to take. The concerns are now not only of gender but also of human rights, not only as members of a society but also as members of a nation.

The women's movement is alive and thriving, but there seems to be a sharp division as activists often relate more to their political affiliation than to the women's cause; a very small percentage of the affluent are visible in it—it remains dominantly a middle-class leadership, even as

it concerns itself with other classes. The positive aspects are a growing awareness in rural sectors, the political awakening facilitated by the
reservation for women at the panchayat level and the temporary coming
together over major concerns. Every now and then a court judgement
either propels the movement forth or results in a setback; every now
and then a law is enacted which attacks the base of gender equality or
religious equality (Khullar 26–27).[27] The complex web of religion, caste
and gender tightens its hold in times of riots, communal disharmony and
even elections.

Wasbir Hussain's documented account of women-headed households
in war-torn Assam, *Homemakers without the Men* (2006), brings home
the extraordinary claims strife makes on the survival instincts of women
as well as the degree of dislocation and subterfuge that enter their lives.
These women are widows, sisters and mothers of the men who are either
dead, crippled, missing or fugitives. These absent men are on the run
or have been killed in 'encounters' or shot dead by unidentified gun-
men (xi). The account stresses several things—the constant pursuit and
persecution, an operation for cleansing the militant-infested areas, on
one hand, and the no-return situation that the fugitives are placed in, on
the other. As each party becomes increasingly brutalised in this run-and-
catch situation, family life is disrupted, earning capacities are affected,
sexual deprivation takes place and the village is constantly under threat.
Hussain observes, 'Marble or concrete memorials by the roadside, list-
ing the names of the dead, were grim reminders of the mindless violence
that the area had witnessed' (xiii). Passersby stop to admire them without
calculating the human loss. These low intensity conflicts are an ongoing drain on human energy, resources and values. Many women (and
other victims) are traumatised, the very humanity of men and women
is assaulted and violated. Hardly any counselling is catered for. State
rehabilitation action is limited, inadequate and characterised by breaks
and interruptions. The women and children are constantly subjected to
harassment. Army trucks roar in, breaking the silence of the night, and

soldiers surround their homes and questioning sessions begin. There are cases of breakdowns, suicides, stress and loneliness. It is not that it is only the women who suffer, but the question is: how do they survive this trauma? Also, are there any ideological forces developing either to control or resist this terrorism?

The Naga underground movement, the long-lasting army presence, the low-intensity conflict and the hide-and-seek that accompanies it, presents a similar scene. Temsula Ao in a collection of short stories, *These Hills Called Home: Stories from a War Zone*, has depicted the tragedies of ordinary lives when dreams are snuffed young, when violence goes berserk and the task of living is interwoven with insecurity. There are multiple problems: the underground movement has its own jealousies, atrocities and barbarity; villages are divided between the underground on one hand and the army on the other; families when they harbour militants, whether their own or someone else's, are persecuted; a sub-nationalism based on hostility to the government and loyalty to the community raises its head, adding to the decades-old problem of identity.

In one of the stories, 'The Last Song', Ao writes about a young girl who 'was born to sing'. Even as a baby, she would join community singing in her 'own version', mostly consisting of loud shrieks and screams. This girl named Apenyo would often embarrass her mother by joining the solo singing in church, so much so that the mother stopped going to church. The child apparently had inherited this talent from her dead father. As she grew up, she did well at school and her singing talents also blossomed. But then the trouble started. As the crescendo of expectations rose with an approaching festival, a raid on the village took place and plans for an attack on the villages were afoot. During a ceremony on the dedication day of a new church, the church was surrounded by soldiers. Apenyo, nevertheless, burst out singing and others accompanied her. At this the soldiers were enraged. The Captain dragged the girl away in order to punish her by raping her. When the mother ran to her rescue, she too was victimised. It degenerated into a gang rape. And when the villagers, after the departure of the soldiers, came to take their limp bodies away, they were hedged in and the church set on fire. This is how crimes are committed and all witnesses are destroyed. The village is as it were, erased, the guns emptied and the house of God destroyed. The Captain appeared to 'have gone mad'. Apenyo's song ended amidst the ashes of the whole congregation. The song continues to haunt the Captain but it can in no way revive the hopes and dreams that lay buried all around. Apenyo's song dwells in the wind. And on a cold December night, 'an old storyteller gathers the young of the land round the leaping flames of the hearth and squats on the bare earth among them to pass on the story of the Black Sunday when a young and beautiful singer sang her last song even as one more Naga village began weeping for her ravaged and ruined children' (33).

Storytelling thus carries on history, creates legends and keeps memories alive. But larger questions as to how can healing take place and whether or not any solutions can be worked out remain unanswered. There is a natural inclination to rake up old memories of both hurt and heroism. Rani Gaidinlui's acts of heroism in the protest movement against colonialism (193) are similarly extolled. But other ways of protest are also there. A woman protestor, Irom Chanu Sharmila, has been on fast since November 2000 for the withdrawal of the Armed Forces Special Powers Act of 1958. She is arrested for a year, then released for twenty-four hours and then arrested again. Briefly she was shifted to New Delhi from the J.N. Hospital, Imphal and put under the care of doctors in All India Institute of Medical Sciences. The move brought her case a greater visibility. Today, nearly nine years into her fast, the body shows the strain even as the spirit is strong. Other movements have sprung up around her fast, thus creating waves of protest.

In addition, there are peace activities that have been initiated by women. Rita Manchanda in *We Do More Because We Can: Naga Women in the Peace Process* (2004) has traced the development of these movements. As mothers, not only is their need for peace more intense than that of men, they also have the sensitivity and the position to spread the message of peace. There is need to recognise this aspect for it signifies a major leap forward in several ways: it aims at reconciliation and restoration to normal life; it projects women in a more active role and stresses their consciousness and responsiveness to more humanistic concerns. From a slightly different perspective, one can recognise that it relocates them in traditionally feminine roles—as mothers and wives. Manchanda has a whole chapter on mother–son relationships and stresses the space of the kitchen as one where communication can take place. Whatever their place in feminism maybe, these peace initiatives are important both at political and personal levels. This is then not passive nurturing but a creative process of nurturing, extending beyond the physical fact of birthing. One needs to re-examine the title of Wasbir Hussain's book. He does not say 'women without men' which would stress gender and sexuality, but 'homemakers'. This home-making now has to move out of the confined space of the home into areas of larger concerns such as survival, development and life itself. Moves such as peace activism thus account for the shift from pure feminist concerns into larger political movements and human rights. They signify an expansion of the women's 'world'.

The Punjab militancy, the 1984 riots, and the Gujarat riots—each one of these happenings has its aftermath. The boundaries between the personal and the political, between personal rights and human rights, even between religion and humanity are being recast. Whether women like it or not, both as citizens and individuals they have to participate in a larger sphere. Having accepted this reality, we need now to move ahead.

Some of the questions which need to be addressed are: Is the movement passing through a crisis? Has it reached its highest point? Is there a backlash as cases of violence multiply? Where do we go from here? With the rise of fundamentalism and rightist politics, the nature of the challenge has changed. The confrontation between orthodoxy and the need for equality is more direct than ever before. Do we identify ourselves with a larger 'Third World feminism' or do we shelve the gender issue

266

in favour of other oppressive social problems like violence and atrocities against the disadvantaged caste prejudices? Does gender have a role in all this? Finally, in what equation does one place the 'self'—initially seen as the male 'self'—to the concept of 'self' a woman in India holds today.

A host of questions, all leading us into different directions, have now risen. Placing gender centre stage, I hope to address some of them in the next chapter, which should also lead me to some kind of conclusion, may be a temporary one, at this point of time.

VII

Tracing the Difference

The word 'trace' has a multiplicity of meanings ranging from a faint mark, a connectivity, a similarity to an absent presence. As children, we were in the habit of tracing maps and floral designs in order to reproduce them, fill them in and give them a fullness. Semiology has lifted both 'trace' and 'difference' into a philosophical, metaphysical plane. Both the terms have Derridean connections—one pointing to the similarity, the other to the difference. But when I used the word, my emphasis was on exploring the cultural constructs, the manner in which they are represented, that is, their nature as signifiers and connecting them with what they signified to examine the manner in which they had changed through social pressures and political interventions. Secondly, by examining the nature of these cultural constructs and the fixity they had acquired or the hollowness that now inhabited them, the aim was to emphasise the difference between the cultural systems between the East and the West.

Further to this, it has been my contention that because of the difference in cultural systems and political histories, the origins and nature of the feminist movement are different in the two worlds. Women, in the Indian context, are opposing different kinds of power structures, not all of which are male, though the construction of many may be patriarchal. They are also carrying on a constant struggle against their own self-image and the cultural construction of femininity. Such struggles even as they are politico-economical are also heavily laced with psychological conflicts. Autobiographies, memoirs or public struggles often do not reveal the depth of these psychological conflicts. The struggle has not been linear or consistently progressive. There have been phases of regression, increased conservatism and orthodoxy. At times, the processes of modernisation have run parallel to the regressive hegemonic controls.

When theory takes over, it often assumes an underlying universality or an underlying difference. One needs to acknowledge that nothing is universally true or universally applicable; similarly, differences too contain some trace of the universal. All categories have the potential of becoming stereotypes. Perspectives differ; realities differ and histories are different as well. They do not flow like parallel lines that do not meet at any point, but there are points when they meet and alter the flow of the other. Cultural encounter, as either an influence or a threat, is a reality and there is no way it can be wished away.

Again, all—and if not all, most—conceptual terms also work within their defining contexts, whether they relate to perception, methodology or periodisation. Modernity, postmodernity and feminism collect a lot of cultural baggage. It is a mistake to shift these concepts in their pristine purity as conceptualised, theorised and historicised in Western thought to other geographical and historical locales without taking into account the difference in inherited philosophical traditions.

Placing the feminist movement against these objectives, one may ask the question: what is it that women in India are striving for? The category again is not simple: women are defined by a variety of roles and classifications—caste, class, urban, rural, tribal, education and its absence, married, abandoned, widowed or divorced, single, dependent or economically independent, barren or productive, lesbian or heterosexual—the list could go on. I have somehow left out (by oversight) the category of religion, which is a dominating factor in India. It controls the socialisation processes, divides women and creates divisive social practices, defines the personal law, is hegemonic and ritualistic; it restricts their freedom but also if they transgress, it leaves them with a sense of guilt. Religion, paradoxically, also governs the way they relate to their bodies—pure or impure, virgin or not, worthy or not—it shapes their self-image as well as their sexuality. Religion is also indirectly responsible for treating Indian culture as a monolithic structure. The presence of Muslims, Christians, Jains, Buddhists and Sikhs is barely acknowledged. Projections of women in the different religious and social structures have shades of difference that need to be made visible and their interventions recognised both for an assessment of reality and for accuracy in history. The transformations which take place when similar concepts find a different habitat are significant factors when we work towards any tentative definition/s.

The term history also begs a question: how do we define it? Krishna Sobti, a noted Hindi writer, prefixed a long poem to her novel *Zindagi Nama*, which means a saga of life. This poem, part of which I am reproducing below, seeks to define history through unwritten narratives, lived experiences, perspectives and voices of the margins (I hesitate to use the word 'margins'; perhaps, 'ordinary' or 'common people' would be a better term). For Krishna Sobti, in *Zindagi Nama*, history comes together through folk traditions, rituals, ceremonies, marriage ties, images of maternity, of birth and nurturing, and continuity:

> *History / what is not*
> *And history / what it is*
> *Not that*
> *Which is secured in*
> *the royal archives with*
> *date and time in the*
> *chronicles.*
> *But that*
> *which flows within the*
> *consciousness of the people's mind*
> *Flows, flourishes and spreads*
> *and lives in the*
> *ordinary people.*[1]

Submerged histories, hitherto ignored histories, once they begin to surface and be heard, alter mainstream perceptions of the past. Nancy Armstrong has observed that the feminisation of cultural information is 'meant to detach it from its active role within a historical field and to ground its meanings in a private sphere of consciousness'. She goes on to add how the directness of history is seen as 'supposedly characteristic of men and literature as embodying the coyness of women' (Armstrong 14–15). There is an obverse side to this—the private sphere of consciousness goes to flow into political action and thus enlarges itself to make history. Urmila Pawar, in her account of the role of women in the Ambedkar struggle, *Amhihi Itihaas Ghadavlaa* (We Also Made History), focuses on the women's participation in the making of history (Pawar and Moon). But a Telugu poet, Shilalolitha, talks about 'rewriting' history in her poem, 'Let Us Rewrite History'. I quote the full text of the poem:

In the inmost lockers of the eyelids
Tear flakes gather and block the throat
And all worries huddle therein!
Around this frozen life
Lie the thorny-fenced
Life impressions!
There is no eraser
That can rub off the marks
Of male scribbling on my forehead—
They are the age-old edicts
You alone can smash
Let us rewrite
Our own History![2]

Shilalolitha simultaneously talks of 'trace' and the need to overwrite the trace, through transgression, resistance and rebellion. *Rewriting* and *retelling* are powerful mediums of alteration (for better or worse). They involve a relocation in time and perspective; they also reveal a continued presence of the past and the need to reflect and rethink on it and proceed to connect with at least two living traditions, one literary, the other cultural. Retellings and rewritings are an evidence of the manner in which cultures flow, change, evolve or are overridden. The words are not exact synonyms. Over and above the fact that one 'tells' and the other 'writes', that is, one claims an oral heritage, the other a more fixed written one, the two also are different in intention. Retelling is constantly concerned with the listener, and then language, communication, emphasis, dramatisation become its natural allies. Rewriting, in addition to the change in context and perspective, is also a conscious attempt to rewrite its meaning; it seeks to dominate the earlier version. Retelling and rewriting both, when they alter the meaning or the perspective, hesitate to add or to imagine beyond the text. They are both acts of evaluation and of re-visioning, creating a hypertext. Other additions that take place are in the nature of transforming a subtext into a mainstream narrative, a sequel or even a departure. In the many retellings and rewritings that have been discussed, more specifically in Chapters 2 and 3, ranging from the Jain version of the *Rāmāyana*, the *Sitayana* to Pratibha Ray's *Yajnaseni* and all other contemporary rewritings, the re-interpretative focus is obvious.

In the history of the feminist movement, progress or evolution has not moved in a linear fashion. Very often, the erstwhile freedoms have been attacked and open spaces have been closed in. Today, the blueprint remains approximately the same as charted out in Figure 7.1.

At least it serves as a reference point, though social realities may have rejected or bypassed them. One could juxtapose the same with a more futuristic (and problematic) structure of contemporary locations and aspirations as in Figure 7.2.

It is more than evident that in every aspiration the personal and the social work within cultural frames, which are not necessarily (perhaps not at all) supportive of them. Thus, they have to be worked for through contestatory frameworks. Women are not necessarily willing to break

Figure 7.1: Patriarchal Structures

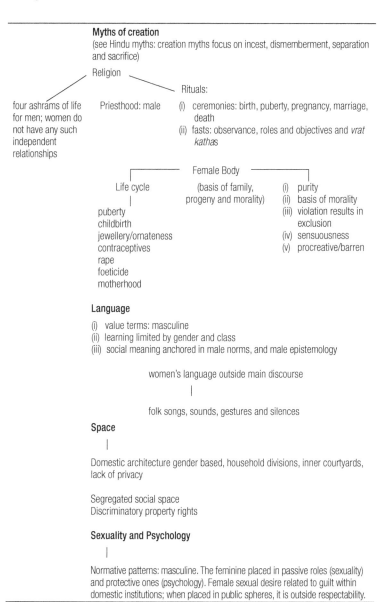

Myths of creation
(see Hindu myths: creation myths focus on incest, dismemberment, separation and sacrifice)

Religion

Rituals:

four ashrams of life for men; women do not have any such independent relationships

Priesthood: male

(i) ceremonies: birth, puberty, pregnancy, marriage, death
(ii) fasts: observance, roles and objectives and *vrat kathas*

Female Body

Life cycle

(basis of family, progeny and morality)

(i) purity
(ii) basis of morality
(iii) violation results in exclusion
(iv) sensuousness
(v) procreative/barren

puberty
childbirth
jewellery/ornateness
contraceptives
rape
foeticide
motherhood

Language

(i) value terms: masculine
(ii) learning limited by gender and class
(iii) social meaning anchored in male norms, and male epistemology

women's language outside main discourse

folk songs, sounds, gestures and silences

Space

Domestic architecture gender based, household divisions, inner courtyards, lack of privacy

Segregated social space
Discriminatory property rights

Sexuality and Psychology

Normative patterns: masculine. The feminine placed in passive roles (sexuality) and protective ones (psychology). Female sexual desire related to guilt within domestic institutions; when placed in public spheres, it is outside respectability.

Source: Author.

273

Figure 7.2: Structure of Contemporary Locations and Aspirations

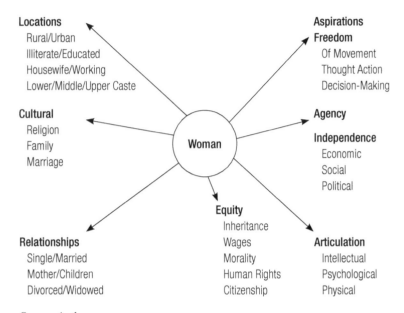

Source: Author.

away from all of them—more specifically the institutional frameworks, such as marriage and family—and with reference to location, the necessary freedom from them is at times not possible. Relocation from caste or locality is difficult. Education is one hope that rulers, reformists, educationists and activists have all alike looked forth to as a solution. But this does not always work. Either social circumstances, cultural prejudices, superstitions or lack of political will intervene. And even educated women find themselves trapped in their circumstances.

Mother–Daughter and Family Relationships

To substantiate this, I shall proceed to analyse two three-generation narratives—one by Mary Roy, a Syrian Christian (and Arundhati Roy's mother), and the other by Nabaneeta Dev Sen, a well-known writer, a

274

Hindu and an independent woman intellectual. Three-generation narratives have a way of travelling across time and social changes, but one is surprised to see that little else changes except the individual's personal courage and perspective. The obstructive social patterns persist; the resistance needs to be an ongoing and continuous process. Forms of oppression and exclusion have become modernised, but are not different in essence. Education, prosperity, upper-middle-class background or travel is no protection against either the feeling of being oppressed or marginalised.

Writing in 1999, Mary Roy begins with her mother's narrative. Mother and daughter live in the same town but have not met because of family differences. Roy's account is stark, bitter and one of familial, community and religious oppression—thus exposing the fixities and indifferences of these institutions. Her highly educated father, who had studied abroad on a Rhodes scholarship was a wife-beater, 'He did not drink, he did not smoke, but he womanised in a frenzied manner. At the age of 7, I can remember his excitement as he stalked new prey' (203). Attempts at legal redress were thwarted and the beatings continued with monotonous regularity. The young 17-year-old bride's talents for music and other activities were destroyed by a husband twice her age, one who made no attempt to understand her or accommodate her interests. Mary has memories of her maternal grandparents' house, which offered them a refuge during their periods of abandonment. But whenever her father returned into their lives, the beatings were resumed. Once, she recalls, her mother was thrown out on a cold, rainy night.

Growing up in such a family, what kind of a person does a child become, with hardly any shared companionship at home and no one interested in nurturing her academic ambitions? Mary wasted a couple of years after her graduation, sitting at home with her mother, with no desire to get out of the 'horrendous lethargy that engulfed' them (207). Finally, she took up a job and went on to accept the first marriage proposal she received. She married a Hindu, Rajib Roy; the best part of the marriage was that no dowry was paid; the worst part, that Roy was an alcoholic. The marriage was not oppressive but it was a negative one. Mary opted out of it and decided to open a school for children.

This was a personal struggle, but soon to become a public one when she decided to go to court against the Travancore Christian Succession Act, an Act which denied daughters any share in intestate property, in 1984. The Act was struck down in 1986 but both the Church and the community felt threatened. It was feared that 'an estimated 20,000 nuns who were not given dowry and therefore wedded to the church, would now demand their share in their father's property' (211). Not only is property protected by marrying daughters to the church, the young girls are also subjected to sexual deprivation. The other side of the story is available in Bama's autobiography *Karukku*, where she critiques the indifference of the nuns. Another question which comes to the mind is: how is this different from the system of the devadasis or the widows who were sent to the ashrams at Mathura and Benaras, or alternatively kept at home to work as domestic drudges. Women may not be surplus where the gender ratio is concerned, but they become surplus if they wish to acquire a full-fledged human status.

The legal battle on a matter of principle may have been won, but not with reference to the details of her personal case. Not only moral laws, but even economic valuations can often be discriminatory. The same property, valued at Rs 1,500 is now valued as Rs 15,000 when the division of property is concerned. Roy writes:

> Thus, two distinct valuations are used by the community, the media, the courts and the government taxation department as two big sticks with which to beat Mary Roy as and when the occasion demands! Unfortunately, in spite of being soundly thrashed, Mary Roy will not go away! (213)

The third generation of the title is Arundhati Roy, her daughter, who at age 18 declared her independence and went on and got married.

276

At the end of the essay, the reader is left with a mixed response. It becomes possible to see how bad marriages affect children, how bad systems erode human will and also how resistance—a continued battle on all fronts—embitters life. One also realises that a discriminatory structure destroys the potential for personal fulfilment. There is need to rethink the meaning of parenting, of success and of family. More than all else, there is the need to rethink the meaning of masculinity—how men think of themselves as protectors or as 'male', a concept which needs to be expanded to include empathy and sensitivity.

Nabaneeta Dev Sen's account travels further back. Her three generations are her grandmother, mother and the writer herself. In her case, the battles are not legal but social and personal. A quick recounting of Sen's narrative reveals that it is not necessary that women who are more naturally socialised into conventional role models are generous and caring. Her grandmother was probably born in 1865 and during Nabaneeta's childhood must have been above 70 or more—perhaps nearly 80. Apparently, this grandmother was not very 'fond of her granddaughters'. What kind of an identity did the old woman have except for having 'borne a dozen offspring' ('The Wind' 221)?

Sen's own mother was widowed young and then went on to marry again. Nabaneeta is the child of this second marriage. She recounts how her mother's second marriage was linked with her own divorce by their spiritual guru. Sen writes:

A decent and an affectionate, a *sanyasi* (ascetic), he wrote a letter to comfort me, stating that it had to happen since I was paying for my mother's sins. It was all Radharani's fault that my husband had deserted me, because when a widow remarries, she loses her chastity and the gravity of the sin affects the following generations. What I should do now to put things right was to give up my worldly desires and choose a life of spiritual enlightenment. Although I was passing through a phase of spiritual inclinations, this letter upset me. (224)

One main reason for Sen to be upset was that the *Sanyasi* was blaming an innocent woman. She wrote back a 20-page letter to him, and this upset her mother who saw it as a 'rebellion' against Gurudev. Strangely enough, her mother did not resent Gurudev's accusation. She felt it was natural for a Hindu holy man to think so. Her mother had been widowed at the early age of 13 when her marriage had not yet been consummated and she remarried 15 years later, when nearly 30. The holy guide apparently saw nothing wrong in a widow's life-denying situation, but everything wrong with her second marriage! Such were the obstacles that women came up against each time they desired to live a fuller life.

Radharani, Nabaneeta Dev Sen's mother, a writer in her own right, had lived a widow's life but her in-laws had encouraged her in every way to fulfil her intellectual interests. She wrote both poetry and fiction and despite the critical appreciation, there were reviewers who felt that the emotions were faked. Being the 'child widow of an aristocratic family', it seemed logical to presume that 'the erotic tension underlying her poetry' was artificially simulated (227).

When she got married to another poet, she did not have the courage to tell her in-laws beforehand. But she went ahead, as in this she had the support of both Rabindranath Tagore and Sarat Chandra Chatterjee. The child Nabaneeta was loved and cared for and had a happy childhood, with a brave, courageous and sensitive mother and a loving, though distant, father. Her childhood is unlike Mary Roy's in several ways. Looking back, Nabaneeta recounts how her mother nurtured ambitions on her behalf, 'She offered me all the opportunities, but no freedom of choice. Being such a possessive and domineering guardian, she rendered me powerless, vulnerable and transparent' (231). Nabaneeta Dev Sen celebrates motherhood—both in the fulsome praise of her mother, who unknowingly made her dependent, and in the overflowing love for her firstborn, which she celebrates in her poetry. In a poem titled 'Antara I', she writes, addressing her baby daughter:

Antara, because of you
I've earned the right to
Enter the tenfold halls of my foremothers
Clutching your baby hands in my fist
I hold the future in my debt forever
Antara, in an instant you have filled all time
By your grace I'm coeval with the earth today. (*Selections* 6)

Broken marriages leave behind heartache, conflict and a total re-viewing of the past. There is also a sudden hostility all around—both from friends and critics. Radharani also initially blamed Nabaneeta for her broken marriage. There is also often the need to review the meaning of trust and reassess the sense of self-assurance experienced earlier. And Radharani was a different kind of grandmother than Sen's own grandmother. How differently do daughters grow! Each moved in diagonal opposition to her own mother. In 'The Wind beneath My Wings', one can see the family support and freedom Radharani's in-laws gave her; one can also sense how the individual (a person like Nabaneeta) has to consciously struggle against domineering family structures to be able to think independently.

Mary Roy and Nabaneeta Dev Sen are near contemporaries, but their experiences of marriage, family life and mother–daughter relationships comment differently on family relationships. Gender differences are apparent and the male distancing from offspring is evident in both the narratives, in one through restraint, in the other (Mary Roy's) through violence.

Oppression, Identity and Self

Oppression is a very abstract term encompassing a wide range of situations. Economic and social oppression can be measured or assessed in some way through percentages, analysis and comparisons, but the emotional depths cannot be measured. The 'oppressed' do not only suffer deprivation, stress, emotional imbalance, helplessness and other related psychological pressures, but also denigrate their self-image. One's sensitivity towards oppressive situations as both a victim and an observer is moulded by a host of other factors. It is not merely a matter of sensitivity. The degree of socialisation of traditional values, the level to which they have been internalised and accepted, cultivated spiritualism, lack of exposure—all go to dull evaluation of oppressive situations or reaction to them, and many are accepted as normal. The feeling of oppression is not simply a matter of comparing visible situations—like economic levels, political rights and legal redressal; it is also not concerned only with the visible atrocities like physical beating or control of movement. Sensitivity to oppression is dependent on both emotion and intellect; on feeling and analysis; on comparison and historicity (comparing in 'time', with a past situation); and on the gap between desire and reality, need and actuality, potential and fulfilment.

The other side of oppression is empowerment, an 'in' word these days; it has strong economic and political associations and is an offspring in today's parlance of development policies. Jane Parpart describes it as a 'motherhood' term 'embraced by development practitioners from World Bank to the smallest NGOs. It seems that empowering the poor (including women) to improve their lives has become a stock practice and an uncritically accepted goal of most of the development community' (Parpart 41). When the word first surfaced in the 1990s, following close on the heels of 'Equality', I happened to be the President of Rajasthan University Women's Association. In that position, very often, I had to speak on the term with rural women, with the media and in other public forums. I all along felt a little uncomfortable with the term. As an attack on poverty, it is justifiable. But as a strategy, it implies a 'giving'. There is a touch of charity about it. Only self-empowerment, the development of a will and an agency, is a methodology that can offer stable and permanent empowerment.

Empowerment is a term used to indicate many things, including a 'fundamental social transformation' (Parpart 41). But in case of its application to development, it needs to be contextualised in a particular social context. In India, we are often engaged in discussing sustainable development, for development can also be a myopic one depleting resources in the long run. The Narmada Bachao Andolan led by Medha Patkar and Vandana Shiva's researches into ecology; the imbalances caused by the green revolution; the exploitation of the Third World in the interests of global development; the use of developing countries as dumping ground; the cultivation of marketable products, livestock and other related things for export at the cost of local interests have all brought about a counter discourse.[3] The development discourse is seen as patriarchal; thus, it connects up with indigenous concerns even as it reflects the equation of women with nature. Is this a regression? Can social structures work through polarities? When binary oppositions form the base of any structure, power always works as unequal. The word em-power-ment is also all about 'power'. Patriarchy, masculinity and hegemony are all power structures. One needs to think beyond polarities in matters of gender, caste and development, because the division caused by polarities appears impassable. In matters of gender now, more than two genders are recognisable even in legal terms. And law is often a slow and a reluctant partner where substantial change is required.

When women activists shift to issues like forest rights, tribal rights and human rights, it is not a shift away from the feminist perspective. Mahasweta Devi is on record for saying that she is not a feminist, but her concern for the tribals is a concern for equality, economic justice, land and forest rights, which cannot be separated from feminist perceptions. When Asma Jehangir (the well-known Pakistani lawyer and human rights' activist) brings her woman's point to examine issues of citizenship, it is also a centre staging of women's perspective, of lifting up women out of an invisibility and marginalisation. Women have now stepped into a movement for equal citizenship. Tzeporah Berman, an eco-feminist activist, has strong objection to the use of women-related language in the environmental discourse. Berman is of the view that many common expressions like the 'rape of the land', 'virgin forest' and 'Mother Earth' 'reinforce patriarchal dualisms and hierarchical traditions which continue to objectify women and Nature, and perpetuate the separation of humans from each other and the non-human world.'[4] The image of the Mother Earth, she goes on to add, gives 'us an image of the Earth as human and female' and 'reinforces the subordination and oppression of women and Nature and perpetuates the patriarchal ideology of domination'.

The point I wish to make here is that, though socio-political and legal structures are necessary for women to achieve equal rights, change in our ways of thinking and our mindsets is equally relevant. Language, images, metaphors and stereotypes all confine. They dominate and die. Dead metaphors only leave behind an echo. A constant renewal of terms and terminologies is required to keep them fluid. The metaphor of rape is aggressive and exposes the vulnerability of the subject/object of this rape. Polarities, linguistic metaphors and stereotypes need to be dismantled and analysed. Feminist research has unearthed a past that sends out different signals to many of us. Once again, it is epistemology that is of significance. How does one know, acquire knowledge, conceptualise, see? How do we think and formulate ideas? In this respect, June O'Conner, in her essay, 'The Epistemological Significance of Feminist Research in Religion', has made a perceptive remark that has a wider application beyond religion. She observes that theories and methods are far more important than goals:

> ... the ideas that have the most powerful hold upon us are not those *we think about*....
> The most powerful ideas are those *we think with*. They are the ideas that lie 'behind' our eyes, enabling us to see; what we see is shaped by them. (47)

Women, in their individual lives and as cultural subjects, have, over the last several centuries, continuously explored and questioned stereotypes and role models as we have seen in the foregoing chapters. There is a continued tradition of resistance at both individual as well as collective levels. In the process, they have expanded the notion of the 'self' as contained in the *Upaniṣad*s. It was not a gendered 'self', yet it did not fully recognise the female of the species. Later rituals evolved strategies of keeping women in secondary and dependent roles, excluding them from access to education and learning, binding them by their bodies and creating fixed images that were subservient to patriarchal institutions. But women worked for redefinitions from within these roles. Draupadi deconstructed the notions of chastity and *sati*; Sītā, of power and motherhood; Kali, of violence; Puru's young wife, of sexuality; the *bhakta* women, of marriage and prayer; and closer to our times, Ramabai, Rukhmabai and a host of other women deconstructed other social structures including widowhood, marriage and power. Identity or self—what were they working for? Which of the two precedes the other?

Identity and self are often treated as synonyms. But they are not. Identities can be dependent on men or on externals like class, status—both economic and married—caste and culture, while self is an internal consciousness of strength, awareness and ability. Women may work for an independent identity or have a visible identity such as caste, dalit or a racial characteristic, a nationality or an occupation. But 'self' is a more significant conduit connecting the inner being with the outer reality—which may more often than not be a patriarchal construct and in constant need of remoulding.

Freedom is again a very wide-ranging term and moves right across a whole gamut of constructs: physical confines to the right of ownership or visibility, right to body and to equal opportunity. What kind of a freedom do the majority of Indian women want? Three of the most basic freedoms are right to education, to body and to space within marriage. There is always a slight feeling of guilt when one discusses freedom when one looks around. What about the young girl who wants to just go for a cycle ride? Is she safe? Is she free to go? And the housewife, whose lowly paid husband brings home the rotting vegetables to be cooked for dinner and on some annual festival gets her two sarees of his choice for the whole year. She has no choice in the food she cooks or eats, or the clothes she wears. There is then the case of the daily charwoman, the domestic help who works throughout the day and when she goes home, her alcoholic husband gives her a good beating, wants her to cook for him and orders that a fresh chilli paste be ground for his food. What degree of freedom, of identity or self, do these women have?

Political battles are also equally uneven. Women in the panchayats have had to struggle against male control and caste hegemony. NGOs (and at times state bodies) have extended external support and have organised training programmes and a number of women are able to take a stand, but at the national level, women MPs are like a sprinkling of salt and either aggressive or convenient 'ideal woman' models projected by their political mentors. The strength, however, is in the grassroots movements where rural women have a role; these movements display a solidarity and team spirit, not always visible in the mainstream. Women's associations, engaged in different tasks and areas, also have a good networking. And their struggles for legal reform are yielding results. In India, the women's movement is a comfortable mix of academics and activism.

Like the rest of the world, we in India too are faced with certain problems: one of globalisation, which prioritises economic development; the second of religious fundamentalism, which seeks to reinstitute control over women's bodies, freedom and morality; and the third of indifference of the metropolitan young woman, who is being fast absorbed by the marketing forces. The fourth, which is an offshoot of medical and technological advancement, is the reorganisation of human reproductivity. Contraceptives and legal abortion provided a right to the body in some measure, but now the fertility centres, which treat the female body as an object, artificial insemination, in-vitro fertilisation and embryo transfers (IVT-ET), and female foeticide are detrimental in their overall effect. As Hélène Rouch has observed, the treatment of infertility as if it were a disease is to 'confuse the survival of the species with that of the individual' and the child becomes the 'very child women wanted to avoid when they fought for liberalizing contraception and abortion'. It equates womanhood with motherhood—'a woman is a woman only if she is a mother': it is politically right-wing and supports a rising birth rate (273). Rising birth rate is often a political issue when it ranges one community against another, and when votes are cast along caste/religion lines. Women are objectified in any such calculation of percentages just as they are erased when female foeticide takes place. Campaigns have been launched in several parts of the country against sex-selective abortions, sex determination and pre-elimination of daughters by a number of non-governmental agencies, taking the battle to the streets and those of the medical profession who are party to it. First against dowry deaths, then sati, followed by agitations against rape and now female foeticide and domestic violence—these are private battles being fought in public space in order to involve societal responsibility and raise the level of consciousness of the other.[5] These lead to legal provisions and a larger participation in the resolution of social problems, but the real battles that effect long-term change are carried on and fought at individual levels— bit by bit—until a dent is made in the value structures around one.

Equating Modernity with 'Values' and Agency

Any tracing of histories, resistance movements and continuities automatically necessitates a discussion on its relationship with 'modernity', a term, which again has been seen through a mono-lens of Western origins. In an earlier book on literary modernism, I have redefined and relocated it in the Indian context (*Contextualising Modernism*). I do not wish to repeat it here but proceed to relate it with the 'values' of agency,

285

transparency and secularism—values which help bypass domination or control and manipulation and narrow religious morality, and thus relocate them amidst a lived world. For substantiating this I move to a 2006 Hindi film, *Dor*, directed by Nagesh Kukunoor. The title could mean anything—'connection', 'strand' or 'thread'—words which signify relationships and a connection with the stream of life.

A story about two girls, one Hindu the other Muslim, *Dor* is set in two different locations, both rural—one the hills of Himachal Pradesh, the other the vast deserts of Rajasthan—and the convergence takes place in two different ways. The husbands of the two girls, Zeenat and Meera, go to Saudi Arabia, meet there and share accommodation. Shankar dies in a mishap for which Aamir is held responsible and placed under a death sentence, unless the wife of the deceased gives a letter of forgiveness. This convergence is in the background and not played out in the film; the second convergence forms the main narrative. Zeenat, who is an orphan, sets out in search of Meera—all alone. On the way, she encounters both kinds of men—those who stalk her and those who help her. But she manages to get along and find Meera with the help of a harmless pickpocket, a *bahrupiya*.

The two girls meet in the premises of a temple, and significantly, this religious space is used for secular purposes. After the usual complications, one realises that Meera, after coming into contact with Zeenat, is beginning to discover herself and her hidden strengths. Briefly, she steps outside the strict household regime and the circle drawn around widowhood. Zeenat helps her to realise that widowhood should not block all desire, that the young body has a rhythm of its own, that one can still dance and eat and think and care. Thus enabled, she is now able to see how her father-in-law plans to use her young body as a bargain for paying off his debts as she overhears him seal the deal with his tenant. There are a couple of very powerful scenes in the film. One where Zeenat advises Meera to allow herself the 'leap of faith', '*emaan ki chlang*', and Meera jumps a step to feel the impact on her inner being. Second, when she tells her father-in-law that he has no right to touch her; it is a right she had conceded only to her husband. There is also a third scene when the grandmother-in-law advises her to follow the voice of her conscience. Meera leaves home to give the letter of forgiveness to Zeenat, who has already boarded a train. The film ends on this note, where one woman extends help to another, and reciprocally, the other extends her hand. Meera rises above the role that her father-in-law is scripting for her as well as the one that Shankar's death has marked for her. She also rises above the conventions of society as she walks out of her house, uncertain of the future.

In the two parallel narratives, the viewer is conscious of the marginality of the religious discourse. Women's identities are constructed more by patriarchy than by religion. Zeenat has some education; she lives alone and works in the post office. She too has had to struggle at every step towards her present sense of self-confidence. But it is Meera's narrative that is foregrounded, her battles are actually being fought, and her moral conflict is a real one just as her fear of the outside is. It is through her experience that feminism is re-viewed, the catalytic forces lying outside her in Zeenat and the grandmother-in-law. When she signs the form granting forgiveness, she moves outside her prison to the railway station, and she does so with a full awareness that the future may be lonely, insecure and uncertain. She also steps outside the moral law imposed upon wifehood into a morality which is more widely applicable. Women have, in almost all cultures, through the agencies of law, philosophy and religion, through Manu and Aristotle, been excluded from a participation in the formations of morality. Male discourses have stressed rationality and have ruled that women are irrational. Moving outside loyalty to the husband, or the family code, Meera moves into a larger moral world where forgiveness is of a higher value than adherence to the idea of revenge.

As Carol Gilligan has observed in her work, *In a Different Voice*, women often bypass legalities and prioritise relationships as they concentrate on activities of care (29–65). The final push towards this larger morality is through the voice of her conscience. She realises that she cannot carry the burden of guilt or be responsible for Aamir's death. Meera's journey to a recognisable agency is marked by a whole re-visioning of both masculinity and femininity. In this, the film stands in sharp contrast to the polarised treatment of tradition–modernity discourse, as it also does by bypassing urban spaces and romantic entanglements. At another level, it also bypasses the primacy of dependency as a wife or a widow. This modernity is infused not by a desire to be like the 'other', but by a desire to recognise the 'self'; it works with value structures and moves towards integrating inner spaces with larger structures of morality and freedom.[6] In this, the film scripts a new narrative for feminism which is more than a voice of protest or questioning. It is moral self-reflection, a conquering of inner fears and a realisation of self-worth, a feminism that does not abandon values or relationships, but goes on to create new ones.

Finally, one has to stop to ask: is this a representation of contemporary reality or a projection of an ideal situation? The minimal attention given to religious difference, the disruption of the association between Meera and Gopal or Krishna by linking Meera with Shankar,[7] and the location of Zeenat in a parallel narrative that encroaches and superimposes itself on the other, carrying within it a new construction of the nation, and interrupts the romantic transcendentalism of the Meera–Krishna relationship.

Encounters, interactions and dialogues apart, the woman's movement in India has a long tradition of resistance in religious and secular, oral and written discourses, in personal lives, and stands in political resistance to domination, and of participation, at various levels in political and economic movement. It is not only in tradition but also in contemporary India that we see activism in all spheres. True, the motives and frameworks may be specific, goal oriented or ideologically committed, but the larger concern is the same. It is not a singular, monolithic movement, but neither are Indian cultural, social or religious constructs. Struggles and conflicts between self-interest and collective interest continue to exist, but two factors—the fact of a colonial past and the framing of culture as a strong anti-discourse to on alien domination—have shaped the movement over the last two centuries. The feminist discourse, despite the generational and spatial shift, is still heavily laced with struggles such as the Salt Satyagraha: 'Who will buy the salt of freedom?' These struggles also account for the difference from Western feminism and the break from male representations of femininity; they work in cultural contexts and against cultural impositions which deny them space and freedom, self and agency.

NOTES

Chapter I

1. *Dharma*, *arth*, *kama*, *moksha* are traditionally identified as the pursuits of human existence ranging from duty, livelihood (economic wellbeing), love and desire to salvation.
2. *Triya jaal*: a term used to describe the tricks a woman employs in order to manipulate others, more specifically her husband. But the strategy may recoil and once having adopted such a strategy, a woman is not likely to be direct or transparent. Thus, it makes an honest, bold relationship difficult to achieve.
3. Mala Khullar has provided a detailed account in her 'Introduction' to *Writing Women's Movement: A Reader* (1–27).
4. The reference is to Jonathan Swift's *Gulliver's Travels*, a classic satire written in mid-eighteenth century.
5. C.S. Lakshmi, in one of her articles, 'Bodies Called Women: Some Thoughts on Gender, Ethnicity and Nation', quoted a popular song of a Tamil film of the 1950s, which describes a 'good' woman as one who must 'Follow everyday/The wise counsel of the father/One who combines timidity, bashfulness, implicit acceptance and/Physical sensibility'.
6. The commentary, however, qualifies that this learning is limited to domestic affairs (336).
7. The section on Sikhism in the present chapter is largely dependent on Grewal's work.

8. See also Pashaura Singh's 'The Place of Sikh Scripture in the Sikh Tradition' in *The Guru Granth Sahib* (especially 274–281).

9. Also refer Uma Chakravarti's *Everyday Lives, Everyday Histories: Beyond the Kings and Brahmanas of 'Ancient' India.* Chakravarti in her essay 'Whatever Happened to the Vedic Dasi?' moves beyond Altekar. She is critical of the 'decline' theory, namely that Muslim invasions brought down the status of women. Instead, she traces it back to brahmanical sources (31). While supporting and agreeing with his main thesis, she points out that he perceives women as 'stock breeders of a strong race' (32). One has to admit that traditionally a woman's body has been valued primarily for its chastity, virginity and fertility. There are two other essays, 'The Social Philosophy of Buddhism' and 'Brahmanical Patriarchy in Early India', in the same volume. Chakravarti is of the view that the Buddha maintained a dual approach, separated the social from the asocial world and did not support any legitimization of inequalities (135–136).

10. Bankim Chandra Chatterjee, in a series of novels in the late nineteenth century, projected very unconventional heroines who through sacrifice, self-control and asceticism emerged as strong women and were consequently able to take an independent stand against family atrocities. Two such heroines are Durgesh Nandini in the novel of that name written in 1865 (refer Hindi translation) and Debi in *Debi Chaudhurani* in 1884 (refer Hindi translation by Ramesh Dixit).

Chapter II

1. Surendranath Dasgupta also points out that Samkhya philosophy differs both from the Jaina and the Vedanta philosophies. In the first, the soul possesses qualities such as *anantasnana, anantdarshana anantasukha* and *anantaviryya*, and the latter holds that the individual souls are but illusory manifestations of one soul or pure consciousness—the Brahman.

2. I have depended primarily on M. Hiriyanna's article, 'The Samkhya' in *The Cultural Heritage of India* and on Surendranath Dasgupta's 'The Samkhya and the Yoga Doctrine of Soul or Purusa' in *History of Indian Philosophy.*

3. See Donna Wilshire, 'The Uses of Myth, Image and the Female Body in Re-visioning Knowledge'. *Gender/Body Knowledge*. Eds. Alison E. Jagger and Susan R. Bordo (New Jersey: Rutgers University Press, 1989) as well as

Carolyn Merchant. *The Death of Nature: Women, Ecology and The Scientific Revolution* (London: Wildwood House, 1982), who discuss in detail the way knowledge systems have been governed by treating Mind and Matter as gender characteristics. I reproduce below a classificatory graph of gender attributes (from Wilshire):

Knowledge (accepted wisdom) / ignorance (occult and taboo)
Higher (up) / lower (down)
Good, positive / negative, bad
Mind (ideas), head and spirit / body (flesh) womb (blood) Nature (Earth)
Reason (the rational) / emotion and feeling (irrational)
Cool / hot
Order / chaos
Control / letting-be, spontaneity
Objective (outside, 'out there') / subjective (inside / immanent)
Literal truth, fact / poetic truth, metaphor, art
Goals / process
Light / darkness
Written text, Logos / oral tradition, enactment, Myth
Apollo as sky-sun / Sophia as earth-cave-moon
Public sphere / private sphere
Seeing, detached / listening, attached
Secular / holy and sacred
Linear / cyclical permanence, ideal (fixed) forms / change / fluctuations, evolution
Changeless and immoral / process, ephemeras (performance)
Hard / soft
Independent, individual isolated / dependent, social connected, shared
Dualistic / whole
Male / Female

4. This can be observed in the process of meditation, especially when there is abstinence from speech and communication and the eyes are closed. Interestingly enough, this philosophy can be related to the practice of observing fasts, which will be discussed at a later stage.

5. Hiriyanna then proceeds to describe the approach to God and the subtle distinctions between the atomistic and the evolutionary explanations, which need not concern us here (49–50); what concerns us is Patanjali's view (50–51).

6. I refer the reader to a very informative and interesting book by Robert Winston, *The Human Mind.*

7. I make a distinction between them. Every man is not a patriarch—the younger male members are also subordinated. But when we grow up in a patriarchal hierarchical structure, the line of authority is perceived as male and our thinking—unless we consciously resist or question it—is framed by the dominant social expectations. Patriarchy could also be divided—if power is divided. Does Bhishma exercise a patriarch's authority or only the moral authority of a senior member? Has patriarchal power been seized by Duryodhana? Extraction of obedience or the ability to do so—does it form a part of it? For a detailed discussion of patriarchy in the modern context, see V. Geetha's *Patriarchy.*

8. The television media, which has a more wide-ranging reach than literature, is surfeit with a projection of 'traditional' values, rituals and elaborate symbols, which locate women in constricted roles—a broad streak of sindhoor, karva chauth, sacrificing mother figures and other behavioural codes. At one level, these projections reinforce rightist ideology.

9. *The Mahabharata*, originally written in Sanskrit, happens to be perhaps the longest epic in the world; K.S. Singh observes that the Constituted Text according to the *Critical Edition of the Mahabharata* (edited by Suthankar, Belvalkar and Vaidya) consists of about 73,000 verses by itself. If verses from the southern and northern versions are added, it would be much longer (K.S. Singh 3).

10. Thapar writes that the *Krta-yuga* extends for 1,728,000 human years, the *Treta-yuga* is 1,296,000 years, the *Dvapara-yuga* is further reduced and is 864,000 years of length and the *Kali-yuga* still further reduced to 432,000 years. They are located in a descending order from best to worst as well as in terms of length. The *Kali-yuga* is often the period of transgressions and deviations from orderly practices.

11. See Karnad's 'In Search of a Theatre', which was written as an Introduction to *Three Plays* published by Oxford University Press. Karnad writes how he was torn between conflicting desires—personal need to travel and explore and an emotional need to stay anchored in family and country. It is at this time that he wrote *Yayati.* Looking back, he realises that the play reflected his anxieties at the moment (179–180).

12. Girish Karnad's *Yayati* was written in 1960 in Kannada. The English edition is a translation by the author. In the Preface to this edition, Karnad refers

briefly to its first staging in Hindi in 1967. This English translation was performed in 2006 and published in 2008.

13. This extract is from her introduction to the 2005 edition of Karnad's *Collected Plays*, but is used almost as an introduction on the very first page of the new English translation of Karnad's *Yayati*.

14. Pooru had also recoiled from the wonderful successes and military feats of his ancestors and the model of masculinity they had projected (Karnad, *Yayati* 35).

15. It also indicates that the ability to create (potency), in itself, is an incomplete power. Christine Battersby in *The Phenomenal Woman* also takes up the aspect of being 'born' as an act important for both the one who is born and the one who gives birth for the identity of the self (2–4). This will be elaborated upon at a later point.

16. Pandu lived his life under a curse that forbade him from sexual pleasure. Thus, his two wives shared the boon granted to Kunti, enabling her to bear children through a divine union. Kunti had four sons—the elder Karna, having been born before her marriage was disowned and discarded, and the other three were Yudhistra, Bhima and Arjun—and Madri gave birth to the twins Nakul and Sahdev.

17. Namely Adi-Parv, Sabha-Parv, Van-Parv, Virat-Parv, Udyog-Parv Bhishma-Parv, Drona-Parv, Karn-Parv, Shalya-Parv, Sauptik-Parv, Stree-Parv, Shanti-Parv, Anushashan-Parv, Ashramedhik-Parv, Ashramvasik-Parv, Mansal-Parv, Mahaprasthanik-Parv, Swargrohan Parv and the final section on how to listen to the story, titled Mahabharat-Shrawan-Vidhi.

18. Continuously referred to as *ekvastr*, a single piece, which women wore during menstruation.

19. With Karna's admiration, the action has come full circle.

20. Mahasweta Devi's story 'Draupadi' has been translated by Gayatri Spivak and is available in several collections. Here the page references are to 'Draupadi' in *Women in Patriarchy*, edited by Jasbir Jain.

21. For more details, see *Encyclopaedia of Indian Cinema* (Revised edition) by Ashish Rajadhyaksha and Paul Willemen.

22. Sattar's perspective is a balanced one, because in India, the literal interpretation of the *Rāmāyana* has led to riots, divisions and social unrest. The Babri Masjid demolition of 6 December 1992, the hysteria that accompanied it and the riots that followed in Mumbai in January 1993 set off an unending chain of hatred and violence. Currently, as I write this, the

controversy surrounding the Ramsetu Bridge has stalled the building of the link between India and Sri Lanka.

23. In fact, all the essays in this collection take it as a starting point. See Preface, xi.

24. For the two passages refer Ramanujan's 'Three Hundred *Rāmāyanas*', 25–31. This particular reference is on page 26.

25. In contrast to these folk narratives, Kamban accounts for Rāvana's immortality by referring to a boon that he would not be killed by a mortal.

26. To jog the non-culture reader's memory, Kunti is the mother of the Pandavas.

27. Earlier in the essay, Lutgendorf elaborates on the *rasik sadhana*—'sadhana' meaning devotion—and writes, 'Its use among Vaisnava devotees reflects the sixteenth-century Gauriya Vaishnava theologians' reinterpretation of classical Sanskrit aesthetic theory in the service of the ecstatic devotionalism promulgated by Krsna Caitanya, the renowned mystic of Bengal' (219).

28. R.K. Narayan in one of his early novels *The Dark Room* (1935) uses this very stratagem for his heroine Savitri, so that she can divert her husband's attention back to her from his growing interest in a younger woman. Refer 186–189 (Valmiki) for Kaikeyi–Bharata meeting and Bharata's indictment of her behaviour.

29. Three sisters—Amba, Ambika and Ambalika—were carried away by Bhishma for his half brother, but Amba told him she was in love with King Shalv. So he let her go, but she was rejected by her lover. The other two sisters were married to his brother but he passed away without leaving behind an heir. The two widows were then asked to produce children through a relationship with the sage Vyas. But terrified of him, one closed her eyes and so her son was born blind; the other paled and her son was born weak and pale.

30. Rāma's mother Kausalya, on learning about the sentence of exile, tells him, 'From the moment you were born seventeen years ago, I have waited anxiously for an end to my sorrows' (Valmiki 129).

31. It should be noted that Tulsidas's *Ramcharitmanas* is the one recited in most homes and temples and thus it is much more widely read and its ideas more easily propagated in Hindi-speaking zones.

32. Edward Said wrote his essay 'Travelling Theories' in order to trace how cultures and history reshape theory. The travels of the *Rāmāyana* lend themselves to a similar analysis.

33. Velcheru Narayana Rao gives a detailed account of the Andhra society. The restrictions imposed on women are, by and large, similar to those imposed in most other regions. Variations are specific to religion, individual histories and economic circumstances. In broad strokes, wherever respectability, lack

of education and orthodoxy join hands, the lot of women is expected to be docile and sexuality limited to procreation, that too preferably of the male child—signifying the importance of patriarchal lineage and of the male desire to see a lost childhood restored.

34. Though this explanation is not there in Valmiki, some later literary versions refer to this (Rao 120).

35. Richman in her introductory essay to the volume refers to the Bharatiya Janata Party (BJP) members filing charges of criminal conspiracy against the organisers of a cultural festival for showing a panel of an earlier Buddhist version, which depicted Sītā and Rāma as siblings (1–2).

36. Oral literature has both a flexibility and freedom. Wedding songs all over the country are often full of slanging matches, mockery and exposure of oppressive customs, dowry demands, female-dominated households and men with a roving eye.

37. The work was brought out as *Jan Janak Janaki*, edited by Sacchidanand Vatsyayan. I have depended on Kishwar's references.

38. This, however, is quite in keeping with Manu's laws.

39. See Richard Schechner's *Performative Circumstances: From the Avant-garde to Ramlila.*

40. Mukul Kesavan, in his novel *Looking Through Glass*, works through the *akhara*, Benaras Ramlila, to a film production of the *Rāmāyana* narrative.

Chapter III

1. The word *stree* carries several meanings, one of them being wife. The title could as well be translated as 'A Wife's Letter'. In fact, Ram Singh Tomar has translated it as such into Hindi as 'Patni Ka Patr'. The word *stree* (woman) is much more encompassing and is both specific as well as generic. A Bengali friend informs me that the Bengali original carries the word '*stree*'. It needs to be pointed out that though the difference between the times of the two translations is approximately 30 years, the target audience and purpose are entirely different. Moreover, the Katha publication is also a 'retelling' and is thus abridged and selective. The original story is much longer, far more detailed and contextualised in the freedom struggle. The Katha publication is meant for adult learners. Suffice it to say that it is abridged but free of distortion, misrepresentation or addition.

2. Refer Wendy Doniger, 'Introduction' to *The Laws of Manu*. 'Probably composed sometime around the beginning of the Common Era or slightly earlier' (xvii).

3. See Kapila Vatsyayan, *Bharata: The Nātyaśāstra*, '…. the composition of the text may have taken place some time between the second century BC to second century AD, but not later' (24).

4. Refer Wendy Doniger (lviii–lix) for Brian K Smith's views and the question of real and ideal.

5. Refer Gauri Vishwanathan, *Outside the Fold: Conversion, Modernity and Belief.*

6. Jotiba Phule, Ranade and several others, including Pandita Ramabai's father, were men who took up the cause of educating their wives despite family and social opposition.

7. Anandibai Joshi went to America for medical studies.

8. For her life story refer to 'An Autobiographical Account', in Kosambi, *Selected Works* (115–118).

9. The 1888 edition of *The High Caste Hindu Woman* carries an introduction by Rachel Bodley. For details refer *The High Caste Hindu Woman* (i–xxiv). This is not included in *Selected Works*. But for the text of *The High Caste Hindu Woman*, I shall refer to Kosambi.

10. The choice for women was limited between an apparent widowhood and ostracism by society or following their husband's decision. Lakshmi Bai Tilak records her experiences in *Smriti Chitra*, translated into English as *I Follow After.*

11. Sathianadhan gives an account of the difficult decision in *Saguna*. See pages 46–54 for details of Harichandra's conversion and 55–60 for the aftermath.

12. Bal Gangadhar Tilak, the editor of *Kesari* and a freedom fighter, who in this particular case adopted a very conservative position.

13. For a debate on this point refer Sudhir Chandra 36–41 and 50–55.

14. See 'An Autobiographical Account' in Kosambi (116–117). Ramabai's was married as a child to a poor boy so that the couple would continue to stay with the bride's parents, but the boy was not interested in studies and ran away from his in-law's house. Ramabai writes, 'This marriage ended in a life of unhappiness for my parents' (117).

15. *Dan* literally means alms or charity; thus *kanyadan*, giving a girl (daughter) away.

16. Dharamvir, an IAS officer, who was instrumental in bringing it to light and has also written an Introduction, wherein he expresses the view that it is

very likely that further research in the holdings of Kanhialal Aalakhdhari may yield more information about the writer (Dharamvir 3).

17. Jewellery has been seen as a compensation, reward, custom and punishment. It is connected with various rituals and indicates a woman's marital status whether wife or widow. In the hot summer of a tropical country, it is often uncomfortable. I once came across a society woman whose daughter was unhappy as her husband was a wife beater. I was shocked to hear her comment, 'So what, he also buys her diamonds!' The ornaments often do resemble the rings and chains with which animals are tied.

18. Tanika Sarkar in *Hindu Wife, Hindu Nation* has dealt at length with Rassundari Devi's life. I have not dwelt on the same aspects.

19. For a very interesting view on the womanly woman and the unbecoming woman, the reader is referred to Parama Roy's 'Becoming Women: The Gender of Nationalism' in *Indian Traffic: Identities in Question in Colonial and Postcolonial India*.

20. See A.K. Singh's *Devadasi System in Ancient India: A Study of Temple Dancing Girls of South India*.

21. Also refer Manmohan Ghosh's 'Introduction' to *The Natyasastra* (ii–liii).

22. See Chandra Rajan's 'Introduction' in Kālidāsa's *The Loom of Time: A Selection of His Plays and Poems* (25–26) and 'Appendix I' of the same volume (307–313).

23. These different explanations have been offered. Kālidāsa's explanation will shortly be taken up for consideration.

24. Some well-known film directors like Bhupen Hazarika, V. Shantaram and Vijaya Mehta have made these. The appeal of Shakuntala is entirely different from that of the *Rāmāyana*. The latter carries a religious appeal. V. Shantaram's film in 1943 symbolised the birth of a new India, via the birth of Shakuntala's son Bharat. See Ashish Rajadhyaksha and Paul Willemen's *Encyclopaedia of Indian Cinema*.

25. See Romila Thapar's *Narratives and the Making of History*.

26. Dancing girls had an equally hard life as *devadasi*s. Mirza Mohammed Hadi Ruswa's novel *Umrao Jan Ada* is a moving account of a courtesan's life. But here I am not going to elaborate upon it. Meenakshi Mukherjee has discussed it in *Realism and Reality* and I have also briefly touched upon it in *Feminizing Political Discourse: Women and the Novel in India*. Among other powerful fictional accounts are Shivaram Karanth's *Woman of Basrur* and Girish Karnad's play, 'Flowers: A Dramatic Monologue'.

27. It has been translated into other Indian languages. Jasbir Jain and Shobha Shinde have recently translated it into English under the tentative title, *I Speak, You Listen* (under publication).
28. Page numbers of the English translation are not available at the moment as it is under publication.
29. I refer to a performance held in Jaipur. The performance was brought here by Ajoka Production, Lahore.
30. See Mirza's *A Woman of Substance: The Memoirs of Begum Khurshid Mirza.*

Chapter IV

1. Samuel Taylor Coleridge's 'Kubla Khan' is a poem written probably in 1797, but published in 1816. 'Kubla Khan' is a poem that lends itself to a wide range of meanings and encompasses different cultures. It creates a strange environment with its rapid transitions from one to another.
2. This is a wide generalisation. Separation between sexuality and romance depends on social circumstances, moral norms, personal will and even caste and economic background. I am not passing any value judgement but the contemporary practice, increasingly gaining social acceptance even in conservative societies, of live-in relationship admits (*a*) the need for an active will and (*b*) the possibility of temporariness.
3. I have partly borrowed this from Sugana Ramanathan's 'Foreword' to the *Songs of Chokhamela* translated by Rohini Mokashi Punekar (vi) and have altered it for my purpose.
4. A dominant movement of rural Maharashtra. The Varkaris go for annual pilgrimages to Pandarpur on foot, singing abhangs (poetical compositions) as they walk. They don't have any elaborate rituals or pujas and do without mediating priests.
5. Sandhya Jain in her work *Adi Deo Arya Devata: A Panaromic View of Tribal Hindu Cultural Interface*, traces the tribal-Hindu continuum, working through the accommodation of tribal gods. Jagannath Puri is one such example where a tribal god is worshipped by all alike. But there is need to look closely at the authoritarian structures that begin to inhabit this accommodation. Bhakti, on the other hand, concentrates on the methods of worship, reducing and erasing distances, moving outside fixities and orthodoxies and above all valuing the human devotee. Hindu-tribal interface, from one point of view shows an

299

assimilative tendency to give marginal projection to the weaker section but concentrates power in the establishment.

6. Translated by Uma Chakravarti and Kumkum Roy in Susie Tharu and K. Lalita's *Women Writing in India: 600 B.C. to the Early Twentieth Century*, Vol. 1. (68). For the background information on Mutta, the same source has been used (67–68).

7. For this account of Mahadeviakka, I have depended mainly on A.K. Ramanujan's essay, 'Talking to God in the Mother Tongue'. This quote is from page 13.

8. See Vijaya Ramaswamy's *Walking Naked: Women, Society, Spirituality in South India* (156–160) for more details.

9. Quoted by Vijaya Ramaswamy in *Walking Naked* (149). The poem itself has been taken from K.V. Zvelebil's *The Lord of the Meeting Rivers—Devotional Poems of Basavanna*.

10. Quoted from Zvelebil.

11. Quoted from Ramanujan, *Speaking of Siva*.

12. Vijaya Ramaswamy cites one contemporary example, when she had the opportunity of interacting with one Kanakamma, a lady in her seventies, in the Ramanashramam at Tiruvannamalai. ' "Why women and spirituality?" she asked and laughed. "I did not know that spirituality can be male or female" ' (*Walking Naked* 1).

13. Another article in the same issue, which deals specifically with Akka Mahadevi is 'Akka Mahadevi' by Vijaya Dabbe and Robert Zydenbos.

14. I have travelled to some of these places and seen them. These belong to the sixteenth century.

15. Chakravarty, however, makes a distinction on the basis of *bhakti*.

16. The poem quoted by Chakravarty has been taken from Vidya Dehejia's *Slaves of the Lord* (124).

17. Refer 'Andal: She Who Rules', based on a manuscript by K. Meenakshi and supplemented by material from Friedhelm Hardy's *Viraha* and Vidya Dehejia's *Slaves of the Lord* (35).

18. For more details see Vidyut Bhagwat's 'Man–Woman Relations in the Writings of the Saint Poetesses'.

19. Translated by Eleanor Zelliot, in her 'Eknath's Bharuds: The Sant as Link between Cultures' (98–99). This poem, addressed to Amba, was reproduced in *Manushi* ('Let Me Live Alone'. The numbers against every couplet mark the couplet and the repetition of the refrain.

20. There is a Punjabi romantic song, where the young girl refuses to go with her younger brother-in-law (he is but a chit of a boy) and her father-in-law (he is too old), but is willing to merrily follow her husband.

21. Translated from Gujarati by Nita Ramaiya, in Tharu and Lalita's *Women Writing in India* (Vol. I, 93).

22. Translated by Zide and Pandey, in Kishwar and Vanita's 'Poison to Nectar' (76). 'Hari', 'Giridhar', 'Govind', 'Shyam', 'Gopal' are other names for Krishna.

23. Ramaswamy spells Varkari with a 'W'. I have retained it within the quotation but have not used it in the text.

24. See Chandra Talpade Mohanty's *Feminism without Borders: Decolonizing Theory, Practicing Solidarity* (223–225).

25. *Hauli* was the women's prison where the women of tax-defaulters were kept. These laws had been made for revenue collection during Allaudin Khilji's rule, but were pursued even in Akbar's rule. Chandrabati's was a protest was against them (Tharu and Lalita 103).

26. The opening passage from Euripides' 'Iphigenia in Tauris':

I am Iphigenia. I am descended
From…Agamemnon.
He was my father; my mother, Clytemnestra.

The story's told how, in that land-locked bay
Of Aulis, where swift eddying gusts of wind,
Ceaselessly churn the dark swirl of Euripus,
My father slaughtered me, for Helen's sake,
A sacrifice of blood to Artemis.
For Agamemnon had assembled there
A thousand Grecian ships of war, resolved
To crown Greek arms in triumph over Troy,
Take vengeance for Helen's ravishing, and restore
Honour to Menelaus. But no wind
Stirred any sail. Disastrous calm drove him
To augury; and Calchas then pronounced:
'Agamemnon, Marshall of the arms of Greece,
You shall see no ship sail till Artemis
Receive your daughter's blood in sacrifice.' (73–74)

27. The verse is very powerful and makes a strong statement in favour of deeper relationships.
28. Tharu and Lalita also support this point (Vol. 1, 8–10).
29. Both *Hind Swaraj* by Gandhi and *The First War of Independence* by Vir Savarkar were banned at about this time (Tharu and Lalita Vol. 1, 10).
30. The whole concept is discussed in detail (viii–xii).
31. There is no dearth of examples on this subject. We have several in the novels of Bengali writers like Bimal Mitra, Sarat Chandra Chattopadhaya and others. Deepa Mehta's *Water* (2006) gives a realistic account of this. Often these widows' homes turned into brothels. Parents sent away young teen-aged, widowed daughters to these ashrams in order to protect their own reputation against a possible elopement or remarriage.
32. This introduction 'A Woman's Journey: From Prison to Paradise' has been privately translated by a friend, Indira Nityanandan, at my request.
33. 'Mast Qalander', a very well-known qawwali, has been sung by different singers at different times—Runa Laila, Abida Parveen, as also Nusrat Fateh Ali Khan. It is religious in nature and is about the Sufi saint Hazrat Lal Shahbaz Qalandar (1177–1274). It has a rhythm that absorbs the listener into an ecstatic experience.
34. English translation is mine.
35. Almost all societies have sanctioned these mystic trances, frenzied dances, hypnosis and healing techniques induced by shamans, methods that allow for intermediation between the natural and spiritual. In some parts of India, the tantric tradition is still alive and village shamans are still popular.
36. This is the answer of a 74-year-old brahmin who was interviewed by Usha Menon and Richard A. Shweder. For more details see their essay 'Dominating Kali: Hindu Family Values and Tantric Power' (85).
37. Cited by Hugh B. Urban in 'India's Darkest Heart' (185).
38. See Ashish Rajadhyaksha and Paul Willemen's *Encyclopaedia of Indian Cinema.* (363).
39. See Ashish Rajadhyaksha and Paul Willemen's *Encyclopaedia of Indian Cinema.* (364).
40. News of witch-persecution (persecution of women on the pretext/belief that they are witches) is reported pretty frequently in rural India, underlying the nurturing of superstition and blind faith. Unfortunately, the electronic media sensationalises these for its own purpose.

Chapter V

1. This is from memory. When I grew up this was a popular verse and I have had this confirmed by others.

2. I'll not dwell on this in detail but it would suffice to point out that the pressures on India and its people were multifold. The Orientalist project on the one hand and Macaulay's language policy, plus the missionary efforts, on the other were increasingly squeezing the space available for native cultures. The imperial power's energies were directed at a psychological reframing of India with its stress on museumification and pageantry so brilliantly traced by Bernard S. Cohn's *Colonialism and Its Forms of Knowledge: The British in India* as well as Ronald Inden's *Imagining India*.

3. For more details see my unpublished essay 'Between Sameness and Difference', presented at the Asiatic Literary Bicentenary, Mumbai.

4. For example, Jotiba Phule and Pandita Ramabai.

5. Refer Sudhir Chandra's *Enslaved Daughters*.

6. Referred to in Chatterjee's 'The Nationalist Resolution of the Women's Question' (235–236).

7. See Jasbir Jain's *Writing Women Across Cultures*.

8. See Partha Chatterjee's 'The Nationalist Resolution of the Women's Question' (245) and Jasbir Jain's 'From Listener to Reader' in *Feminizing Political Discourse: Women and the Novel in India*.

9. Nishadin, apparently, is a tribe. Later on in the story, other tribes are also mentioned. Nishadin is used for females, Nishad for men. A slight variation in spellings—Nishidin—would convey the meaning of demon and demonic. In Hindu mythology, the distinction between gods and demons is worked out through *karma*.

10. Fasts are observed on full moon day, or for particular days of the week, in honour of different gods, like Monday for Shiva, Tuesday for Ganesha, Friday for Santoshi Maa. These fasts, commonly referred to as *vrat*s are accompanied by *vrat katha*s, stories that moralise on the rewards and punishments for observance and non-observance of these fasts. Though men also observe some of them, a large majority are observed by women for procuring a good virile husband, for the well-being of the family, for the long life of the husband (as Karva Chauth) or as penance for widowhood (Ekadasi). *Vrat katha*s are discussed in greater detail in the next chapter.

11. Translated into English as *Perfecting Women: A Partial Translation of Bihisti Zewar* by Barbara Daly Metcalf.

12. The official educational policy has consistently stressed the importance of female education for the family, to make women good housewives and good mothers. The slogan has been, 'If you educate a man, you educate one person; if you educate a woman, you educate a whole nation.' Thus, from family, to society, to nation, then it has moved to education for employment, that is, economic independence. In 1986, the New Education Policy, for the first time, stressed female education for equality. Thus, it is remarkable that women themselves could think of these things (no matter how subtly worded or cloaked) and seek to spread the message to other women, calling upon them to take the initiative.

13. When she moved a resolution in the All India Women's Conference of 1936, 'asking the government to supply necessary information to those seeking contraceptive advice', it was passed amidst great controversy. J. Devika in an explanatory footnote (128), comments this resolution was 'on entirely feminist grounds raising precisely the issue of women's control over their bodies.'

14. In *Sultana's Dream and Padmarag.* 'Sultana's Dream' was published in 1905 and 'Padmarag' in 1924. Her essays on 'purdah' are available in a collection *Inside Seclusion: The Avarodhbasini of Rokeya Sakhawat Hossain.*

15. The term *madi* means purity. *Madi* women are required not to touch others.

16. All translations from this text are mine.

17. This episode has been written about by other writers as well, such as K.B. Sreedevi, who has a full-length novel titled *Yagnam* (Sacrifice), and Matampu Kunjukuttan, who in his novel *Outcaste–Bhrishtu* provides a male perspective which is far more sympathetic towards Tatri and the Namboodri women's lot than the hesitant sympathy offered by the women writers.

18. All quotations from this text are my translations.

19. Faiz Ahmed Faiz is a very well-known Urdu poet.

Chapter VI

1. See *Subaltern Studies* (a series on subaltern historiography initiated in 1982 by Ranajit Guha; earlier published by Oxford University Press, the project has now shifted to Orient Longmans). The several volumes unfold the past

in a different way, providing details of an absent history and filling up the gaps in the existing knowledge.

2. See Judy Simons' *Diaries and Journals of Literary Women*. Simons comments at length on the silence that women maintain.

3. How does one conceptualise the self? It is a very slow process and not necessarily a conscious one. One may never be able to do it, and very often it may be a constant play between self-image, self-expression, tradition, role models and the expectations of the other around one.

4. Refer Robert Winston's *The Human Mind* (251–257). Winston points out the physiological differences in the brains of men and women. Women have a smaller hypothalamus, the corpus callosum—the bridge that connects the left and right hemispheres—is thicker in women, thus allowing a better shunting of information from the feeling area to the analytical, vocal one. Again, age affects their brains differently. Winston also takes up the effect of trauma on memory as well as on memory recall. It is possible for people to 'bury' traumatic memories, and at times 'false' memories can also be created (296–297). It is not always easy to process emotions, 'a further argument is that the stress hormone cortisol may interfere with the process of long-term potentiation' (297).

5. Pawar has written a full-length work on women's role in the Ambedkar movement, which is titled *Amhihi Itihas Ghadavlaa* (We Also Made History). The SPARROW interview which carries a similar title is marked with inverted commas.

6. Gandhi's whole insistence on spinning was part of this concept of self-respect. E.V. Ramasamy Naicker Periyar, himself of a lower caste, led a movement in the late 1920s and early 1930s (of the twentieth century) which is known as the Self-Respect Movement. This movement, like Ambedkar's, was in opposition to Gandhi's inclusion of the 'untouchables' (Harijans, children of god, as he referred to them) in the category of Hindus.

7. These details are very useful for anthropological purposes and their actual medical effects need to be explored. In this connection, also refer to the story 'Septic' by Sivashankari, in *Growing Up as a Woman Writer*, edited by Jasbir Jain.

8. Refer Rajender Singh Bedi's *Ek Chadar Maili Si*. Translated into English by Khushwant Singh as *I Take This Woman*, it was filmed in 1986 by Sukhwant Dhadda.

9. Upper caste women took to the streets in the anti-Mandal agitation, in favour of their potential husbands, who may remain unemployed in case of reservations for the backward caste.

10. Chakravarti comments on the 'honour' killings of upper caste women marrying lower caste boys. In contemporary India, several cases have taken place where not only the women but also the men are killed; very often, the couple is pursued and persecuted. Caste panchayats meet and sentence them to death and the concept of private justice prevails.

11. Though the opinion Lata expresses and the account she gives of Ambedkar's resentment at the stalling of the Hindu Code Bill and the delegation of All Indian Women's Associations meeting with him needs to be looked at critically. For more than two decades now, women have been trying to bring in a Uniform Civil Code. The support for it slackened only when the BJP came to power in a coalition government, primarily because they were hijacking the issue for the ideology of the Rightist Movement. It also needs to be juxtaposed with other accounts available in biographies of other leaders. Nevertheless, it is clear that history needs to be sifted over and over again and the various accounts examined.

12. See Partha Chatterjee's *The Nation and Its Fragments* (174–175).

13. See Arjun Dangle's story 'Promotion'.

14. The Urmila–Lata discourse reflects the contemporary situation.

15. Refer Sharan Kumar Limbale's *Hindu* for a depiction of power politics and caste divisions.

16. The anthology put together by Arjun Dangle in *Poisoned Bread* (has several essays. In addition, Shrawan Kumar Limbale has written a full-length book on dalit aesthetics. Non-dalits have also intervened in the process of reshaping and evaluating dalit aesthetics.

17. For an elaborate discussion see Jasbir Jain's *Beyond Postcolonialism*, especially the chapter, 'Classical and Experiential Aesthetics'.

18. R. Von Deth and Walter Vandereycken have worked together in their research on religion, eating disorders and anorexia. They have published extensively in this area. A well-known work is *From Fasting Saints to Anorexic Girls: The History of Self Starvation*.

19. From 'Will Not Women Awake?' in Devika's *Her*-Self. Women got the voting right in Travancore in 1919. They began to contest elections, but such women had to face many obstacles. For many decades, the policy of nominating women members to sit on various committees and councils persisted (see page 111 of Devika, notes 1 and 2).

20. For more details see Radha Kumar's *The History of Doing* (32–52).

21. 'Exile' and the other stories discussed in this section are from the Bhalla anthology and page references are to the one-volume edition (which brings all the 3 volumes together).

22. '…Partition is often seen in metaphysical terms…. A loss of a world rather than a loss related to prestige' (Sengupta, 'An Afterword' 189).

23. Kamaladevi Chattopadhyaya's recollection, quoted by Radha Kumar (78).

24. See for more details the references to Aruna Asaf Ali's role in the freedom struggle (Kumar, *The History of Doing* 63) and for Kamaladevi Chattopadhyaya's (Kumar, *The History of Doing* 55). Sarojini Naidu's marriage was both inter-caste and inter-lingual and she had her own set of problems to contend with (56–57). Radha Kumar has provided an account of these women who joined the national struggle and contributed to it in different ways in her chapter 'Organisation and Struggle'. Sucheta Kripalani had to withstand Gandhi's opposition when she decided to marry J.B. Kripalani. Gandhi didn't object to marriage but advised her to marry someone else. In refusing to submit to Gandhi's almost dictatorial interference in her life, she showed a tremendous amount of courage, which also displaced the image of the docile and obedient woman (for details see Kumar, *The History of Doing* 84). Gradually the conventional image of a traditional woman was being displaced in politics and a new image of woman as an activist was taking its place (Radha Kumar analyses this process in the chapter 'Constructing the Image of a Woman Activist').

25. Also see pages 235–237 where they discuss the question of Western influence (or otherwise) in fair amount of detail.

26. They refer to Renuka Ray's and Romola Sinha's work. In Rajasthan itself, the Rajasthan University Women's Association was founded in 1971 with the specific aim of working for women's causes: better working conditions for working women, crèches at the workplace, a home for destitute women and running counselling services. The state welfare schemes were also supportive of such activities.

27. The Shah Bano case is one such example where the judgement was set aside by subsequent legislation. See for more details 'Changing terms of Political Discourse' by Indu Agnihotri and Vina Mazumdar in *Writing the Women's Movement: A Reader*, 62–63.

Chapter VII

1. Translation mine.

2. The poem has been translated by K. Swarnalatha who teaches at Warangal. It was made available to me by her. I acknowledge the debt.

3. See Vandana Shiva's *Staying Alive: Women, Ecology and Survival in India.* Shiva has a chapter on science in which she discusses modern science as patriarchy's project, which leads to mal-development (14–26).

4. See Tzeporah Berman's 'The Rape of Mother Nature? Women in the Language of Environmental Discourse' (internet source, pages not numbered).

5. For details, see *Whose News? The Media and Women's Issues,* edited by Ammu Joseph and Kalpana Sharmaand *45 Million Daughters Missing: A Compendium on Research and Intervention on Female Foeticide and Infanticide in India* by USAID India. Collective resistance against gender discrimination of any kind marks a different approach. But, at some point the solution lies and often comes from individual resistance.

6. See Steven Connor's 'The Necessity of Value' (8).

7. The *bhakta* Mirabai worshipped Krishna. Girdhar Gopal is another of the many names Krishna is called by. Shankar is one of the names of Shiva, whose female consort is Parvati. In Hindi films, we often have names of gods and goddesses (which is also true in real life) used for ordinary mortals, and the romantic couple carries the symbolisation forward as Ram and Janaki (another name for Sita), or Radha (Krishna's paramour) and Govind (another name for Krishna). In *Dor,* however, Meera's husband carries the name of Shankar and thus breaks this coupling.

BIBLIOGRAPHY

Aboobacker, Sara. 'A Muslim Girl Goes to School'. Aboobacker, *Breaking Ties* 87–105.

———. *Breaking Ties* (Kannada). Trans. Vanamala Visivanatha. Chennai: Macmillan India Limited, 2001.

———. 'Growing up as a Woman Writer'. J. Jain, *Growing Up As a Woman Writer* 29–35.

Agnihotri, Indu and Vina Mazumdar. 'Changing Terms of Discourse: Women's Movement in India 1970–1990, 1869–1879'. *EPW* 30(29). 22 July 1995. Also in Khullar, *Writing Women's Movement: A Reader* 48–79.

Altekar, A.S. *The Position of Women in Hindu Civilization*. Delhi: Motilal Banarsidass Publishers (1956), 2005.

Amma, Kochattil Kalyanikutty. 'Some Obstacles in the Way of Equality between the Sexes'. *Her-Self: Gender and Early Writings of Malayale Women. 1898–1938*. Trans. and ed. J. Devika. Kolkata: Stree, 2005. 174–178.

Amur, G.S., ed. *Listen Janamejaya and Other Plays* by *Adya Rangacharya*. New Delhi: Sahitya Akademi, 2005.

Ansal, Kusum. *Uski Panchvati* (Hindi). New Delhi: Hindi Book Prakashan, 1996.

Antherjanam, Lalithambika. 'A Leaf in the Storm'. Bhalla 161–171.

———. 'A Writer is Born'. Antherjanam, *Cast Me Out If You Will* 144–150.

———. 'An Account of a Performance'. Antherjanam, *Cast Me Out If You Will* 165–171.

———. *Cast Me Out If You Will*. Calcutta: Stree (1998), 2000.

———. 'Lessons From Experience'. Antherjanam, *Cast Me Out If You Will*. 157–164.

Antherjanam, Lalithambika. 'Sesame Seeds, Flowers, Water'. Antherjanam, *Cast Me Out If You Will* 172–183.

———. 'The Goddess of Revenge'. Trans. Gita Krishnakutty. Antherjanam, *Cast Me Out If You Will.* 18–30.

———. 'The Mother of Dhirendru Mazumdar'. Translated from Malayalam by T. Murlidharan. Bhalla 511–519.

———. 'We Cast Away Our Umbrellas', part of 'Childhood Memories'. Antherjanam, *Cast Me Out If You Will* 133–143.

Ao, Temsula. 'The Last Song'. Temsula, *These Hills Called Home* 23–43.

———. *These Hills Called Home: Stories from a War Zone.* New Delhi: Penguin in association with Zubaan, 2006.

Armstrong, Nancy. 'The Gender Bind: Women and Disciplines'. *Genders 3*, Fall, 1988: 1–23.

Arora, Sudha., ed. *Dehleez ke us Paar* (Hindi). Mumbai: SPARROW, 2003.

———, ed. *Pankhon ki Udaan* (Hindi). Mumbai: SPARROW, 2003.

Badrinath Chaturvedi. *The Mahabharata: An Inquiry in the Human Condition.* Hyderabad : Orient Longman Pvt. Ltd. 2006.

Baisantri, Kaushalya. *Dohra Abhishaap* (Hindi). New Delhi: Parmeshwari Prakashan, 1999.

Bagchi, Jasodhara. 'Freedom in an Idiom of Loss'. Available at http://www.india-seminar.com/2002/510/510%20jasodhara%20bagchi.htm (accessed on 6 August 2006).

Bama. *Karukku* (1992). Translated from Tamil by Lakshmi Holmström. Chennai: Macmillan, 2000.

Battersby, Christine. *The Phenomenal Woman.* New York: Routledge, 1998.

Bedi, Rajinder Singh. *Ek Chadar Maili Si* (1963). Translated from Urdu by Khushwant Singh as *I Take This Woman* (1967). New Delhi: Orient Paperbacks, 1994.

Berman, Tzeporah. 'The Rape of Mother Nature? Women in the Language of Environmental Discourse'. *Trumpeteer* 11.4 (1994): 173–178. Available at http://trumpeter.athabascau.ca/index.php/trumpet/article/view/805/1171 (accessed on 6 August 2008).

Bhabha, Homi. *The Location of Culture.* London: Routledge, 1994.

Bhagwat, Vidyut. 'Heritage of Bhakti: Sant Women's Writings in Marathi'. *Culture and the Making of Identity in Contemporary India.* Eds. Kamala Ganesh and Usha Thakkar. New Delhi: SAGE Publications, 2005. 164–173.

———. 'Man–Woman Relations in the Writings of the Saint Poetesses'. *New Quest* Vol. 82, July–August (1990): 223–232.

Bhalla, Alok, ed. *Stories about the Partition of India.* 3 vols. 1994. single volume, New Delhi: Harper Collins, 1999.

Bharata Muni. *Nātyaśastra*, Translated into English by Manmohan Ghosh. Vol. 1. Chapters I–XXVII. Calcutta: Manisha Granthalaya Private Ltd., 1967

Bharati, Dharamvir. *Andha Yug.* (1953) Translated from Hindi by Alok Bhalla. New Delhi: Oxford University Press, 2004.

Bhattacharya, Haridas, ed. *The Cultural Heritage of India.* Calcutta: The Ramakrishna Mission (1937). 1953.

Bhattacharya, Malini. 'Introduction'. Bhattacharya and Sen 1–16.

Bhattacharya, Malini and Abhijit Sen, eds. *Talking of Power: Early Writings of Bengali Women.* Kolkata: Stree, 2003.

Bhattacharya, Rimli. 'Afterword: Binodini Dasi to Nati Binodini'. B. Dasi, *My Story and My Life as an Actress.* New Delhi: Kali for Women, 1998. 188–243.

———. 'Introduction: Binodini Dasi and the Public Theatre in Nineteenth Century Bengal'. B. Dasi, *My Story and My Life as an Actress* 3–46.

———. 'Afterword: Notes on the Bengali Public Theatre'. B. Dasi, *My Story and My Life as an Actress* 159–185.

Buck, William. *Ramayana: King Rama's Way*, with an Introduction by B.A. Van Nooten. New York: Mentor, New American Library (1976), 1978.

Bulle Shah. *Bulle Shah.* Eds. Harbhajan Singh and Shoab Naqvi. New Delhi: Hind Pocket Books, 2006.

Butalia, Urvashi. *The Other Side of Silence: Voices from the Partition of India.* New Delhi: Viking, 1998.

Caldwell, Sarah. *Oh Terrifying Mother: Sexuality, Violence and the Worship of Kali.* Delhi: Oxford University Press, 1999.

Chakravarty, Uma. 'The World of the Bhaktin in South Indian Traditions—The Body and Beyond'. *Manushi.* Special: Tenth Anniversary Issue. Nos 50–52, 1989: 18–29.

Chakravarti, Uma. 'Brahmanical Patriarchy in Early India'. Chakravarti, *Everyday Lives, Everyday Histories* 138–155.

———. *Everyday Lives, Everyday Histories: Beyond the Kings and Brahmanas of 'Ancient' India.* New Delhi: Tulika, 2006.

———. 'The Social Philosophy of Buddhism'. Chakravarti, *Everyday Lives, Everyday Histories* 119–137.

———. 'Whatever Happened to the Vedic Dasi?' Chakravarti, *Everyday Lives, Everyday Histories* 3–38.

———. *Gendering Caste.* Kolkata: Stree, 2003.

Chandra, Sudhir. *Enslaved Daughters: Colonialism, Law and Women's Rights.* New Delhi: Oxford University Press (1998), 2008.

Chandrika, B. 'In Search of Infinity: The Parallel Strands in Women's Fiction in Malayalam'. J. Jain, *Growing Up as a Woman Writer* 343–353.

Chandy, Anna. 'On Women's Liberation' (1929). *Her-Self: Gender and Early Writings of Malayalee Women.* Trans. and ed. J. Devika. Kolkata: Stree, 2005. 113–129.

Chatterjee, Bankim Chandra. *Debi Chaudhurani* (1884). Hindi trans. Ramesh Dixit. Delhi: Sanmarg Prakashan, 1984.

———. *Durgeshnandini* (1865). Hindi translation. Delhi: Bharti Bhasha Prakashan, 1989.

Chatterjee, Minoti. 'Creatures of the Subworld: Nineteenth Century Actress of Bengali Stage'. Ramaswamy, *Researching Indian Women.* Section 6, 337–352.

Chatterjee, Partha. 'The Nationalist Resolution of the Women's Question'. Sangari and Vaid 233–253.

———. *The Nation and Its Fragments: Colonial and Postcolonial Histories.* Delhi: Oxford University Press, 1997.

Chatterjee, Sarat Chandra. *Pather Dabi* (1926). Translated into English as *Right of Way* by Rimli Bhattacharya. Kolkata: Shreesti, 2002.

Chattopadhaya, Bankim Chandra. *Anand Math* (1882). Hindi translation. Delhi: Hind Pocket Books, 1992.

Chokhamela. *Songs of Chokhamela.* Trans. Rohini Mokashi Punekar. New Delhi: The Book Review Literary Trust, 2002.

Chughtai, Ismat. 'In the Name of Those Married Women'. Chughtai, *Kagzi Hain Pairahan* 24–43.

———. 'Lihaf'. Trans. Syed Sirajuddin. Tharu and Lalitha Vol. 2, 129–138.

———. *Kagzi Hain Pairahan.* New Delhi : Rajkamal Prakashan, 1998, 2000.

———. 'Roots'. Trans. Vishwamitter Adil and Alok Bhalla. Bhalla 574–588.

———. *The Crooked Line.* Translated from the original Urdu into English by Tahira Naqvi. New Delhi: Kali for Women, 1995.

Cirlot, J.E. *A Dictionary of Symbols.* Translated from Spanish by Jack Sage. London: Routledge (1962), 1988.

Cohn, Bernard S. *Colonialism and Its Forms of Knowledge: The British in India.* Delhi: Oxford University Press, 1997.

Connor, Steven. 'The Necessity of Value'. *Theory and Cultural Value.* Oxford: Blackwell, 1992. 8–33.

Coomaraswamy, Radhika. 'Preface'. *'Honour': Crimes, Paradigms and Violence Against Women*. Eds. Lynn Welchman and Sara Hossain. New Delhi: Zubaan, 2006. xi–xv.

Dabbe, Vijaya and Robert Zydenbos. 'Akka Mahadevi'. *Manushi* Nos. 50–52, 1989. 39–44.

Dahejia, Vidya. *Slaves of the Lord*. [Delhi: Munshiram Manoharlal, 1988] *Manushi* Nos 50–52 (1989).

Dangle, Arjun. 'Promotion'. Trans. Lalita Paranjpe. Dangle, *Poisoned Bread* 168–172.

———, ed. *Poisoned Bread: Translations from Modern Marathi Dalit Literature*. Hyderabad: Orient Longman (1992), 1994.

Das, Veena. *Critical Events: An Anthropological Perspective on Contemporary India*. New Delhi: Oxford University Press, 1995.

———. 'The Mythological Film and Its Framework of Meaning: An Analysis of *Jai Santoshi Maa*'. *India International Quarterly* 9.1 (1981): 43–56.

Dasgupta, Surendranath. 'The Samkhya and the Yoga Doctrine of Soul or Purusa'. Dasgupta, *History of Indian Philosophy* Vol. 1, 238–247.

———. *History of Indian Philosophy*, 5 vols. Delhi: Motilal Banarsidass Publishers (1922), 1975.

Dasi, Binodini. 'My Life as an Actress'. Written in Bengali in 1924/25. B. Dasi, *My Story* 127–158.

———. 'My Story'. Written in Bengali in 1912. B. Dasi, *My Story* 47–126.

———. *My Story and My Life as an Actress*. Ed. and trans. by Rimli Bhattacharya. New Delhi: Kali for Women, 1998.

———. 'Preface'. B. Dasi, *My Story* ix–xii.

Dasi, Girindramohini. 'A Terrible Problem' (1894). Trans. Jasodhara Bagchi. Bhattacharya and Sen 69–76.

Dermott, Racher Fell and Jeffrey J. Kripal, eds. *Encountering Kali: In the Margins, at the Center, in the West*. Delhi: Motilal Banarasidass Publishers, 2005.

Desai, Anita. *Clear Light of Day*. New Delhi: Allied, 1980.

———. *Fasting, Feasting*. London: Chatto and Windus, 1999.

Deshpande, Shashi. 'Hear Me, Sanjay'. *The Stone Women and Other Stories*. Kolkata: Writers Workshop, 2002. 42–51.

———. *The Binding Vine*. [London: Virago Press, 1993] New Delhi: Penguin, 1993.

———. *The Stone Women and Other Stories*. Kolkata: Writers Workshop, 2002.

Deshpande, Sudhavna. 'Excluding the Petty and Grotesque: Depicting Women in Early Twentieth Century Marathi Theatre'. Ramaswamy, *Researching Indian Women* 353–372.

Deth, R. Von and Walter Vandereycken. *From Fasting Saints to Anorexic Girls: The History of Self Starvation*. New York: New York University Press, 1994.

Devi, Ashapurna. *Bakul Katha*. Trans. Hanskumar Tiwari. New Delhi: Bhartiya Jnanpith Prakashan, 1979.

———. *Pratham Pratishruti* (1977). Trans. Hanskumar Tiwari. Noida: Mayur Paperbacks, 1992.

———. *Suvarnlata* (1977). Translated into Hindi from the original Bengali by Hanskumar Tiwari. New Delhi: Bhartiya Jnanpith Prakashan, 1979.

Devi, Bamasundari. 'What are the Superstitions that must be Removed?' Translated by Malini Bhattacharya. Bhattacharya and Sen 17–24.

Devi, Kailashbasini. 'The Woeful Plight of Hindu Women'. Translated by Kumar Deb Bose. Bhattacharya and Sen 25–51.

Devi, Kusumkumari. 'A Letter'. Trans. Chandrajee Niyogi. Bhattacharya and Sen 52–55.

Devi, Mahasweta. 'A Tribute to Jaidev'. Pankaj K. Singh 83–84.

———. 'The Witch'. *Bitter Soil: Stories by Mahasweta Devi*. Trans. Ipsita Chanda. Calcutta: Seagull Books, 1998. 57–123.

———. 'Draupadi'. Translated from the original Bengali into English by Gayatri Chakravarty Spivak. J. Jain, *Women in Patriarchy* 95–110.

———. 'Kunti and the Nishadin. Pankaj K. Singh 85–96.

Devi, Rassundari. *Amar Jiban.* Trans. Enakshi Chatterjee. Calcutta: Writer's Workshop, 1999.

Devi, Sarala. 'Nanari Dabi–The Rights of Women' (from *The Rights of Women*, 1934). Trans. Sachidanandan Mohanty. S. Mohanty 153–160.

Devika, J., ed. *Her-Self: Gender and Early Writings of Malayalee Women.* Kolkata: Stree, 2005.

Dharamvir. 'Introduction'. *Simantni Updesh* (1882). Ed. Dharamvir. Noida: Shesh Sahitya Prakashan, 1988.

Dharwadker, Aparna Bhargava. 'Introduction'. Girish Karnad, *Collected Plays of Girish Karnad.* 2 vols, New Delhi: Oxford University Press, 2005. vii–xxxix.

Divakaruni, Chitra Banerjee. *The Palace of Illusions*. New York: Doubleday Broadway Publishing Group, 2008.

Doniger, Wendy. 'Introduction'. *The Laws of Manu*. Translated by Wendy Doniger and Brian K. Smith. New Delhi: Penguin India, 1991. xv–lxxviii.

Easwaran, Eknath.Trans. *Dhammapada*, with a general Introduction and chapter Introductions by Stephen Rupenthal. New Delhi: Penguin (1986), 1996.

Euripides. 'Iphigenia in Tauris'. *Alcestis and Other Plays*. Trans. Philip Vellacott. Middlesex: Penguin, 1953. 73–120.

Foucault, Michel. *Discipline and Punish: The Birth of a Prison.* (1975). Trans. Alan Sheridan. New York: Pantheon, 1977.

Franco, Fernando, Jyotsna Macwan and Saguna Ramanathan. *The Silken Swing.* Calcutta: Stree, 2000.

Fuller, Marcus B. *The Wrongs of Indian Womanhood*, with an Introduction by Rukhmabai. Edinburgh: Oliphant Anderson and Ferrier, 1900.

Gandhi, M.K. *Hind Swaraj or Indian Home Rule* (1909). Ahmedabad: Navjiwan Publishing House (1938), 1996.

Geetha, V. *Patriarchy*. Calcutta: Stree, 2007.

Geetha, V. and E.V. Rajadurai. 'Interrogating "India"—A Dravidian Viewpoint'. Available at http:/www.tamilnation.org/heritage/aryan_dravidian/interrogating_India.htm (accessed on 5 August 2009).

Ghosh, Girishchandra. 'How to Become an Actress'. B. Dasi, *My Story and My Life as an Actress* 208–209.

———. 'Srimati Binodini and the Bengali Stage'. B. Dasi, *My Story and My Life as an Actress* 210–212.

Ghosh, Manmohan. 'Introduction'. *The Natyasastra.* Calcutta: Granthalaya Private Limited. Revised second edition, 1967.

Gilligan, Carol. *In a Different Voice: Psychological Theory and Women's Development.* Cambridge, Massachusetts: Harvard University Press, 1982.

Gilman, Charlotte Perkins. 'The Yellow Wallpaper'. J. Jain, *Women in Patriarchy* 29–46.

Goldberg, Naomi. 'The Return of the Goddess'. *Religion and Gender*. Ed. Ursula King. Oxford: Blackwell, 1995. 147–163.

Goldman, Sally J. Sutherland. 'The Voice of Sita in Valmiki's Sunderkanda'. Richman, *Questioning Rāmāyaṇas.* 223–238.

Granoff, Phyllis. ed. *The Forest of Thieves and the Magic Garden: An Anthology of Medieval Jain Stories*. Trans. Granoff. New Delhi: Penguin Books, 1998.

Grewal, J.S. *Guru Nanak and Patriarchy*. Shimla: Indian Institute of Advanced Study, 1993.

Hardy, Friedhelm. *Viraha Bhakti: The Early History of Krsna Devotion in South India*. New Delhi: Oxford University Press, 2001.

Hariharan, Githa. 'Foreword'. Mythily Sivaraman, *Fragments of a Life: A Family Archive*. New Delhi: Zubaan, 2006. vii–viii.

Hashmi, Jamila. 'Exile'. Bhalla. 50–67.

Haslanger, Sally and Nancy Tuana. 'Topics in Feminism'. *Stanford Encyclopedia of Philosophy*. Entry Feb. 7 2003 rev. March 15 2004. Available online at http://plato.stanford.edu/entries/femenism_topic (accessed on 5 August 2009).

Hiriyanna, M. 'The Samkhya'. H. Bhattacharya 41–52.

Hosain, Attia. 'After the Storm'. Bhalla 395–399.

———. *Sunlight on a Broken Column*. New Delhi: Arnold Heinemann (1961), 1979.

Hossain, Rokeya Sakhawat. 'Sultana's Dream' (1905). *Sultana's Dream and Padmarag*, with an Introduction by Barnita Bagchi. Trans. Bagchi. New Delhi: Penguin, 2005. 1–14.

———. 'The Worship of Women'. ['Nari Puja'. *Mahila* Dec. 1905–March 1906.] Trans. Barnita Bagchi. Bhattacharya and Sen. Kolkata: Stree, 2003. 105–115.

———. *Inside Seclusion: The Avarodhbasini*. Ed. and trans. Roushan Jahan. Dacca: Women for Women, 1981.

Hussain, Wasbir. *Homemakers without the Men*. New Delhi: Indialog Publications, 2006.

Iliaih, Kancha. *Why I am not a Hindu*. Calcutta: Samya (1996), 2002.

Inden, Ronald. *Imagining India*. Oxford: Basil Blackwell,1990.

Indira, M.K. *Phaniyamma* (1976). Translated from the original Kannada into English by Tejaswini Niranjana. New Delhi: Kali for Women, 1989.

Indra, C.T. 'Introduction'. Rajam Krishnan, *Lamps in the Whirlpool*. Chennai: Macmillan, 1995. vi–xv.

Iravati. *Performing Artists in Ancient India*. New Delhi: D.K. Printworld (P) Ltd., 2003.

Jain, Jasbir. 'Purdah, Patriarchy and the Tropical Sun'. *The Veil*. Ed. Jennifer Heath. Berkeley: University of California, 2008. 231–247.

———. *Beyond Postcolonialism: Dreams and Realities of a Nation*. Jaipur: Rawat Publications, 2006.

———. *Contextualising Modernism: The Novel in India 1880–1950* (Punjabi). Ludhiana: Chetna Prakashan, 2000.

Jain, Jasbir. ed. *Creating Theory: Writers on Writing.* Delhi: Pencraft International, 2000.

———. *Feminizing Political Discourse: Women and the Novel in India.* Jaipur: Rawat Publications, 1997.

———, ed. *Growing Up as a Woman Writer.* New Delhi: Sahitya Akademi. 2009.

———. *Writing Women Across Cultures.* Jaipur: Rawat Publications, 2003.

———, ed. *Women in Patriarchy.* Jaipur: Rawat, 2005.

Jain, Jasbir and Avadhesh Kumar Singh. *Indian Feminisms.* New Delhi: Creative Books, 2001.

Jain, Sandhya. *Adi Deo Arya Devata: A Panaromic View of Tribal Hindu Cultural Interface.* New Delhi: Rupa and Co., 2004.

Joseph, Ammu and Kalpana Sharma, eds. *Whose News? The Media and Women's Issues.* New Delhi: SAGE Publications (1994), 1997.

Kabir. *Love Songs of Kabir.* Trans. G.N. Das. New Delhi: Abhinav Publications (1992), 2003.

Kakar, Sudhir. *The Inner World: A Psycho-Analytical Study.* Delhi: Oxford University Press, 1981.

Kale, Kishore Shantabai. *Chora Kolhati Ka.* Translated into Hindi from the original Marathi by Arundhati Devasthale. New Delhi: Radhakrishan Paperbacks, 1997.

Kālidāsa. 'Abhijnānāśakuntalam'. Kālidāsa, *The Loom of Time* 165–281.

———. *The Loom of Time: A Selection of His Plays and Poems.* Ed. and trans. Chandra Rajan. New Delhi: Penguin, 1989.

Kamban. *The Kamban Rāmāyana.* Trans. P.S. Sundaram. Ed. N.S. Jagannathan. New Delhi: Penguin, 2002.

Kamble, Baby. 'Interview given to Maya Pandit'. *The Prisons We Broke.* Hyderabad: Orient Black Swan, 2008. 136–157.

———. *Jeevan Hamara.* Translated from the original Marathi into Hindi by Lalita Asthana. New Delhi: Kitab Ghar, 1995.

———. *The Prisons We Broke.* Translated from the original Marathi *Jina Aamcha* into English by Maya Pandit. Hyderabad: Orient Black Swan, 2008.

Kapadia, Kundanika. 'Introduction'. *Seven Steps in the Sky* (Gujarati edition). Trans. Indira Nityanandan. Private circulation.

———. *Seven Steps in the Sky* (1982). Translated from Gujarati by Kunjbala and William Anthony. Bombay: Navbharat Sahitya Mandir (1994), 2004.

Karanth, Shivaram K. *Woman of Basrur* (1970). Translated from the original Kannada by H. Y. Sharada Prasad. New Delhi: Ravi Dayal Publishers, 1997.

———. *Collected Plays*, Vol. 2. New Delhi: Oxford University Press, 2005.

Karnad, Girish. 'Flowers: A Dramatic Monologue'. Karnad, *Collected Plays*, Vol. 2 243–260.

———. 'In Search of a Theatre'. *Three Plays.* Oxford University Press. Reproduced in *Creating Theory: Writers on Writing.* Ed. Jasbir Jain. Delhi: Pencraft International, 2000. 178–195.

———. *Talé-Danda.* Delhi: Ravi Dayal Publishers, 1993.

———. *Yayati.* Trans. Karnad. New Delhi: Oxford University Press, 2008.

Karve, Iravati. *Yuganta: The End of an Epoch.* Hyderabad: Disha Book, an Imprint of Orient Longman Ltd. (1969) 1999.

Kesavan, Mukul. *Looking Through Glass.* Delhi: Ravi Dayal Publishers, 1995.

Khan, Sorayya. 'Where Did She Belong?' Bhalla.

Khandekar, V.S. *Yayati.* Translated from the original Marathi into English by Y.P. Kulkarni. New Delhi: Hind Books, (1959) 1978.

Khote, Durga. *I, Durga Khote: An Autobiography.* Translated from Marathi into English by Shanta Gokhale (1976). New Delhi: Oxford University Press (2006), 2007.

Khullar, Mala. 'Introduction: Writing Women's Movement'. Khullar, *Writing Women's Movement: A Reader* 1–43.

Khullar, Mala, ed. *Writing Women's Movement: A Reader.* New Delhi: Zubaan, 2005.

Kishwar, Madhu and Ruth Vanita. 'Poison to Nectar: The Life and Work of Mirabai'. *Manushi* Nos 50–52 (1989): 75–93.

Kishwar, Madhu. 'Yes to Sita. No to Ram: The Continuing Hold of Sita on Popular Imagination in India'. Richman, *Questioning Rāmāyanas* 285–308.

Kosambi, Meera, ed. *Pandita Ramabai through Her Own Words: Selected Works.* New Delhi: Oxford University Press, 2000.

Krishnakutty, Gita. 'Introduction' Antherjanam, *Cast Me Out If You Will* xiii–xxix.

Krishnan, Rajam. *Lamps in the Whirlpool* (1987). Translated from the original Tamil by Uma Narayanan and Prema Seetharam. Chennai: Macmillan, 1995.

Kumar, Radha. 'Constructing the Image of a Woman Activist'. Kumar, *The History of Doing* 74–95.

———. 'Organization and Struggle'. Kumar, *The History of Doing* 53–73.

Kumar, Radha. *The History of Doing: An Illustrated Account of Movements for Women's Rights and Feminism in India 1880–1990*. New Delhi: Zubaan, an imprint of Kali for Women, 1992.

———. 'Towards Becoming "The Mothers of the Nation"'. Kumar, *The History of Doing* 32–52.

Kunjukuttan, Matampu. *Outcaste*. Translated from the original Malayalam *Brushte* by Vasanthi Shankaranarayanan. Madras: Macmillan India Limited, 1996.

Lakshmi, C.S. 'Bodies Called Women: Some Thoughts on Gender, Ethnicity and Nation'. *Economic and Political Weekly* 32.45 (15–21 Nov. 1997): 2953–2962.

———. *The Face behind the Mask: Women in Tamil Literature*. New Delhi: Vikas Publishing House, 1984.

Lambert-Hurley, Siobhan. *Muslim Women, Reform and Princely Patronage*. London: Routledge, 2007.

Leslie, Julia. *Roles and Rituals for Hindu Women*. London: Pinter Publishers, 1991.

Liddle, Joanna and Rama Joshi. *Daughters of Independence: Gender, Class and Caste in India*. New Delhi: Kali for Women, 1986.

Limbale, Sharan Kumar. *Hindu*. Translated from the original Marathi by Surya Narayan Ramsubhe. New Delhi: Vani Prakashan, 2004.

Lutgendorf, Philip. 'The Secret Life of Ramchandra of Ayodhya', Richman, *Many Rāmāyanas* 217–234.

———. *The Life of a Text: Performing the Ramcharitmanas of Tulsidas*. Delhi: Oxford University Press, 1994.

Mahadeviakka. 'Mahadeviakka's Vachanas'. Trans. A.K. Ramanujan. *Manushi* Nos 50–52 (1989): 15–17.

Manchanda, Rita. *We Do More Because We Can: Naga Women in Peace Process*. Kathmandu, Nepal: South Asia Forum for Human Rights, 2004.

Mani, Braj Ranjan. *Debrahmanising History: Dominance and Resistance in Indian Society*. New Delhi: Manohar Publication, 2005.

———. 'Introduction'. Mani, *Debrahmanising History* 13–44.

Mansfield, Katherine. *The Aloe* (1918). London: Virago, 1930.

Manu. *The Laws of Manu*, with an Introduction and Notes. Trans. Wendy Doniger and Brian K. Smith. New Delhi: Penguin India, 1991.

Markandaya, Kamala. *A Silence of Desire*. New York: Doubleday, 1960.

Mattoo, Neerja. 'Transforming the Gaze: Some Kashmiri Women Poets'. J. Jain, *Growing Up As a Woman Writer*. 331–342.

Mayo, Katherine. *Mother India*. London: Jonathan Cape, 1927.

319

Meenakshi, K. 'Andal: She Who Rules'. *Manushi* Nos 50–52: 35–38.

Mehta, Narsi. *Devotional Songs of Narsi Mehta*, with an introduction by Sivapriyananda. Trans. Swami Mahadevanand. Delhi: Motilal Banarasidass Publishers (1985), 1995.

Menon, Ramesh. *The Ramayana: A Modern Translation*. New Delhi: Harper Collins (2003), 2008.

Menon, Ritu. 'Structured Silences of Women: Culture, Censorship and Voice in a Globalized Market'. *EPW* 35.18 29 April–5 May, 2000, WS3–WS6. [Also included in *Word: On Being a (Woman) Writer*. Ed. Jocelyn Burrel. New York: Feminist Press, 2004.]

Menon, Usha and Richard A. Shweder. 'Dominating Kali: Hindu Family Values and Tantric Power'. Dermott and Kripal 80–99.

Merchant, Carolyn. *The Death of Nature: Women, Ecology and the Scientific Revolution*. London: Wildwood House, 1982.

Metcalf, Barbara Daly. *Perfecting Women: A Partial Translation of Bihisti Zewar*. Delhi: Oxford University Press, 1992.

Mirza, Khurshid. *A Woman of Substance: The Memoirs of Begum Khurshid Mirza*, with a Foreword by Gail Minault. Ed. and comp. Lubna Kazim. New Delhi: Zubaan, 2005. ix–xxv.

Mitra, Saoli. 'Five Lords, Yet None a Protector'. *Five Lords, Yet None a Protector & Timeless Tales: Two Plays*. Translated from the original Bengali by Rita Datta, Ipshita Chanda and Moushumi Bhowmik. Kolkata: Stree, 2006. 1–71.

Mohanty, Chandra Talpade. *Feminism without Borders: Decolonizing Theory, Practicing Solidarity*. Durham: Duke University Press, 2003.

Mohanty, Sachidananda., ed. *Early Women's Writings in Orissa 1898–1950: A Lost Tradition*. New Delhi: SAGE Publications, 2005.

Mukherjee, Meenakshi. 'Gender and Nation: Iconography of the Past'. Pankaj K. Singh 117–130.

———. *Realism and Reality*. New Delhi: Oxford University Press, 1988.

Mukta, Parita. 'Mirabai in Rajasthan'. *Manushi* Nos 50–52 (1989): 94–99.

Muktabai. 'Songs of the Door' Trans. Ruth Vanita. *Manushi* Nos 50–52 (1989): 52–53.

Nagarkar, Kiran. *Cuckold*. New Delhi: Harper Collins (1997), 1998.

Nair, Janaki. *Women and Law in Colonial India: A Social History*. New Delhi: Kali for Women, 1996.

Nandy, Ashis. 'A Report on the Present State of Health of the Gods and Goddesses of South Asia'. *Dissenting Knowledges, Open Futures: The Multiple Selves and*

Strange Destinations of Ashis Nandy. Ed. Vinay Lal. Delhi: Oxford University Press, 2000. 129–156. [Also in *Time Warps: Silent and Evasive Pasts in Indian Politics and Religion*. London: Hurst and Company, 2002.]

Nandy, Ashis. 'Foreword: The Days of the Hyaena'. Sengupta, *Mapmaking* n.p.

Narayan, R.K. *The Dark Room*. Mysore: Thought Publication, 1935.

'National Policy on Education 1986'. New Delhi: Ministry of Human Resource Development, 1986. Available at http://www.education.nic.in/cd50years/g/t/49/toc.htm (accessed on 7 December 2010).

Nawaz, Mumtaz Shah. *The Heart Divided* F.P. Lahore 1957. New Delhi: Penguin, 2004.

Nevile, Pran. *Nautch Girls of the Raj*. New Delhi: Penguin, 2009.

Nilsson, Usha. 'Grinding Millet but Singing of Sītā: Power and Domination in Awadhi and Bhojpuri Women's Songs'. Richman, *Questioning Rāmāyanas* 137–158.

O'Connor, June. 'The Epistemological Significance of Feminist Research in Religion'. *Religion and Gender*. Ed. Ursula King. Oxford: Basil Blackwell, 1995. 45–64.

O'Flaherty, Wendy Doniger. *Hindu Myths*. Harmondsworth, Middlesex: Penguin, (1975), 1978.

O'Hanlon, Rosalind. 'Introduction'. *Stree-Purush Tulana*. Translated into English as *A Comparison between Women and Men*. Madras: Oxford University Press, 1994. 1–71.

Palit, Dibyendu. 'Alam's Own House'. Sengupta, *Mapmaking* 59–86.

Parikh, Salome. 'The Blessed and the Damned'. *Express Magazine*. (19 Feb. 1984): 3.

Parpart, Jane. 'Lessons from the Field: Rethinking Empowerment, Gender and Development from a Post-development Perspective'. *Feminist Post-Development Thought: Rethinking Modernity, Post-colonialism and Representation*. Ed. Kriemild Saunders. London: Zed Books, 2004. 41–56.

Pawar, Urmila. 'Hum Nein Bhi Itihaas Racha Hai'. *Dehleez Ke Us Paar*. Ed. Sudha Arora. Mumbai: SPARROW, 2003. 49–100.

———. 'My Four Enemies'. J. Jain, *Women in Patriarchy* 297–308.

Pawar, Urmila and Meenakshi Moon. *Amhihi Itihaas Ghadavlaa* (Marathi, 1989). Translated into English as *We Also Made History*. New Delhi: Zuban, 2008.

Phule, Jotiba. *Mahatma Jotiba Phule Rachnavali*. Ed. and trans. Dr L.G. Meshram 'Vimal Kirti' 2 vols. New Delhi: Radhakrishnan Prakashan, 1995.

Pirandello, Luigi. *Six Characters in Search of an Author* (1933). Trans. Eric Bentley, 1952. Included in *Naked Masks: Five Plays* by Pirandello. Ed. Eric Bentley. New York: E.P Dutton, 1958: 211–276.

Pritam, Amrita. *Pinjar* (Hindi). Delhi: Hind Pocket Books, 1997.

Pukhraj, Malka. *Song Sung True: A Memoir.* Ed. and trans. Saleem Kidwai. New Delhi: Kali for Woman, 2003.

Radhakrishnan, S. *The Principal Upanisads.* New Delhi: Harper Collins (1951), 2005.

Rajadhyaksha, Ashish and Paul Willemen. *Encyclopaedia of Indian Cinema.* Revised Edition. New Delhi: Oxford University Press (1999), 2002.

Rajan, Chandra. 'Introduction'. Kālidāsa, *The Loom of Time* 21–102.

Ramabai, Pandita. *Selected Works.* Ed. and comp. Meera Kosambi. New Delhi: Oxford University Press, 2000.

———. *The High Caste Hindu Woman*, with an Introduction by Rachel Bodley. Philadelphia 1888; Reprinted New Delhi: Inter-India Publications, 1984.

Ramanujan, A.K. 'Talking to God in the Mother Tongue'. *Manushi* Nos 50–52 (1989): 9–14.

———. 'Three Hundred *Rāmāyanas*'. Richman, *Many Rāmāyanas* 22–49.

———. *Speaking of Siva.* London: Penguin, 1973.

Ramaswamy, Vijaya. *Walking Naked: Women, Society, Spirituality in South India.* Shimla: Indian Institute of Advanced Study, 1997.

———, ed. *Researching Indian Women.* New Delhi: Manohar, 2003.

Rangacharya, Adya. *Sanjivani.* Trans. Usha Desai. Amur 187–250.

Rao, Abanti. 'Abhibhasana: To the Women of Orissa'. Trans. Aurobindo Behera. S. Mohanty 41–46.

Rao, Velcheru Narayana. 'A Ramayana of Their Own: Women's Oral Tradition in Telugu. Richman, *Many Rāmāyanas.* 114–136.

Ray, Pratibha. *Yajnaseni.* Translated from the original Oriya into English by Pradeep Bhattacharya. New Delhi: Rupa, 1995.

Ray, Rajat Kanta. *Exploring Emotional History: Gender, Mentality and Literature in the Indian Awakening.* New Delhi: Oxford University Press (2001), 2003.

Richman, Paula, ed. *Many Rāmāyanas: The Diversity of Narrative Tradition in South Asia.* New Delhi: Oxford University Press (1992), 1994.

———, ed. *Questioning Rāmāyanas: A South Asian Tradition.* New Delhi: Oxford University Press (2000), 2003.

Rouch, Hélène. 'New Reproductive Techniques: From Difference to Inequality'. *French Feminism: An Indian Anthology.* Eds. Danielle Haase-Dubosc et al. New Delhi: Sage Publications, 2003.

Roy, Mary. 'Three Generations of Women'. *Indian Journal of Gender Studies* 6.2 (1999): 203–220.

Roy, Parama. 'Becoming Women: The Gender of Nationalism'. *Indian Traffic: Identities in Question in Colonial and Postcolonial India.* New Delhi: Vistaar Publications, 1998. 128–151.

Rukhmabai. 'Introduction', *The Wrongs of Indian Womanhood.* Ed. Marcus B. Fuller. Edinburgh: Oliphant Anderson and Ferrier, 1900.

Ruswa, Mirza Mohammed Hadi. *Umrao Jan Ada* (1899). Translated from the original Urdu by Khushwant Singh and M.A. Hussaini (1980). Hyderabad: Sangam Books, 1987.

Said, Edward. 'Travelling Theories'. *The World, the Text and the Critic.* Cambridge: Harvard University Press, 1982. 226–242.

Sangari, Kumkum and Sudesh Vaid, eds. *Recasting Women: Essays in Colonial History.* New Delhi: Kali for Women, 1989.

Sarkar, Tanika. 'Foreword'. Bhattacharya and Sen. ix–xiv.

———. *Hindu Wife, Hindu Nation.* New Delhi: Permanent Black, 2001.

———. 'The Women's Question in Nineteenth Century Bengali Culture'. *Women and Culture.* Eds. Kumkum Sangari and Sudesh Vaid. Bombay: SNDT Women's University, 1985. 157–172.

Saroagi, Alka. *Shesh Kadambari* (Hindi). New Delhi: Rajkamal Prakashan (2001), 2002.

Sarojini. 'Womanliness'. Trans. J. Devika. Devika 52–60.

Satthianadhan, Krupabai. *Saguna* (1895). Ed. Chandani Lokuge. Delhi: Oxford University Press, 1998.

Sattar, Arshia. 'Introduction'. Valmiki, *The Rāmāyana* xvii–lviii.

Schechner, Richard. *Performative Circumstances: From the Avant Garde to Ramlila.* Calcutta: Seagull, 1983.

Segal, Zohra. *Stages: The Art and Adventures of Zohra Segal*, written with Joan L. Erdman. New Delhi: Kali for Women, 1997.

Sen, Amiya P. *Hindu Revivalism in Bengal 1872–1905: Some Essays in Interpretation.* New Delhi: Oxford University Press, 1993.

Sen, Mala. *India's Bandit Queen: The True Story of Phoolan Devi.* New Delhi: Harper Collins, 1993.

Sen, Nabaneeta Dev. 'Antara'. *Selections*. Calcutta: 2004. 6.

———. 'The Immortality Trap'. Jain and Singh 13–20.

———. 'The Wind Beneath My Wings'. *Indian Journal of Gender Studies* 6.2 (1999). 221–240.

———. *Selections*. Kolkata: Bhalo Bhasa, 2000.

Sengupta, Debjani. 'Afterword'. Sengupta, *Mapmaking* 185–195.

———, ed. *Mapmaking: Partition Stories from the Two Bengals*. Kolkata: Shristi Publishers, 2003.

Sheikh, Mallika Amar. *Mala Udhvasth Vahachai* (in Marathi). Mumbai: Majestic Bookshop, 1984.

Shilalolitha, 'Let Us Rewrite History'. Trans. K. Swarnalatha. *An Anthology of Feminist Poetry*. Hyderabad: Vipla Computer Services, 1993.

Shinde, Tarabai. *Stree-Purush Tulana* (Marathi). Translated into English as *A Comparison Between Women and Men: Tarabai Shinde and the Critique of Gender Relations in Colonial India* by Rosalind O'Hanlon. Madras: Oxford University Press, 1994.

Shiva, Vandana. *Staying Alive: Women, Ecology and Survival in India.* New Delhi: Kali for Women (1988), 1992.

Shri Ravisheshnacharya. *Sri Padma Purana*. Trans. Kavivar Pandit Daulatramji. Abridged version, Singhai Shri Parmanand Master. Muzaffarnagar: Arihant Sahitya Sadan, n.d.

Shukla, Sonal. 'Traditions of Teaching—Women Sant Poets of Gujarat'. *Manushi* Nos 50–52 (1989).

Shulman, David. 'Fire and Flood: The Testing of Sītā in Kampan's *Iramavataram*'. Richman, *Many Rāmāyanas* 89–113.

Simons, Judy. *Diaries and Journals of Literary Women.* London: Macmillan Press Ltd, 1990.

Singh, A.K. *Devadasi System in Ancient India: A Study of Temple Dancing Girls of South India.* Delhi: H.K. Publishers and Distributors, 1990.

Singh, Avadhesh Kumar. 'Towards an Indian Theory of Postcolonialism'. *Contesting Postcolonialisms*. Eds. Jasbir Jain and Veena Singh. Jaipur: Rawat Publications, 2000. 40–58.

Singh, K.S. 'The *Mahabharata*: An Anthropological Perspective'. K.S. Singh, *The Mahabharata in the Tribal and Folk Traditions of India* 1–12.

———, ed. *The Mahabharata in the Tribal and Folk Traditions of India*. Shimla: Indian Institute of Advanced Study and Anthropological Survey of India, 1993.

Singh, Madhu. 'Mahasweta Devi's "Kunti and the Nishadin": A Re-visionist Text'. *Journal of the School of Language, Literature and Culture Studies*, Spring (2007): 7–15.

Singh, Pankaj K., ed. *The Politics of Literary Theory and Representation: Writings on Activism and Aesthetics*. New Delhi: Manohar, 2003.

Singh, Pashaura. *The Guru Granth Sahib: Canon, Meaning and Authority*. New Delhi: Oxford University Press (2000), 2007.

———. 'The Meaning of Gurbani: A Focus on Hermeneutic Techniques'. P. Singh, *The Guru Granth Sahib* 239–261.

———. 'The Place of Sikh Scripture in the Sikh Tradition'. P. Singh, *The Guru Granth Sahib* 265–281.

Sivaraman, Mythily. 'Preface'. *Fragments of a Life: A Family Archive.* New Delhi: Zubaan, 2006.

Sivashankari. 'Septic'. J. Jain, *Growing Up as a Woman Writer* 143–149.

Sobti, Krishna. 'Where Is My Mother?' Bhalla 433–439.

———. *Zindagi Nama.* New Delhi: Rajkamal Prakashan, (1979) 1994.

Somadeva. *Tales from the Kathāsaritsāgara.* Trans. Arshia Sattar. New Delhi: Penguin Books India (P) Ltd. 1994.

Sreedevi, K.B. *Yagnam* (in Malayalam). Kottayam: N.B.S National Bookstall, 1976.

Srinivasan, K.S. *The Ethos of Indian Literature: A Study of Its Romantic Tradition*. Delhi: Chanakya Publication, 1985.

Sundari, P. Usha. 'Draupadi in Folk Imagination'. K.S. Singh, *The Mahabharata in the Tribal and Folk Traditions of India*. 254–259.

Suraiya, Qasim. 'Where Did She Belong?' Bhalla 404–414.

Suthankar, V.S., S.K. Belvalkar and P.L. Vaidya, eds. *Critical Edition of Mahabharata*, 18 volumes. Poona: Bhandarkar Oriental Research Institute, 1967.

Tagore, Rabindranath. *Char Adhaya* (1934). Translated into English as *Four Chapters*. New Delhi: Rupa and Co., 2002.

———. *Home and the World.* Trans. Surendranath Tagore. Madras: Macmillan (India), 1919.

———. 'Patni Ka Patra'. *Rabindranath ki Kahaniyan* (3 Volumes). Trans. Ram Singh Tomar. New Delhi: Sahitya Akademi (1961), 2002. Vol.1, 357–372.

———. 'Sakuntala: Its Inner Meaning'. English translation of an essay originally written in Bengali in 1907. *Modern Review* 9 (1911): 171ff.

———. 'Stree Ka Patra'. Translated and retold in Hindi by Deepanvita and Ruchi Lahiri. New Delhi: Katha (1991), 2004.

Tarlekar, G.H. *Studies in the Natyasastra.* Delhi: Motilal Banarsidass Publishers, (1975), 1999.

Thapar, Romila. 'The Tradition of Historical Writing in Early India'. Thapar, *Ancient Indian Social History* 237–258.

———. 'Interpretations of Ancient Indian History'. Thapar, *Ancient Indian Social History* 1–22.

———. *Ancient Indian Social History: Some Interpretations.* New Delhi: Orient Longman Pvt. Ltd (1978), 2003.

———. *Narratives and the Making of History: Two Lectures.* New Delhi: Oxford University Press, 2000.

———. 'Śakuntalā: Histories of a Narrative'. Thapar, *Narratives and the Making of History: Two Lectures* 1–23.

———. *Time as a Metaphor of History: Early India.* New Delhi: Oxford University Press, (1996) 2006.

Tharu, Susie and K. Lalita. eds. *Women Writing in India: 600 B.C. to the Early Twentieth Century* 2 vols. Delhi: Oxford University Press, 1993 (Vol. 1), 1995 (Vol 2).

Thomas, K. Mary. 'Women's Independence' (1927). Devika 106–108.

Tilak, Lakshmibai. *Smriti Chitra.* Translated from the original Marathi into English as *I Follow After* by E. Josephine Inkster (1950), New Delhi: Oxford University Press, 1998.

Towards Equality: Report on the Status of Women in India. A report prepared by the India Committee on the Status of Women under the Chairmanship of Puirenu Guha, 1974. New Delhi: Ministry of Education and Social Welfare, Government of India, 1975.

Tulsidas. *Shri Ramcharitmanas,* commentary by Hanuman Prasad Poddar. Gorakhpur: Gita Press, 2002.

Turner, Victor. *From Ritual to Theatre: The Human Seriousness of Play.* New York: Performing Arts Journal, 1982.

Urban, Hugh B. 'India's Darkest Heart'. McDermott and Kripal. Delhi: Motilal Banarasidas Publishers, 2005. 169–195.

'UN Resolution on International Women's Day', 1977. Resolution No. 322/142. Available at http://www.womenaid.org/events/iwd/iwd.htm (accessed on 6 December 2010).

USAID India. *45 Million Daughters Missing: A Compendium on Research and Intervention on Female Foeticide and Infanticide in India.* IFES/Ekatra, n.d. supported by United States Agency for International Development.

Valmiki. *The Rāmāyana*. Abridged and translated by Arshia Sattar. New Delhi: Penguin (1996), 2000.

Van Nooten, B.A. 'Introduction'. Buck n.p.

Vanita, Ruth. 'Three Women Saints of Maharashtra: Muktabai, Janabai, Bahinabai'. *Manushi*. Nos 50–52 (1989): 45–61.

Vatsyayan, Kapila. *Bharata: The Nātyaśāstra*. New Delhi: Sahitya (1996), 2003.

Vatsyayan, Sacchidanand. *Jan Janak Janaki*. New Delhi: Vatsal Foundation, 1986.

Viswanathan, Gauri. *Outside the Fold: Conversion, Modernity and Belief*. Delhi: Oxford University Press, 1998.

———. 'Preface', Viswanathan xi–xvii.

Volga. 'Confluence'. J. Jain, *Growing up as a Woman Writer* 221–230.

Vyas, Ved. *Mahābhārata*. 2 volumes. Abridged and translated by Jai Dayal Goendka. Gorakhpur: Gita Press, 2003 (Samvat 2060, 28th Reprint).

———. 'Sabha Parv'. *Mahābhārata* (Vol. 1). Abridged and translated by Jai Dayal Goendka. Gorakhpur: Gita Press, 2003 (Samvat 2060, 28th Reprint). 164–170.

Wadkar, Hansa. *Sangyte Aika* (Marathi) Pune: Rajhans Publications (1970), 2003.

Wadley, Susan S. '*Vrats*: Transformer of Destiny'. *Essays on North Indian Folk Traditions*. New Delhi : Chronicle Books, 2005. 36–52.

Wilshire, Donna. 'The Uses of Myth, Image and the Female Body in Revisioning Knowledge'. *Gender/Body Knowledge*. Eds. Alison E. Jagger and Susan R. Bordo. New Jersey: Rutgers University Press, 1989. 92–114.

Winston, Robert. *The Human Mind*. London: Bantam Books (2003), 2004.

Woolf, Virginia. *A Room of One's Own* (1929) Flamingo: Harper Collins Publishers, 1994.

Zaheer, Noor. *My God is a Woman*. New Delhi: Vitasta Publishing Pvt. Ltd., 2008.

Zelliot, Eleanor. Trans. 'Eknath's Bharuds: The Sant as Link Between Cultures'. *The Sants: Studies in a Devotional Tradition in India*. Eds. Karme Schomer and W.H. Mcleod. Berkeley Religious Studies Series. Delhi: Motilal Banarsidass, 1987. 91–109.

———, trans. 'Let Me Live Alone'. *Manushi*. Nos 50–52 (1989): 60.

Zvelebil, K.V. *The Lord of the Meeting Rivers—Devotional Poems of Basavanna*. Delhi: Motilal Banarsidass, 1984.

Filmography

Bandit Queen. Dir. Shekhar Kapur. Prod. Kaleidoscope & Channel Four Films, Perf. Seema Biswas, Aditya Srivastava and Agesh Markum. 1995.

Bhumika. Dir. Shyam Benegal. Prod. Lalit M. Bijlani, Perf. Smita Patil, Amol Palekar, Anant Nag, Amrish Puri and Naseerudin Shah. 1976.

Challia. Dir. Manmohan Desai. Prod. Subhash Desai, Story: Inder Raj Anand. Perf. Raj Kapoor, Nutan, Pran and Shobana Samarth, 1960.

Devi (Bengali). Dir. and Script. Satyajit Ray. Prod. Satyajit Productions. Perf. Chabbi Biswas, Soumitra Chatterjee, Sharmila Tagore and Anil Chatterjee. 1960.

Dor. Dir. Nagesh Kukunoor. Prod. Elahe Hiptoola and Subhash Jha. Perf. Ayesha Takia, Gul Panag and Shreyas Talpade. 2006.

Khamosh Pani. Dir. Sabiha Sumer. Prod. Vidhi Films, Arte and Flying Film Production. Perf. Kirron Kher and Aamir Malik. 2005.

Meera. Dir. Gulzar. Prod. Premji. Perf. Hema Malini, Vinod Khanna and Vidya Sinha. 1979.

Meghe Dhaka Tara (Bengali). Dir. and Script. Ritwik Ghatak. Prod. Chitrakalpa. Perf. Supriya Chaudhary, Anil Chatterjee and Bijon Bhattacharya. 1960.

Pinjar. Dir. Chandra Prakash Dwivedi. Prod. Lucy Film Entertainment. Story: Amrita Pritam. Perf. Urmila Matondkar, Manoj Bajpai, Sandali Sinha and Priyanshu Chatterjee. 2003.

Shaheed-e-Mohabbat Boota Singh (Punjabi). Dir. Manoj Punj, Prod. Manjeet Mann and Anil Pandit. Perf.. Gurdas Mann and Divya Dutta. 2004.

Water. Dir. Deepa Mehta. Prod. David Hamilton. Perf. Seema Biswas, John Abraham, Lisa Ray, Manorama, Waheeda Rehman, Raghuveer Yadav. 2006.

INDEX

329

ABOUT THE AUTHOR

Jasbir Jain is director of the Institute for Research in Interdisciplinary Studies (IRIS), Jaipur. Formerly of the University of Rajasthan, she has headed the Department of English and has worked in various capacities including the directorship of the Academic Staff College.

Jain has travelled extensively and has been the recipient of several awards. Amongst them are the Sahitya Akademi Fellowship as Writer in Residence (2009), UGC Fellow (2005–2007), Emeritus Fellow (2002–2004) and K.K. Birla Fellowship for Comparative Literature (1998–2000). Elected life-member of Clare Hall, Cambridge, she has also availed of the Fulbright Fellowship and of the American Council of Learned Societies. In 2008, the South Asia Literary Association conferred on her the SALA Award for her work in Feminist and South Asian Studies and her distinguished scholarship. Earlier in 2004, she was awarded the Indian Association of Canadian Studies (IACS) Award in recognition of her outstanding contribution to Canadian Studies. The American Association of Colleges and Universities nominated her a Global Fellow for 2003.

Her publications include three volumes on the Indian novel covering the period 1860–2000 and, interrogating the periodisation thrust on it, she went on to work on the connectivity across languages. Her current interests are in theory and narratology and in exploring traditions. Her recent work includes *Gendered Realities* and *Beyond Postcolonialism: The Dreams and Realities of a Nation* and a forthcoming work is *The Writer as Critic.*

Lightning Source UK Ltd.
Milton Keynes UK
UKHW040010051120
372813UK00001B/17

9 788132 104391